KU-395-437

Hertfordshire
COUNTY COUNCIL
Community Information

au 12.4.2003

1 5 DEC 2007

06/07/15

Please renew/return this item by the last date shown.

So that your telephone call is charged at local rate, please call the numbers as set out below:

	From Area codes 01923 or 020:	From the rest of Herts:
Renewals:	01923 471373	01438 737373
Enquiries:	01923 471333	01438 737333
Minicom:	01923 471599	01438 737599

L32   www.hertsdirect.org

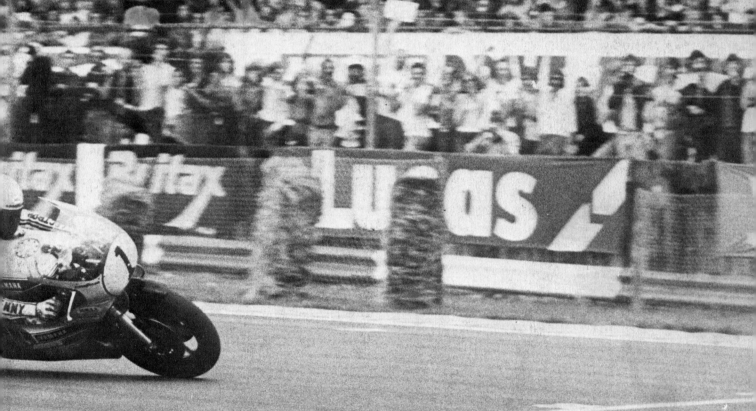

THE RACING MOTOR CYCLE
VIC WILLOUGHBY

Hamlyn
London·New York·Sydney·Toronto

CONTENTS

6746P

The publishers are grateful to the editor of
Motor Cycle Weekly for permission to reproduce the
majority of illustrations in this book, and also to:
Peter Clifford; Edisport, Milan; Wolfgang Gruber;
Jan Heese; Yori Kanda; Dr Helmut Krackowizer; Don
Morley, All Sport; Louis Pauzin; Ulrich Schwab;
and Lawrie Watts.

HERTFORDSHIRE
COUNTY LIBRARY
796.75
9769891

796 7509(04)
21271 482x   3.94

Published by The Hamlyn Publishing Group Limited
London · New York · Sydney · Toronto
Astronaut House, Feltham, Middlesex, England
Copyright © Victor Harold Willoughby 1980
First published 1980
All rights reserved. No part of this publication may be
reproduced, stored in a retrieval system, or transmitted,
in any form or by any means, electronic, mechanical,
photocopying, recording or otherwise, without the permission of
The Hamlyn Publishing Group Limited and the copyrightholder.

ISBN 0 600 36342 2

Printed in Hong Kong

PREFACE

IN the rich kaléidoscope of motor-cycle sport, classic road racing stands supreme both for its aura of glamour and for its technical fascination. As a contest of courage, skill and calculated risk on the track, allied to intense technical endeavour in the race shop, the world championships present a fierce challenge to rider and engineer alike.

Down the years that challenge has attracted men of enormous talent and character. Essentially, these are men of adventure – whether physical, intellectual or both – for whom life without challenge would be empty. And it is their glorious achievements both in riding and engineering that have brought, and continue to bring, so much colour and excitement to our sport.

Almost from the beginning, arguments have raged as to the primary function of classic road racing. Is its chief purpose to "improve the breed" (machines of course) through competition? Or is the sport simply a commercial spectacle?

In the industry's infancy, when machines were primitive, unreliable and unsafe, the accent was undoubtedly on improvement of the breed. Racing forced the pace of design and touring machines benefited enormously. Anyway, the spectacle could hardly have been exploited commercially for vast crowds were unknown at the early races.

Nowadays the emphasis has swung the other way. Design in general is vastly improved and racing and touring machines are much more specialised. Hence the technical spin-off from racing is less than it was, although by no means absent. At the same time, permanent tracks and grandstands cater for grand-prix crowds numbering hundreds of thousands. It would be a pity for either function to overwhelm the other. With wise guidance by the FIM (Fédération Internationale Motocycliste) – by no means a certainty – there is no reason why both functions should not co-exist to the benefit of the sport. It is sometimes argued that racing design has had a bad influence on roadster machines. Where this has been so, the fault lies not with racing but with sales policies.

It has been my delight not only to participate in racing as a private rider/tuner but also, as a journalist, to meet many of my predecessors, contemporaries and successors – riders and engineers alike, including the world's best – and to try out many exotic grand-prix machines. In this book I hope I have managed to capture something of the deep and lasting fascination that draws men of the highest calibre irresistibly to racing.

VHW

HALF A CENTURY OF PROGRESS

TO put the classic scene in perspective, we have to look back not only to the start of the world championships in 1949 but also to the decade preceding the Second World War, when the championships were confined to Europe and decided, for the most part, on the results of a single, selected, event each year. It was 1938 before an overall points system was introduced. Basically, road racing now is much the same as it was then. But in detail there is scarcely an aspect of the sport that has not changed enormously.

The grands prix of the early 1930s were dominated by British and Irish riders on British single-cylinder machines. Indeed, for several years the works Norton team (under Joe Craig) monopolised the 500 and 350 cc classes so emphatically as to seem utterly invincible. At the same time Rudge, New Imperial and Excelsior between them kept a similar stranglehold on the 250 cc class, although hard pressed by Moto Guzzi. It was enough to strike despair into the hearts of the Continental opposition.

Nowadays only a minority of the championships fall to British riders, who are matched by the best from other West European countries, North and South America and the Far East. Nor does Britain supply any title-winning machines. Most of them are Japanese, the rest from the European mainland.

It was in design rather than riding that Britain's double dominance of racing first faltered. By the mid-1930s, vee-twins from Husqvarna and Moto Guzzi surpassed the Nortons for speed. Indeed, with Stanley Woods' dramatic Senior TT win in 1935, Moto Guzzi's rear-sprung 500 cc 120-degree twin foreshadowed the demise of the unsprung frame as well as the single-cylinder engine. Although the single quickly shrugged off the challenge, a greater one soon loomed. It was supercharging.

There was at that time no ban on forced induction and both Germany and Italy decided to exploit it and so bypass the engine capacity limits. First the blown BMW flat-twins humiliated the big Nortons, then the blown Gilera four leapfrogged the Bee-Ems – in both cases with their own national riders, Georg Meier and Dorino Serafini respectively. But BMW and Gilera alike found a substantial advantage in engine power necessary to offset the superior handling and cornering of the unblown British singles. In the 250 cc class, where a similar power advantage was necessary to compen-

Mike Hailwood winning the 1964 Senior TT for MV Agusta

sate for a prodigious thirst, the blown DKW split-single two-strokes did a similar demolition job on the smaller British singles. And a doubled-up version (a split twin) threatened to vanquish the Velocette singles and extend DKW supremacy to the 350 cc class by 1940 – but war intervened in September 1939.

When classic racing restarted some eight years later, this runaway trend was stopped dead by an FIM ban on supercharging. The prewar Gilera fours and BMW twins were outlawed, likewise the 250 and 350 cc DKWs. So too were a host of other exciting blown models – for blowing had spread like wildfire.

From this postwar technical upset Britain came out very well. For the ban on supercharging robbed BMW, Gilera and DKW of the tremendous power advantage that was the cornerstone of their prewar dominance. And since the development of unblown multis had scarcely begun, the ban amounted to a new lease of life for the single. This type of machine was already well advanced in development for power and its superior handling enabled it to remain competitive until the multis had once again established a considerable power advantage.

With the exception of Velocette – where worthwhile technical progress had come to a full stop in mid-1939, when meningitis tragically killed the brilliant Harold Willis – the big British singles seized their postwar

opportunity. Continuing prewar technical trends, Norton and AJS followed the traditional double highroad to increased power. First they stepped-up their brake mean effective pressure (the effectiveness of each individual engine cycle). Second they raised their peak rpm (the engine speed at which peak power is produced).

A substantial boost in bmep came from painstaking attention to port shapes and downdraught angles; valve sizes and included angles; inlet and exhaust resonances; and squish forms and surface/volume ratios in the combustion chamber. Peak revs were raised by higher bore/stroke ratios and cam forms designed to match valve-spring characteristics. Handling, too, was further enhanced, notably by Norton's adoption of the so-called featherbed frame – a duplex-loop structure designed by Irishman Rex McCandless. And backing all this technical endeavour was a concerted effort on the track by a new breed of British stars, of whom Geoff Duke was the brightest, together with a handful of prewar top-notchers, such as Harold Daniell, Freddie Frith and Bob Foster, gleefully shedding their wartime frustrations while the brief chance remained.

But it was a last desperate fling. Technical stagnation put Velocette on the sidelines after Frith and Foster had taken the first two world 350 cc championships (1949 and 1950). For the next two years Norton depended entirely on impeccable handling and Duke's incomparable skill to offset the extra power and speed that Piero Taruffi had grafted into the big Gilera fours. Once Duke acknowledged the writing on the wall and threw in his lot with the Italians in 1953, the 500 cc single became a dodo so far as the world championship was concerned. For Duke's liaison with Taruffi soon added other raceworthy qualities to the Gilera's immense power and until the factory pulled out of racing late in 1957, the howling red-and-white four never looked like being beaten.

In the 350 cc class, however, the situation was entirely different – thanks to the refreshing genius of Moto Guzzi's race chief Giulio Carcano. Persuaded by Fergus Anderson to scale up the factory's highly successful two-fifty, he produced a string of incredibly light and beautifully streamlined horizontal singles that kept the much more powerful fours at bay for the next five years – until Moto Guzzi, too, quit the sport.

More than any other engineer, Carcano

The very essence of endeavour. Jimmie Guthrie, one of the mainstays of Norton invincibility in the early 1930s, cheats the wind on the short straight between Quarter and Braddan bridges while winning the 1934 Junior TT at record speed

understood that a racing machine is much more than a mobile engine. Waging war on weight, he pared his low-slung singles to 216 lb (including the full frontal fairing!), thus giving his riders not only better all-round handling than their rivals but also, as a consequence, much more confidence in their physical mastery of the machine.

Anderson (1953 and 1954), Bill Lomas (1955 and 1956) and Keith Campbell (1957) virtually laughed their way through a Moto Guzzi monopoly of the world 350 cc championship in the last five years of the factory's involvement in classic racing.

The lightweights

For the first few years after the war, the 125 and 250 cc classes, too, were dominated by the Italians. Typically high-revving double-knocker singles (125 cc FB Mondial, Moto Morini and MV Agusta, 250 cc Benelli

and Moto Guzzi) carried all before them until NSU – seeking prestige to back their mopeds, scooters and lightweight roadsters – made a brief, Teutonically thorough and completely shattering assault on the smaller championships.

Their one-two-five (the Rennfox) was also a single – virtually one pot from an abandoned 500 cc four. But no machine did more than the sensational 250 cc Rennmax parallel twin to put the unblown multi firmly on the world-championship map. Its 39 bhp at 11,500 rpm put it streets ahead of its rivals (indeed, it was often quicker

Opposite: *postwar Nortons, old and new. No. 12 is Artie Bell, with a "garden gate" frame having plunger rear springing. No. 43 is Geoff Duke with one of the earliest featherbed frames*

Above: *Geoff Duke on the 500 cc Gilera four – this combination made Norton's big single a dodo in classic racing*

Right: *typical exhibition of Moto Guzzi's 350 cc supremacy in 1954 – in the Italian GP at Monza, Ken Kavanagh leads Enrico Lorenzetti, Fergus Anderson and Dario Agostini into the first Lesmo turn. Anderson won the race (from Lorenzetti, Kavanagh and Agostini) and the world championship*

than the winning three-fifty on the same day) while valve control up to 15,000 rpm made it virtually unburstable. Werner Haas easily won both titles for the factory in 1953, and Rupert Hollaus (125 cc) and Haas (250 cc) rammed the message home the following year. Then, while the lightweight opposition were still reeling from the impact, NSU withdrew as abruptly as they had come in.

Surprisingly, in view of the German example, most of the Italian machines that then resumed the squabble for lightweight supremacy were singles. Notable exceptions were MV, who fielded twins as well as singles in the 250 cc class; Gilera, who brought out a delightful little 125 cc twin; and Ducati, whose audacious desmodromic one-two-five went from one cylinder to two, and would

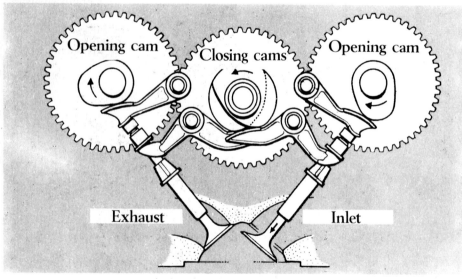

Above: *stars of NSU's brief but shattering impact on the world lightweight championships. Left to right: Rupert Hollaus (winner of the 125 cc title in 1954 on a Rennfox), "Happy" Müller (who took the 250 cc crown on a Sportmax single in 1955, after the factory had withdrawn) and Werner Haas (who won the 250 cc title in 1953 and 1954 on a Rennmax twin, besides the 125 cc championship in 1953*

Left: *the Ducati desmodromic valve gear that made return springs old-fashioned overnight – until Honda reinstated them with paired valves. In this triple-knocker layout, the valve-closing cams are on the middle shaft*

Opening cam
Closing cams
Opening cam
Exhaust
Inlet

have gone to four had the factory not curtailed its racing policy just when desmodromic valve gear was poised for supremacy.

It was Ducati's desmodromic single, indeed, that provided the first major upset in the lightweight ranks since NSU. And what an upset! Recognising valve float as the Achilles heel of the high-revving, high-compression, two-valve single, Ing Fabio Taglioni perfected his triple-knocker valve gear, in which the extra camshaft closed both the inlet and exhaust valves – so dispensing with valve springs (and the consequent loss of valve control at ultra-high revs), as well as permitting higher valve lift for extra power.

A foretaste of the engine's potential came on its debut in the 1956 Swedish Grand Prix, when Degli Antoni trounced the opposition so thoroughly as to lap every other finisher. But the full impact of desmodromic valve gear came two years later. After threatening the haughty MVs in the TT, the Ducatis humiliated them so badly in Belgium and Sweden that sheer pride forced MV to stake everything on a last-race comeback in the Italian GP at Monza. In front of thousands of screaming race fans, they were annihilated. Four desmodromic singles and a twin took the first five places. Carlo Ubbiali and Tarquinio Provini blew up the best two MVs in the forlorn chase – and the only one to finish (sixth) was lapped.

Ducati's subsequent change of policy not only let valve springs back in contention; it also prevented what could have been a fascinating technical struggle a few years later – between desmodromic valve gear and Honda's use of paired valves to solve the very same problem, valve float. I suspect the outcome would have been the same, for the four-valve head has the extra advantages of better breathing and turbulence, a more compact combustion space and a shorter flame path.

Shadow of the two-stroke

While top Italian engineers were waging a valve-gear war in the lightweight classes in the late 1950s, MZ in East Germany were sowing the seeds of an engine type that was eventually to swamp the four-stroke altogether. Virtually alone, Ing Walter Kaaden recognised the immense possibilities of harnessing the gas resonances on which an unblown two-stroke relies, and the fundamental advantage of a disc inlet valve over piston control in bypassing the restrictions of symmetrical port timing.

Working on a shoestring budget compared with Western factories, Kaaden slowly and systematically evolved the formula that laid the foundations of two-stroke supremacy – although it was by chance he stumbled on one of its most crucial features. That was the auxiliary transfer port (or ports) opposite the exhaust port, which he introduced to ease the lot of the overheated, under-oiled small-end bearing. That it did, by drawing some cool, oily gas over the bearing on its way from crankcase to cylinder. But it also brought an unexpected 10 per cent boost in power.

By 1960 MZ were potential champions.

British desmodromic valve gear that never got beyond the practising stage. On a 500 cc Norton single, the valve opening cams worked through hollow tappets, the closing cams through rockers

Had they been able to offer star riders western currency; had Gary Hocking not been bought by MV Agusta following his scintillating run of MZ wins late in 1959; had Ernst Degner not defected to the West in 1961 with the 125 cc title only a race away; and had Mike Hailwood's brilliant rides on the East German two-strokes been regular, not spasmodic, then MZ riders must have won more than one world championship.

As it was, Degner's unexpected flight from communism presented Honda with the first of their many world titles (125 cc, Tom Phillis), then pointed Suzuki's two-stroke race engineers in the right direction. Soon the MZ engine formula was copied, not only by Suzuki but by Yamaha too. With incomparably better resources, both factories were able to retain world-class stars on long-term contracts and to refine Kaaden's formula, although they could not improve it basically by one iota.

So it was that the Japanese inherited from East Germany the formidable task of dislodging the four-stroke from the perch it had proudly occupied in all classes for the 13 years of the postwar championships. Cylinder distortion and borderline lubrication render the racing two-stroke vulnerable to instant piston seizure and crankshaft failure, while local overheating can hole the piston crown without warning.

And as if these inherent problems were not handicap enough for Suzuki and Yamaha, the four-stroke nut became much harder to crack with the advent of the howling Hondas.

Confrontation

Almost immediately, the two-stroke/four-stroke confrontation boiled up into six years of the most exquisite technical rivalry, with the advantage going first this way, then that. With four-valve cylinder heads (abandoned by European race engineers before the war) and tinier cylinders than anyone else dreamed of, Honda set new standards of performance. And whenever the two-stroke challenge became too strong, they scaled cylinder size down and peak revs up still farther. Titles galore fell to Jim Redman and Mike Hailwood (250 and 350 cc classes), Luigi Taveri (125 cc) and Ralph Bryans (50 cc).

Yet, with Honda's 16-valve 250 cc four riding high in 1963, Redman well-nigh lost his title, not to a two-stroke but to the fiery Tarquinio Provini on a two-valve double-knocker Moto Morini single. Like the invincible 350 cc Moto Guzzis six and more years earlier, the Morini was short on sheer power (38 bhp). But it gained in being low, light, slim and superb to handle. And it showed uncanny reliability at the seemingly suicidal speed – for a two-valve 250 cc

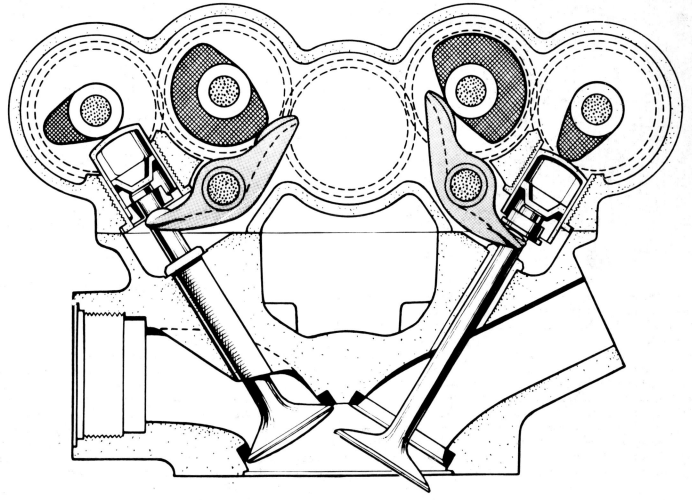

single – of 11,000 rpm. It was a pity Morini did not exploit the single's potential even farther by laying the cylinder down.

Fifties point the way

Strangely, it was the introduction of the 50 cc championship in 1962 that put the two-stroke engineers on the track of the improved stamina they needed to be really competitive. Spending so much more time flat out, the tiny new engines were expected to register a new low in the reliability stakes. They did just the opposite, and it was clear that their smaller pistons ran cooler, their cylinders distorted less and their big ends were not so highly stressed.

The lesson was rammed home when cylinder size was halved as Suzuki switched from 50 cc singles to twins and improved both stamina and power (the latter from higher peak rpm). And soon the adoption of water cooling (forced, not thermo-siphon), by equalising temperatures around the cylinder port belt, reduced the incidence of piston failures still further, besides giving crisper torque (from closer clearances) and eliminating high-temperature fatigue (the drop in peak power when a two-stroke gets hot).

Quite early in the struggle the two-strokes

had been competitive for speed, not just in the 50 cc class but in the 125 and 250 cc classes too. But the necessary stamina took longer to work its way up the capacity scale. This was best seen in the 250 cc class in the mid-1960s when Phil Read, on an air-cooled disc-valve Yamaha twin, played cat-and-mouse with Jim Redman's 16-valve Honda four in most of the grands prix, before romping past in the closing laps to win. But in the TT, on the most demanding circuit ever used for a grand prix, the Yamaha frequently showed its speed only to crack up early on.

So Yamaha changed to water cooling. First they perfected a 125 cc twin, then doubled that up into a 250 cc vee-four and finally scaled that down into one of the most phenomenal two-strokes ever – the 125 cc vee-four immortalised by Read and little Bill Ivy, and the only bike of its size to lap the TT Mountain course at 100 mph.

Meanwhile, Honda had been cutting cylinder size, too, although only for power – they had no reliability problem. After proving 25 cc cylinders in a 50 cc twin peaking at close to 20,000 rpm, they went to five cylinders for the one-two-five and six for the two-fifty (later bored out to 297 cc to scoop the 350 cc class). Winning all five manufacturers' solo championships in 1966, they

remained enormously competitive. And the great technical disappointment of the 1960s was their withdrawal from classic racing at the end of 1967, which gave victory to the two-stroke by default rather than on merit – or at least some years earlier than it would otherwise have achieved it on merit.

Crippling limit

Just 12 months after Honda's withdrawal left Yamaha unchallenged at the top of the lightweight heap, they too pulled out in anticipation of the FIM's crippling limit of two cylinders and six gears for one-two-five and two-fifties (one cylinder and six speeds for fifties) imposed at the end of 1969. Arguing that the complexity of the top designs was unfair to the smaller factories (since when have brains been synonymous with wealth?), the FIM imagined the new

Opposite, top: the lone wolf who almost robbed Jim Redman and Honda of the world 250 cc championship in 1963 – Tarquinio Provini wins the Italian GP at Monza on the phenomenal Moto Morini single

Opposite, below: cat and mouse. With speed to spare, Phil Read (Yamaha twin) shadows Jim Redman (Honda four) before passing him to win the 1964 West German GP at Solitude

First of the victorious fifties – the Suzuki two-stroke single on which Ernst Degner won the 1962 world championship. Tiny cylinders proved unexpectedly reliable and put designers on the track of stamina

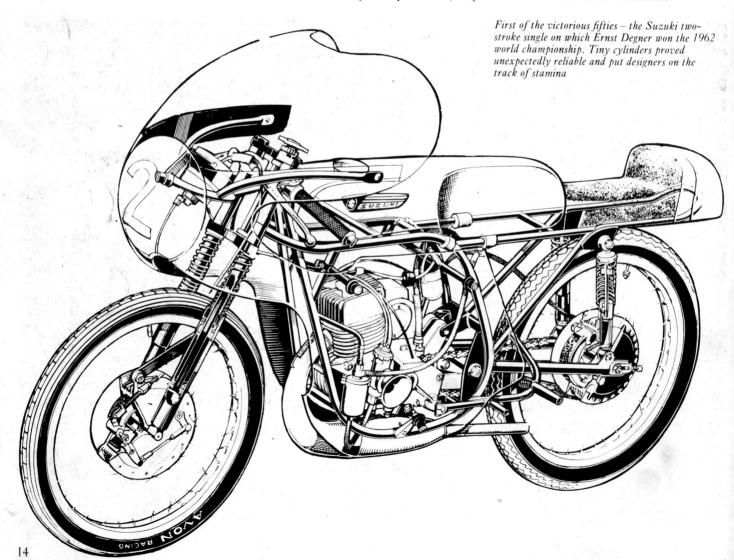

Taking over the 250 cc Honda six in 1966, Mike Hailwood plays cat to Phil Read's Yamaha-four mouse in the Czech GP. Mike won the race and went on to rob Phil of his world title

limits would broaden factory participation in classic racing.

On the contrary, interest in the lightweight classes has never been so keen since. Honda's withdrawal completely blunted the white-hot rivalry that had enlivened lightweight racing for so long. And the FIM's arbitrary restrictions severely curtailed designers' scope for initiative. Some reverted to MZ-style disc-valve parallel twins with side-facing carburettors. Others followed Yamaha who, with the heat off, were able to hold their own for some years with racing versions of sports twins having rear-facing carburettors and piston-controlled induction.

With its edge in peak power and torque spread, the disc-valve engine eventually got the upper hand, through Morbidelli and Kawasaki's tandem twins (discs were never challenged in the 50 cc class). But not before Yamaha had exploited the smaller width of their piston-ported 250 cc twin for minimum frontal area and maximum cornering clearance, and done a remarkable job with induction resonances to curb the blowback inevitable with long-duration symmetrical timing – although inevitably sacrificing tractability as compared with disc-valve engines.

Italian pull-out

The overall effect of Honda's 1967 withdrawal and the subsequent FIM clampdown on design was very much akin to that in the 350 and 500 cc classes more than a decade earlier, when Gilera, Moto Guzzi and FB Mondial pulled out at the end of 1957 and the FIM simultaneously banned full frontal ("dustbin") fairings for solos, but not for sidecar outfits.

Although that ban achieved its aim of preventing over-enthusiastic amateurs from getting themselves blown off the road in high, slab-sided fairings cobbled in the backyard, it regrettably put an end to aerodynamic research into such elegant and efficient dustbins as those on the Moto Guzzi singles, which might well have had a valuable spin-off for roadsters.

As to the big Italian pull-out, since the three factories involved had cornered all four solo championships in 1957, their withdrawal left MV Agusta – no more than second-best at the time – without much serious opposition. In seizing the opportunity, they not only re-established their superiority in the lightweight classes for the next three years (until dislodged by Honda), they also initiated an unparalleled run of 350 and 500 cc successes spanning some 15 years and interrupted only by Honda's dominance in the mid-1960s.

At first Count Domenico Agusta was derided for carrying on regardless of the lack of worthy opposition. In the circumstances, folk said, MV's victories were hollow. And so, at first, they were. But that view does much less than justice to John Surtees, an extremely determined and thoughtful rider with a great flair for development. Pioneering the hanging-in style of cornering to keep his wide four-cylinder engine from grounding, he notched up a phenomenal string of 350 and 500 cc grand-prix successes and world championships.

Building on this firm foundation, MV subsequently signed such rising stars as Gary Hocking, Mike Hailwood and Giacomo Agostini. And by the late 1960s and early 1970s, with Honda no longer competing, Ago and MV seemed unassailable as defenders of the four-stroke faith in the 350 and 500 cc classes.

By then, although two-stroke dominance was accepted in the lightweight classes, there seemed scant chance of its extending farther up the capacity scale. After all, the two-stroke owed its superior performance to disc valves with side-facing carburettors,

On the way to the first of his four world sidecar championships, Eric Oliver dominates the Swiss GP with the help of passenger Denis Jenkinson

and its stamina to tiny cylinders with water cooling. Since side-facing carburettors restrict cylinder coupling to two-abreast, a five-hundred built on those proven principles would need anything from four to ten pairs of cylinders in tandem – hardly a practical layout for a solo.

But four-stroke confidence was misplaced. Diligent two-stroke development put stamina into larger cylinders – and Agostini joined Yamaha. MV, who had earlier gone to three cylinders to cut width, and to four-valve heads to boost power and reliability, switched back to four cylinders (still with four valves) in a desperate bid to stem the tide of two-stroke power.

Beyond a brace of 500 cc titles by Phil Read in 1973 and 1974, it did not work. First Yamaha (through Agostini) then Suzuki (through Barry Sheene) toppled MV off their remaining perches. Yet the exciting Suzuki RG 500 – the disc-valve square four on which Sheene's 500 cc mastery was based – was virtually a quartet of MZ cylinders on a common crankcase, with the identical specific power (200 bhp/litre at 10,800 to 11,000 rpm) that Walter Kaaden had put at Ernst Degner's disposal in the 125 cc championship no fewer than 15 years earlier. In engine design, it was abundantly clear where the credit belonged – although tyres and suspension, with air springing

front and rear, had made great progress since the MZ days.

Clean sweep

Thus, well within 30 years of the start of the world championships, the unblown two-stroke had risen from complete obscurity to dominance of all five solo classes. It remained only for it to take over the 500 cc sidecar class too. And this it did in 1975, when Rolf Steinhausen, driving an outfit powered by a König flat-four disc-valve outboard engine, finally put an end to the greatest monopoly ever established in the world championships – BMW's incredible stranglehold on the sidecar class.

In spite of the greater straight-line speed of the early postwar Gilera fours, single-cylinder Norton outfits had scooped the first five world championships, four titles falling to the indomitable Eric Oliver (who pioneered the kneeler to reduce overall height, hence frontal area) and one to Cyril Smith. Then it was the turn of BMW who, from 1954, took 19 consecutive manufacturer's titles and 19 individual titles, the latter punctuated only by Helmut Fath's heroic win on his home-built Urs four in 1968 and Horst Owesle's championship on the same outfit three years later.

In addition to a brilliant string of German

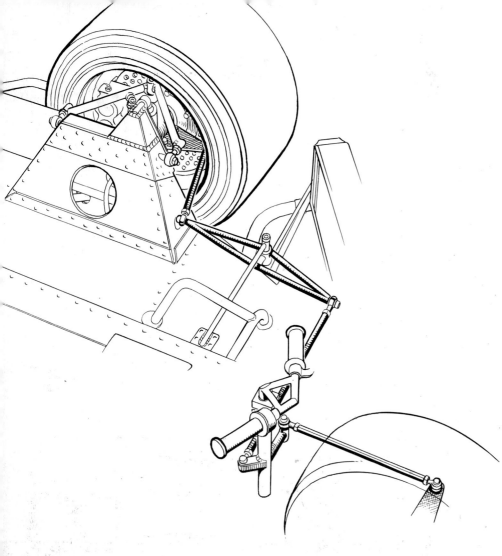

Sidecar-wheel steering on Alain Michel's Seymaz chassis. Both front and sidecar wheels are linked to the steering stem but the sidecar wheel turns less than the front

and Swiss drivers, BMW's trump card was an engine and transmission layout particularly suited to sidecar racing. With no banking involved, the transverse cylinders were no handicap (as they can be in a solo) and the engine could be slung extremely low, so reducing roll and facilitating drifting. The exposure of the cylinders gave ideal cooling and the enclosed shaft drive was more than a match for the arduous duty.

Only an outfit with an equally low centre of gravity and more power could beat the BMW – and that was the secret of Fath's success with the Urs, as it was of the two-stroke's subsequent takeover. Indeed, two-strokes would have taken over sooner had catalogue outfits been available. As it was, crews had to cobble their own outfits from a separate engine, transmission and chassis – and the two-stroke's initial onslaught was blunted by transmission failures.

Once two-stroke power was established in the sidecar class, development switched to the chassis. Telescopic front forks had long since given way to the pivoted type, which bypassed the "stiction" due to side loading in bends. Now, solo-type front and rear forks were abandoned altogether in favour of car-

type suspension with ultra-wide tyres and hub-centre steering.

Although this robbed cornering of much of the popular spectacle of passenger acrobatics, it was a logical move for a twin-track vehicle, keeping the wheels upright regardless of body roll and so allowing faster cornering. Another development, aimed at reducing passenger antics still further, hence reducing wind resistance, was to move the sidecar wheel forward far enough to prevent bike-over-chair loops, then counteract the consequent understeer by linking the sidecar wheel to the steering gear.

Radical sidecar development

But the most radical sidecar development of all occurred in 1978, when Swiss driver Rolf Biland sparked off a fierce controversy with his Beo outfit. In this, apart from helping to push-start, the passenger was virtually no more than human ballast, sitting in a kart-type seat with neither need nor opportunity to perform any acrobatics.

The Beo's underlying principle was simplicity itself. Biland decided to apply the conventional left-hand cornering technique – driving the bike round the airborne sidecar wheel – to right-handers as well. In other words, on right-hand bends the rear

and sidecar wheels swopped roles, the sidecar wheel driving and the rear wheel lifting.

Obviously, this necessitated driving both wheels, so the Yamaha four-cylinder engine was placed between the rear and sidecar wheels, which were driven by half-shafts from the opposite ends of a large-diameter cross-shaft that was chain-driven from the gearbox sprocket.

The internals of the cross-shaft were secret but were clearly concerned with the problem of initiating a turn in either direction. Once the inner wheel is airborne and the outer one still driving, there is no problem. But if the cross-shaft were solid it would be almost impossible to start a turn because the two-wheel drive, with wide tyres, would tend to keep the outfit on a straight course, with the front tyre scrubbing, whenever the handlebar was turned.

An ordinary differential would have spun the inside wheel as soon as it lifted and so cut the drive. Although a limited-slip differential might have solved that problem, Biland begrudged the power loss and extra weight (at upward of 500 lb, the outfit was already embarrassingly heavy).

Naturally, hub-centre steering was used and all the wheels (13 in, with 10 in and 8 in tyres) had car-type suspension – indeed, a stiff anti-roll bar connected the rear and sidecar wheels. The net result was faster cornering in both directions, easy drifting, absence of wheelspin and better braking from the two March Formula 2 ventilated discs with four-piston calipers (the rear brake was inboard, on the cross-shaft).

However, no sooner had Biland and his passenger Kenny Williams proved the Beo's superiority by winning the 1978 world championship than the FIM, at a mere two months' notice, banned their outfit – and not only theirs but any others with ultra-wide tyres, car-type suspension, sidecar-wheel steering or hub-centre steering.

Ostensibly, the FIM justified the immediacy of the ban on the grounds of safety – a farcical claim, since the prohibited design features (transverse suspension, wide tyres, hub-centre steering, sidecar-wheel steering and two-wheel drive) actually enhance stability as well as boosting cornering speeds.

Not surprisingly, the reaction of the progressive crews and constructors was swift and hostile – so much so that the FIM felt obliged to convene a special meeting in Geneva. There, they produced a face-saving compromise that seemed only to compound the farce. It was to run two world championships – one under the old rules, the other under the new!

Foresight

Enormous as all these changes were, not one of them was unpredictable. But hind-

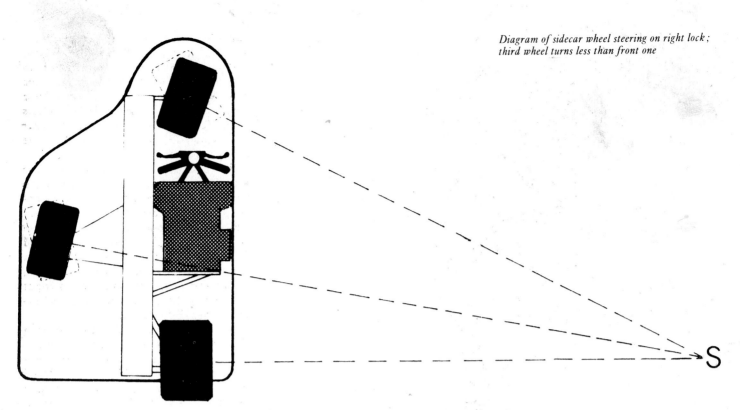

sight never won a championship, and the wisest manufacturers were those who used foresight instead. Long before the war it was well known that more gas could be pumped into a cylinder than the piston could draw in unaided, and that the consequent gain in power would more than offset that spent in driving the blower. Yet many years passed before blowing invaded the GPs.

It was never a secret that air drag is the greatest thief of engine power in racing, increasingly so as speed climbs. Yet more than 20 years elapsed between proof of the speed-boosting effect of streamlining in record breaking and its adoption in classic racing, with the added bonus of rider protection in the event of a spill.

In the earliest days of the internal combustion engine, the brilliant Dr Fred Lanchester proved mathematically that the specific power potential of a cylinder (its bhp/litre) goes up as its size goes down. Hence, for a given total engine capacity, a twin can be more powerful than a single, a four more than a twin, and so on. The lighter pistons, connecting rods and valves enable the smaller cylinders to operate safely at higher speeds and so breathe and burn their fill of gas more often. Also, breathing is enhanced by the relatively larger size of the ports (whether two-stroke or four-stroke) in a smaller cylinder. As cylinder size is increased the area of the ports goes up as the square of the linear dimensions, whereas the volume to be filled goes up as the cube.

True, Lanchester's theories also showed that the process of boosting engine power by using more and smaller cylinders is subject to the law of diminishing returns, because of increasing friction losses and increasing gas drag in narrower passages. But when Honda

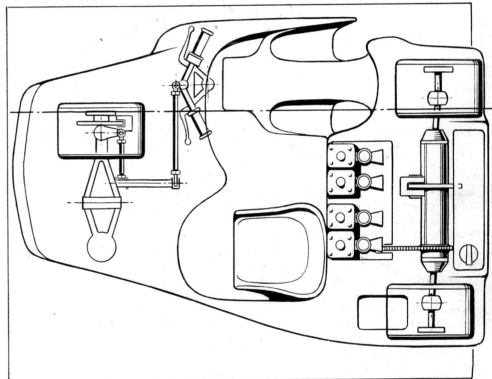

and Suzuki quit racing at the end of 1967 they were both about to replace their 50 cc twins with more-powerful threes. Notwithstanding diminishing returns, that suggests that the gains still offset the losses, in the search for power, at least down to a cylinder size of 16 cc.

Similarly, paired valves had long been known to cut reciprocating weight, so operating reliably at higher speeds, and to enhance breathing by providing a greater "window" area. Nor was there ever any doubt of their additional advantages – greater turbulence, a more compact com-

Layout of the Beo outfit on which Rolf Biland (kneeling) and Kenny Williams (sitting) won the 1978 world sidecar championship. Note the hub-centre steering with transverse suspension; the central position of the Yamaha engine, with chain drive from the gearbox to a cross-shaft from which half-shafts drive the rear and sidecar wheels. The rear disc brake is mounted on the cross-shaft, the front wheel is considerably offset to the left, and the fuel tank is at the rear

This low-level shot from Quarter Bridge in the 1978 Sidecar TT illustrates the Beo's cornering advantage. The rear wheel is airborne while the sidecar wheel continues to drive the outfit – the opposite of normal left-hand cornering. The radiator is in the front left-hand corner

bustion space and the shorter flame path from a central plug.

As to the two-stroke, despite its unpredictable temperament, there was early evidence for its eventual takeover. Indeed, I predicted it in my TT Technical Review for *Motor Cycle* several years before it came about. This I did by annually comparing the best four-strokes and two-strokes on the basis of bhp/litre/1,000 rpm – a yardstick recommended to me by Australian Phil

Irving, one of the shrewdest of engineers.

In the early 1960s, although the higher-revving four-stroke had the edge in sheer power, the equivalent two-stroke was consistently better off by 2-3 bhp/litre/1,000 rpm. Once the bearing problems of the two-stroke could be solved, thereby closing the gap in peak rpm, it would have a substantial power advantage over the four-stroke.

Prejudice

Why, then, were multis, four-valve heads and two-strokes so long in asserting themselves? What kept the big two-valve single-cylinder four-stroke ahead for so long? Largely, the prejudice of one man – Norton

race chief Joe Craig, whose phenomenal concentration on the engine type of his choice offset the theoretical advantages of more advanced designs for many years.

Early in the war, I attended a Sunbeam Club talk by Joe Craig, in which he denounced multis, paired valves and two-strokes for racing, whereas in retrospect their successes were inevitable. Another delaying factor was the lag between engineering theory and engineering practice – it took time to acquire the art of building compact powerful multis.

The riders

As in soccer, British successes in the earliest

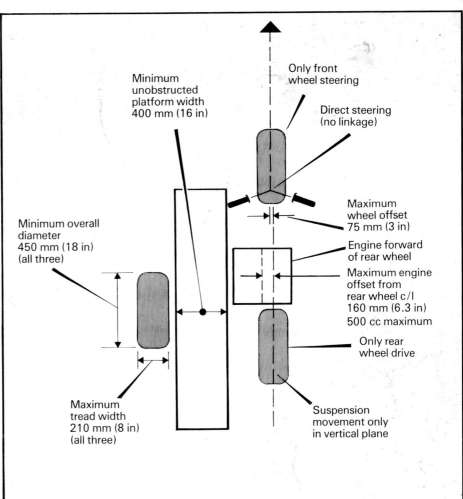

Minimum unobstructed platform width 400 mm (16 in)

Only front wheel steering

Direct steering (no linkage)

Minimum overall diameter 450 mm (18 in) (all three)

Maximum wheel offset 75 mm (3 in)

Engine forward of rear wheel

Maximum engine offset from rear wheel c/l 160 mm (6.3 in) 500 cc maximum

Only rear wheel drive

Maximum tread width 210 mm (8 in) (all three)

Suspension movement only in vertical plane

Restrictions introduced by the FIM at the end of 1978 to curb racing sidecar design. Driver reaction was so hostile that the FIM quickly backed down and separated the world sidecar championship into two classes – an arrangement that proved almost equally unpopular

days of classic racing fostered the notion that natives of the British Isles and Commonwealth were blessed with some special ingredient in their make-up that assured them of everlasting superiority on the track. Dash without foolhardiness, perhaps? A unique blend of courage and self-discipline? Sang-froid and skill under the stress of fierce competition? Certainly there was no denying the calibre of the early British stars – the exquisite grace and razor-sharp tactical sense of Stanley Woods; the superhuman dedication of Jimmie Guthrie, who blossomed at an age when most riders ´retired; the fluent artistry of Wal Handley; the sheer dynamism of Jimmy Simpson – first to lap the TT course at 60, 70 and

80 mph – and likewise Freddie Frith, first to lap it at 90.

Nor was there any doubting the superiority of Britain's postwar top-notchers – Les Graham, Geoff Duke, Fergus Anderson, Ray Amm, John Surtees, Bob McIntyre, Bill Lomas, Gary Hocking, Jim Redman, Mike Hailwood, Bill Ivy, Phil Read and Barry Sheene. They were all eminently worthy of their successes.

But whereas prewar British chauvinists once sought to explain occasional foreign victories by saying that the lucky riders were "blessed with a British temperament" or living on borrowed time – or that their machines had an overwhelming edge in speed – no such excuses were possible after the war.

Riders from so many countries made their mark in the world championships, especially in the smaller classes, that it was clear that top talent was a world-wide phenomenon. To mention only a few, there were Dario Ambrosini, Enrico Lorenzetti, Carlo Ubbiali

and Tarquinio Provini from Italy; Werner Haas from West Germany; Ernst Degner from East Germany; Luigi Taveri from Switzerland; Santiago Herrero from Spain; Fumio Ito and Takazumi Katayama from Japan; Johnny Cecotto from Venezuela and Jarno Saarinen from Finland.

But the rider who did most to demolish the myth that British, Irish and Commonwealth riders had an exclusive corner in the championships was the Italian idol Giacomo Agostini. Taking over the works 250 cc Moto Morini from Tarquinio Provini in 1964, he gave instant evidence of world class by skittling Provini's Italian lap records and robbing him of the national championship. Joining the MV team the following year, he made an immediate impact on the world 350 and 500 cc championships and eventually won a record 15 of them before retiring at the end of 1977 – by which time American riders, too, such as Kenny Roberts, Steve Baker and Pat Hennen – were showing championship class.

For some obscure reason this worldwide spread of talent never infected the sidecar class. Once Willie Noll (BMW) took over from Eric Oliver (Norton) in 1954, the title stayed in German or Swiss hands until George O'Dell (Yamaha) put Britain briefly back on top in 1977.

Three golden eras

Various influences have caused peaks and troughs in the popularity of classic racing and there have so far been three golden eras. The first, in the late 1930s, was curtailed by the war – but for which there would have been a fierce battle between a fascinating assortment of supercharged machines in all classes.

The blown 500 cc Gilera four had already deposed the BMW twin. And the water-cooled AJS vee-four had challenged the Gilera late in 1939 by notching the first 100-mph lap in the Ulster Grand Prix. Ajay's spike-finned Porcupine twin was originally designed for blowing, although converted after the war. The most exciting British challenge in the class, however, was the Velocette Roarer twin, with geared crankshafts, one driving the blower, the other the shaft-drive transmission.

Those two blown twins were testimony to a prewar spirit of enterprise and initiative that could well have been the salvation of the British industry when it collapsed 30 years later.

In the 250 cc class DKW were already developing a 40 bhp split-single (with eccentric-vane compressor) to supersede the 30 bhp one (with piston-type pump) that gave Ewald Kluge the 1938 and 1939 European championships. But Benelli's beautiful little water-cooled four, reputed to give

52 bhp at 10,000 rpm, would surely have given the DKWs something to think about. Anyway, Benelli had hedged their bets by hanging a supercharger on the left-hand end of the crankshaft of their very fast double-knocker single, while Moto Guzzi had long since succeeded in blowing their flat single and had recently given it fuel injection.

With a split-twin version of their new eccentric-vane job, DKW had every intention of staying on top of the 350 cc class. But NSU were patiently eliminating the bugs from a blown parallel twin that proved its straight-line potential after the war by breaking the world 350 and 500 cc speed records – the larger machine being the first to top 200 mph (in 1956).

The second golden era spanned the mid-1950s, when every European factory of note fielded a star-studded team on the finest machines its engineers could produce. The big single was fighting desperately to stay ahead of the fours, yet there were also twins from NSU, BMW and AJS, a three from DKW and a vee-eight from Moto Guzzi.

Streamlining was introduced and progressed rapidly from steering-head cowls to full-frontal dustbins. MZ had only just started to develop the disc-valve two-stroke – but in Ingolstadt Helmut Görg so effectively converted a 250 cc DKW parallel twin, with a cylindrical rotary valve, into a 350 cc three with piston-controlled induction that

Les Graham on the Mountain road in the fateful 1953 Senior TT. The Earles-type pivoted front fork was later abandoned, as were the siamesed exhaust pipes

his machines were a match for the phenomenal Moto Guzzi flat singles and were beaten only by the superior riding ability of the Italian team, with British and Commonwealth riders.

Finally, in spite of Walter Zeller's courage and skill, BMW failed to regain the solo supremacy their power surplus had given them in 1938, and concentrated instead on exploiting their fundamental superiority in the sidecar class. This wonderful era came to an end when the individual withdrawals of NSU, Norton, AJS, BMW and DKW were supplemented by the massive Italian pull-out of Gilera, Moto Guzzi and FB Mondial in 1957.

Underlying the third golden era, in the mid-1960s, was the all-out technical struggle between two-stroke and four-stroke. For the most part this was an all-Japanese confrontation for the simple reason that it was fought out in the 50, 125 and 250 cc classes, with Suzuki and Yamaha mounting the two-stroke challenge against the four-stroke Hondas. Four-stroke supremacy in the larger classes, through MV Agusta, was to continue for several years beyond the end of this era, which came with Honda's withdrawal in 1967.

FROM SIMPLE TO COMPLEX
PREWAR FOUR-STROKES

TODAY'S world-championship machines are out-and-out grand-prix specials, built with scant regard to cost and bearing little or no resemblance to catalogue roadsters. It was not always so. When the European championships started in 1924, racing machines were still virtually hotted-up versions of standard models. And since the motor-cycle market then was even more cost conscious than it is now, most catalogue sports machines, hence most racers, were simple four-stroke singles with pushrod-operated overhead valves.

It was no secret even then that multi-cylinder engines had a greater power potential. But the single had long been the industry's bread and butter and several able engineers had lavished intensive development on it. So long as it won races and championships there was no incentive to design exotic machines.

Indeed, at that time overhead valves had not completely dislodged side valves. Light-alloy pistons and cylinder heads were something of a novelty, as was dry-sump oiling – and engine compression ratios averaged only about 6:1. True, there were some outstanding examples of technical foresight. For example, the Moto Guzzi that won the first European 500 cc title (at Monza) combined such advanced features as oversquare cylinder dimensions (88 × 82 mm), a four-valve head and a bevel-driven overhead camshaft – besides the horizontal cylinder, backward-rotating crankshaft and integral transmission with gear primary drive that still characterised the factory's world-beating three-fifties more than 30 years later.

But it was to be a few years yet before overhead camshafts became a *sine qua non*; a few more before paired valves enjoyed their first brief taste of glory; and more years still before undersquare (long-stroke) cylinders went out of fashion. Meanwhile the pushrod two-valver was the bike to beat and typical examples were the 500 cc Sunbeam, 350 cc AJS and 250 cc New Imperial.

Of these, none was closer to catalogue specification than the superbly engineered Sunbeam, for the works racing machines were simply Model 90 sportsters meticulously prepared, and the Model 90 itself was no more than a high-performance version of the elegant Model 9 roadster. The company had switched from a highly competitive side-valve unit only just in time for the

Lightweight TT win for Bob Foster (250 cc New Imperial) in 1936 while on his honeymoon

introduction of the European championships but there was nothing exotic in the new ohv design – simply first-class engineering practice, execution and design.

At first the engine had a single exhaust port, long converging pushrods and three concentric springs for each valve, while the separate gearbox crossed the drive over from left to right (as did the integral box on the Moto Guzzis). But for 1925 Sunbeam switched to their better-known twin-port layout, dry-sump oiling and an overhead camshaft. At the same time they were among the pioneers of hairpin valve springs designed to bypass the destructive surge of coil springs.

Alas, the ohc engine lacked the pep of its predecessor, for the absence of pushrod flexure made nonsense of a cam form designed to take account of it. So pushrods were back for 1926 (parallel this time) and the single hairpin springs were doubled up to set a fashion that became almost universal so long as valve gear was exposed and there was no restriction on space. Even when full valve enclosure took over, some manufacturers stuck to hairpins (occasionally overlapped to save space); many years were to pass before cam and spring design were well enough matched for coil springs to function reliably at racing revs.

It was that conventional, reliable parallel-pushrod design – with hefty flywheels and a deep cluster of cooling fins between the

exhaust ports of the cast-iron head – that brought Sunbeam their greatest renown in classic road racing, from 1926 to 1929. That was no mean feat, for the team's top two riders were poles apart physically – Graham Walker as burly as they come while the tiny Charlie Dodson weighed a mere 119 lb, 13 lb below today's minimum weight limit! Indeed, Dodson's specially tailored riding position would have suited no one else, so close to the saddle did the footrests, knee-grips and handlebar have to be grouped.

If the big Sunbeam exemplified the merits of straightforward engineering superbly executed, the 350 cc AJS reflected the sheer pace and diversity of experiment in the years when it won the title – 1924, 1926, 1927 and 1929. To start with it was already a bit distinctive, for the exhaust pipe was uncommonly fat ($2\frac{3}{4}$ in outside diameter) – hence the catalogue name Big Port – while the cylinder head was secured by a transverse stirrup and two long tie rods. What is more, when slightly undergeared in the 1924 Junior TT, it had revved up to the then-outrageous speed of 7,000 rpm, although the valves and their seats had protested against such cruelty by disintegrating.

For the next five or six years, however, extreme flexibility characterised all aspects of its design. Lubrication went from the new-fangled dry sump back to total loss (with a foot-operated pump) then to dry sump again. Valves switched from being identical in size to a larger inlet and back again before settling down to the accepted differential. Relative port sizes did a similar shuffle.

Rocker material changed from steel to duralumin and back. Pushrods were forsaken for overhead camshafts, then reinstated before being finally abandoned. Transmission made the transition from three speeds to four not once but twice. Brakes, at first coupled, went to independent control by left and right pedals before conforming to the present hand and foot layout. And front suspension, originally by girder fork, had a brief flirtation with leading links before reverting to girders again.

From all this frenzied activity eventually emerged a four-speeder with chain-driven overhead camshaft that was to form the basis of both the prewar and postwar 7R models.

The 250 cc New Imperial that made its mark on the European championship from 1926 to 1935 started, as did several other

Left: *technical foresight. The Moto Guzzi flat-single on which Guido Mentasti won the first European 500 cc championship (in 1924) had oversquare cylinder dimensions (88 × 82 mm), a bevel-driven overhead camshaft, four valves, dry-sump oiling, an integral gearbox and a backward-rotating crankshaft*

Left, below: *in the 500 cc Moto Guzzi vee-twin, even firing intervals were obtained by spacing the crankpins at 120 degrees. The caged-roller big-end bearings were split and the two crank throws were separated by a middle main bearing*

uphold New Imperial's reputation.

Shortly after the factory switched to integral construction of engine and gearbox on some of its roadsters, the 250 cc racer followed suit. To provide proper lubrication for the primary drive, and rigid alignment of the shafts, the crankcase and gearcase were cast in one, with the engine running backward and driving the clutch through a pair of gears. A gallon of oil was contained in a ribbed compartment hugging the front of the crankcase and the bottom of the gearbox. To save weight, magnesium was used for the casting.

The top half of the engine was unchanged, with an iron cylinder liner in an aluminium muff, an aluminium-bronze head giving a compression ratio of 10·5:1, and hairpin valve springs. For all its straightforwardness, there was no doubting the efficiency of the design. For, at a time when the New Imp's rivals were exploiting such advanced trends as rear springing, overhead camshafts, four-valve heads, twin carburettors and supercharging, it kept up its strong challenge to the blown DKW split singles and, in Bob Foster's hands, won the 1936 Lightweight TT – the last of the Isle of Man classics to fall to a pushrod engine. Alas, New Imperial quit classic racing at the end of that year.

Paired valves

Very few engineers nowadays would contemplate designing a racing four-stroke without paired valves – they were so patently an essential ingredient in both the performance and the reliability of the world-beating Hondas of the 1960s. Before the war, though, the four-valver was the exception in classic racing, not the rule.

Rudge Whitworth were the chief exponents and much the most successful. They started with the valves in parallel pairs in a pent-roof head (now the accepted arrangement), switched to an ingenious radial layout in a part-spherical head and even used a combination of the two in the 500 cc engine – parallel inlets for deep breathing, radial exhausts for cool running. Excelsior took the fully radial theme a stage further by giving each inlet valve an independent port and carburettor.

Considering the spectacular successes of paired valves in the early 1930s – Rudge

eminent designs, with a decision to break free from dependence on proprietary engines, in this case JAP. A straightforward long-stroke pushrod job, the new engine was one of the first to be fitted with a rev counter. Reasonably competitive right from the start, it soon acquired dry-sump oiling, four speeds, downdraught induction and the then-fashionable pistol-grip petrol tank.

In the early 1930s, while still a match for

the best in classic racing, it spread its fame to Brooklands, where it was the first two-fifty to establish world records at more than 100 mph. Doubled up into a 60-degree vee-twin, it won the *Motor Cycle* cup for the first British multi to tuck 100 miles into an hour, then lifted the 500 cc lap record to 115·82 mph. But the twin's handling was never a match for its speed and, in road racing, it was left to the 250 cc single to

alone won European championships in all three solo classes and put up some shattering TT performances, some of them straight from the drawing board – the failure of the four-valve layout to catch on then, rather than 30 years later, reflects the extent to which designers were mesmerised by Joe Craig's gospel of two-valve superiority.

The benefits of paired valves are twofold – thermo-dynamic and mechanical. Under the first heading there is more complete cylinder filling because of the larger total "window" area of two inlet valves, while turbulence is increased as the gas streams impinge on one another. Then, since the smaller head sizes allow the angle between the stems to be reduced, there is a much more compact combustion space, especially if squish segments are incorporated front and rear. Finally the sparking plug can be put in the middle of the head (impossible with two large valves), so shortening the flame path and speeding combustion.

On the mechanical side, the great reduction in individual reciprocating weights makes it possible for springs of reasonable poundage to keep valve motion under proper control (following the cam contour faithfully, not flinging off the peak of the lobe) much farther up the rev scale. This brings two advantages. First, by suitably extending the valve timing and increasing carburettor size, the designer can exploit the freer breathing at higher engine speeds and so get more power. Second, the better valve control lessens the likelihood of

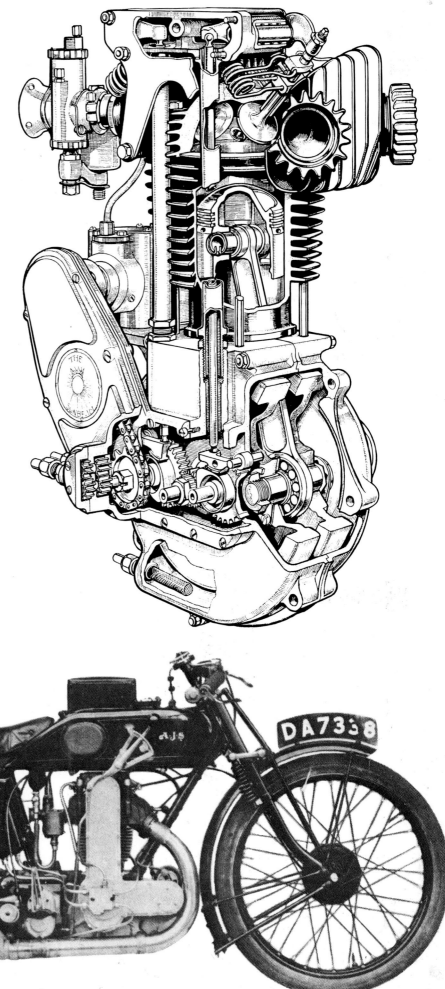

Right: Typical pushrod two-valve engine of the late 1920s, the 493 cc (80 × 98 mm) Sunbeam. Note the hairpin valve springs, deep exhaust finning, three plain piston rings and double gear-type oil pump outboard of the magneto drive

Below: in a period of fluid design and considerable success during the late 1920s, this was the first 350 cc AJS with a chain-driven overhead camshaft. Dry sump lubrication was used. The valve rockers are in duralumin. Magneto is chain driven in front of crankcase

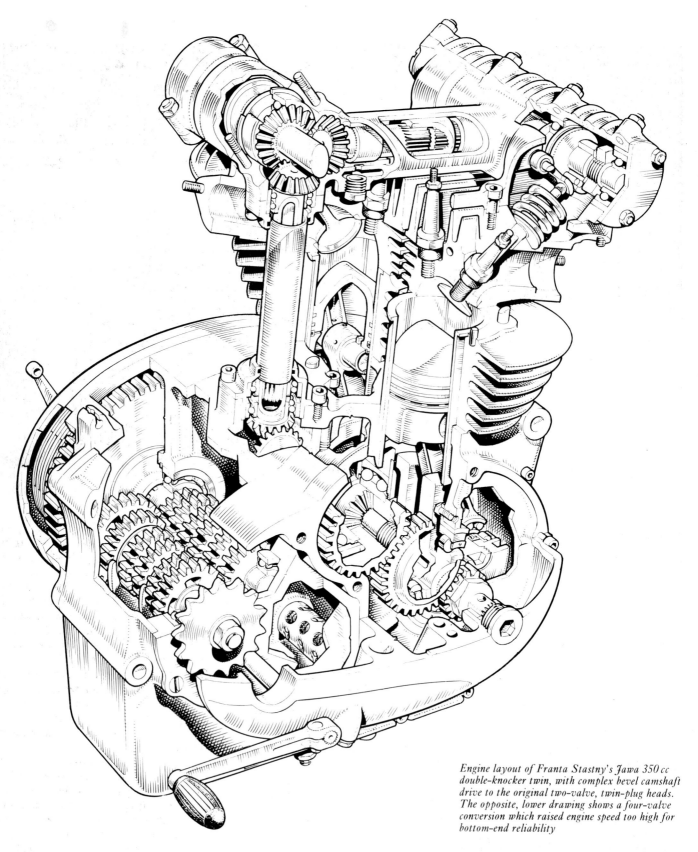

Engine layout of Franta Stastny's Jawa 350cc double-knocker twin, with complex bevel camshaft drive to the original two-valve, twin-plug heads. The opposite, lower drawing shows a four-valve conversion which raised engine speed too high for bottom-end reliability

serious engine damage during an inadvertent bout of over-revving.

Incidentally, smaller valves are stronger and the exhausts run cooler because their seat area (through which they dissipate heat) is larger relative to their head area (through which they absorb it).

But although all these four-valve benefits were there to be exploited in the 1930s no less than in the 1960s, the emphasis of the Rudge/Excelsior approach was different

from Honda's. Whereas Honda went the whole hog, pushing peak revs to undreamed-of heights by using tiny cylinders and double overhead camshafts to cut reciprocating weights to the absolute minimum, Rudge and Excelsior stuck to single cylinders, pushrods and rockers and concentrated rather on the combustion advantages.

Indeed, had they switched to double knockers on their four-valve singles, the valve gear would most likely have proved

"too fast for the big end". This problem beset Jawa in 1963, when they followed Honda's lead to paired valves. They converted the heads on their very fast works double-knocker 350cc twin, so boosting peak revs from 10,600 rpm to 11,400, and immediately ran into failure of the big ends, which must already have been pretty near the safe limit with the two-valve heads. For that size of engine, Honda never used fewer than four cylinders and finished up with six.

Bob Foster rounds Ballacraine in winning the 1936 Lightweight TT on a works 250 cc New Imperial. With gear primary drive, the engine ran backward and the one-gallon magnesium oil sump hugged the front of the crankcase and the bottom of the integral gearbox

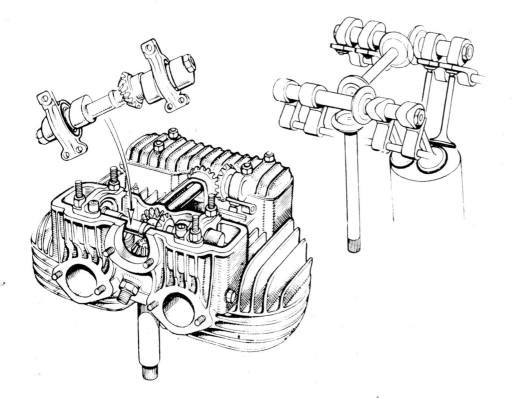

Three ways to do it

Rudge first made an impact on the European championships in 1927, after development engineer George Hack splayed the previously parallel exhaust ports of the 500 cc (85 × 88 mm) engine for better cooling, and enlarged all port sizes to boost peak power to 28 bhp at 5,200 rpm and top speed to 100 mph. Yet it was not until 1930, when Hack introduced radial valves on a new three-fifty (70 × 90 mm), that they won the title chase (in Belgium) – not only in that class with the new design but in the 500 cc division too, with the parallel-valve layout.

The debut of the radial-valver was sensational. Three machines were completed only just in time for the Junior TT (the toughest 350 cc grand prix of them all) and there was time only for bench testing and a brief gallop up the road by Tyrell Smith before they were shipped to the Isle of Man. In training, the pistons proved crack-prone and spares were scarce.

Estimating that brand-new pistons would just about last the race (264 miles in those days), George Hack gambled on saving the last three for race day. His estimate proved uncannily accurate, for those pistons barely survived and the three Rudges massacred the field at record speed with Tyrell Smith first, Ernie Nott second and Graham Walker third. Four days later Wal Handley and Graham Walker pulled off a one-two in the rain-drenched Senior TT, so proving that the old four-valve layout was as much a race-winner as the new.

The following year (1931) Rudge scaled down the new engine to 250 cc and, in the Lightweight TT, practically duplicated the previous year's Junior clean sweep, being robbed of third place by a slack tappet in

Spearheading a Rudge 1-2-3, Jimmy Simpson rounds Ramsey Hairpin on the last four-valver to win a TT for 27 years – the 1934 Lightweight

the last lap, but again setting lap and race records. And they went on to take the European 250 and 350 cc titles in France.

Most remarkable of all, radial-valve Rudges finished first, second and third in the 1934 Lightweight TT more than a year after the factory had found racing too costly and pulled out. The winning team – Jimmy Simpson, Ernie Nott and Graham Walker – was a private syndicate formed by Walker himself. That sad withdrawal by Rudge helped the two-valve disciples bury the four-valve concept for more than 25 years. For, although Excelsior hopped on the radial-valve band wagon in 1933, they failed to capitalise on their initial spectacular success.

Rudge's radial valve operation was ingenuity itself, for it differed from the established layout only at cylinder-head level. Up to the top of the pushrods the layout was conventional, but there were no fewer than six roller-bearing rockers on the head. The first two, operated by the pushrods, did not open the right-hand valves directly. Instead,

they depressed the right-hand ends of a pair of transverse rockers that opened the valves. The left-hand ends of those transverse rockers lifted the inner ends of another pair of transverse rockers that opened the left-hand valves.

Later on, an H-shaped contact pad was interposed between the second and third rocker in each train to give a pure rolling motion but the contact between the first and second rockers, which lay at right angles to one another, was not so happy. A further advantage of the radial disposition of the valves was that it allowed more metal between the exhaust valve seats, so reducing the risk of cracks developing.

Incidentally, Rudge led the way with four-speed transmission a year before the championships started. (The gearbox was notorious for its prolific use of rollers between pinions and shafts, which made assembly a nightmare.) Another Rudge hallmark that anticipated much later developments was coupled brakes with a pressure-limiting coil spring in the rear-brake rod.

The two-carburettor way

With two or three years to think things over,

Excelsior decided to upstage Rudge in radial valves, enlisting the design talents of Ike Hatch, chief engineer for Burney and Blackburne. The Excelsior engine, too, had a part-spherical combustion chamber and central plug. But whereas the Rudge had a single carburettor feeding a horizontal tract split right and left, Ike Hatch settled for two entirely separate tracts, splayed and down-draught, and each with its own Amal carburettor. That complication and even more elaborate valve gear earned the engine the nickname of the Mechanical Marvel.

There were two camshafts, high in the crankcase mouth front and rear. From each, a steeply sloping pushrod reached up to operate a piston sliding in a bronze bush in a separate rocker housing. Side by side on the flat top of each piston, bore the inner ends of a pair of rockers, making rolling line contact. Each rocker was supported in three roller bearings and its outer arm, with threaded adjuster, actuated one valve tip.

Lubrication of the valve gear was a strange mixture: grease gun for the 12 rocker bearings; main oil supply for the rocker boxes themselves; and an adjustable drip feed of a different oil for the valve guides. The rest of the engine was both

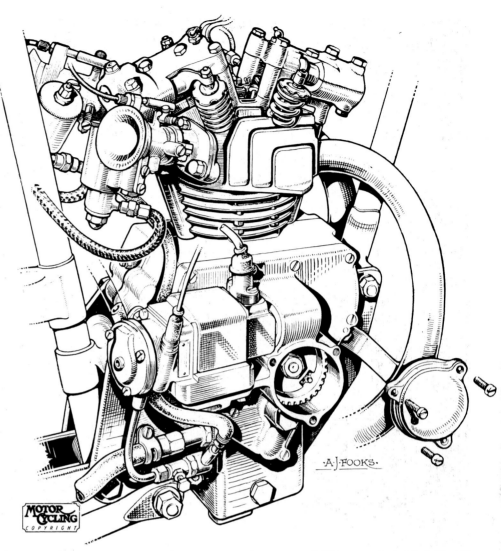

The 1934 version of the Excelsior Mechanical Marvel engine had Bowden carburettors with butterfly throttles. The BTH magneto was driven by skew gears from the intermediate timing pinion

robust and up-to-date, with a light-alloy connecting rod, needle-roller big end, and forged piston.

Like the first radial Rudge, the Mechanical Marvel virtually went straight from the drawing board to the Isle of Man, where it scored a record-breaking win in the 1933 Lightweight TT (Sid Gleave, 71·59 mph) and would have come second, too, if Wal Handley's engine had not failed with only half a lap to go. Alas, it was a flash in the pan, for Excelsior had scant success in the European championship (third place by Leo Davenport at Saxtorp, Sweden) and the close season was spent hunting for higher performance.

Yet, for all the 30 lb slashed off the weight, the change to Bowden carburettors (with butterfly throttles) and the lengthening of the connecting rods, the Mechanical Marvel proved much less competitive in 1934 than it had been initially. In desperation the makers raced conventional overhead-camshaft two-valvers in 1935, although without success, then crossed the two engine types for 1936.

Made in two sizes (250 and 350 cc) that hybrid four-valver had an aluminium-bronze head with a single overhead camshaft and six Rudge-style rockers. In the Excelsior engine, however, the flanged pad was placed between the first and second rockers in each train, since that awkward contact seemed in most need of improvement. With Tyrell Smith's victory in the European 250 cc championship in Saxony, results perked up a bit, but not enough to justify the complexity, for reliability was below par and speed no higher than that of rival two-valvers. Excelsior had had enough and the four-valver faded from the prewar classic scene.

Camshafts get a hold

Notwithstanding Moto Guzzi's inspired example, overhead camshafts did not really come into their own in classic racing until the late 1920s, when first Velocette (1926 Junior TT) then Norton (1927 Senior) won gruelling long-distance races with new designs incorporating bevel drive to a central camshaft and rockers from there to the two valves. In both cases Alec Bennett was the rider.

Statistically, the Norton proved the more successful in the long run. But in engineering terms there are good reasons for awarding Velocette at least an equal share of the credit – and not just because they made their ohc impact first. Norton had previously campaigned a pushrod five-hundred with considerable success – including record-breaking Senior TT wins in 1924 (Bennett) and 1926 (Stanley Woods) – so their conversion to overhead camshafts can virtually be seen as merely a change in valve operation.

Velocette, by contrast, took a bolder and much bigger step forward when, in 1925, they switched straight from small two-strokes to an ohc three-fifty that soon achieved spectacular success – winning the Junior TT not only in 1926 but again in 1928 (Bennett) and 1929 (Freddie Hicks), meanwhile taking second place in 1927 (Harold Willis) and second and third places (behind Jimmy Simpson, ohc AJS) in that year's European 350 cc championship on Germany's tortuous Nürburgring.

Moreover, the Norton team's phenomenal string of classic successes, both before and after the war, owed as much to superior riding talent as to any technical edge. Just how much that edge was exaggerated can be seen from the results of the 1936, 1937 and 1938 Senior TTs when Stanley Woods, who had earlier won five TT races for Norton, rode for Velocette. On each occasion he finished second to the winning Norton – a mere 18 seconds behind Jimmie Guthrie in 1936, 15 seconds behind Freddie Frith the following year and 15·2 seconds behind Harold Daniell in 1938.

Yet that was the period when Norton were reaching their landmark of 50 bhp from 500 cc, whereas Velocette never claimed more than 38. Exaggeration by Norton? Modesty or camouflage by Velocette? A bit of both maybe. But in hard-fought races of three hours' duration such slender margins certainly do not reflect a difference of 12 bhp in engine power.

In basic design (the work of Percy Goodman) the ohc Velocette was distinctive from the start, for the primary drive was inboard of the secondary. This brought several advantages. First, the crankcase was unusually narrow and stiff, with the two lipped roller main bearings directly in line with both crankcase and cylinder walls, so giving really rigid support to the slim flywheel assembly. Second, since the engine sprocket was hard up against the left-hand main bearing, shaft flexure under load was kept to a minimum. Third, the gearbox final-drive sprocket could quickly be changed to alter the overall ratios, and only the secondary chain had to be adjusted to suit.

In the camshaft drive, the upper and lower vertical bevels had different numbers of teeth, so as to spread the load while achieving the overall reduction of 2:1. The bevels were connected by a slotted shaft and two tongued couplings.

The soundness of the design is shown in the lack of fundamental change from the time of its first Junior TT victory in 1926 to its last before the war (Stanley Woods, 1939), including the European 350 cc titles in 1935 (Wal Handley, Ulster) and 1938 (Ted Mellors by a handsome points margin). During all that time, changes were confined mostly to details and materials.

In the dry-sump lubrication system, for example, oil was scavenged at various times from the cambox and bottom bevel housing (as well as the crankcase) to compensate for increases in the circulation rate. On the delivery side, a system of different-size jets

was eventually introduced to squirt oil where it was most needed, to the big-end bearing, the cam/rocker contact and the mesh of the upper bevels.

Positive-stop gear control, with an external ratchet mechanism, was pioneered in 1928 and superseded by an internal mechanism in 1932, when four speeds replaced the previous three. Hairpin valve springs were adopted in 1932. The iron cylinder head was changed to aluminium-broze in 1934, then to light alloy (with rocker enclosure) a year later. Twin camshafts were tried on the bronze head in 1936 and quickly abandoned when a coupling sheared.

With the return to a single camshaft, the rocker box was integrated with the light-alloy head and the valve gear enclosed

completely, with clearance adjustment provided by eccentric rocker spindles. That layout was then developed into the famous 9 in-square head of the Mark 7 KTT engine (1938) and the Mark 8 a year later, with compression ratios of 8·75:1 and 11:1 respectively. Meanwhile, pivoted rear springing was introduced on the works machines in 1936 and catalogued in 1939. In both cases the suspension struts (made by Dowty) had air springing and oil damping, some 40 years before the principle was revived by the Japanese.

Early in this development period Velocette anticipated the later rush to supercharging, notwithstanding the difficulty of marrying a steady blower delivery to a pulsating cylinder requirement. In 1931 the Foxwell blower, with six-blade eccentric rotor, blew through the carburettor – an unhappy arrangement that necessitated pressurising both the float chamber, to maintain the depression over the jet, and the tank, to maintain the flow into the float chamber!

That machine, which rejoiced in the nickname of Whiffling Clara, was tested but not raced. The following year (1932) the lay-out was greatly simplified by having the blower suck through the carburettor while still feeding a large gas reservoir alongside the rear wheel. To obviate a consequent lag in throttle response (while the engine emptied or filled the reservoir) the throttle slide was put between the reservoir and the inlet valve.

That version of Whiffling Clara had an uncannily versatile performance, combining deceptive docility with unprecedented acceleration, but trivial troubles eliminated it from both the Junior and Senior TT races. So Velocette, a tiny concern to undertake such ambitious projects, shelved super-charging until 1939, when they showed enormous courage in designing the Roarer – a 500 cc blown twin with geared crankshafts and shaft drive, on which Stanley Woods planned to play David in 1940 to the Goliath of the almighty BMW twins and Gilera fours.

Although less adventurous technically than Velocette, Norton achieved even quicker success with their first ohc design, for it made its début with Alec Bennett's emphatic Senior TT win in 1927. Designed by Walter Moore (who later went to Germany and produced a similar-looking NSU) the cast-iron engine had a bore and stroke of 79 × 100 mm, a compression ratio of 7:1, separate (adjustable) cams on the one shaft, the hunting-tooth principle in the

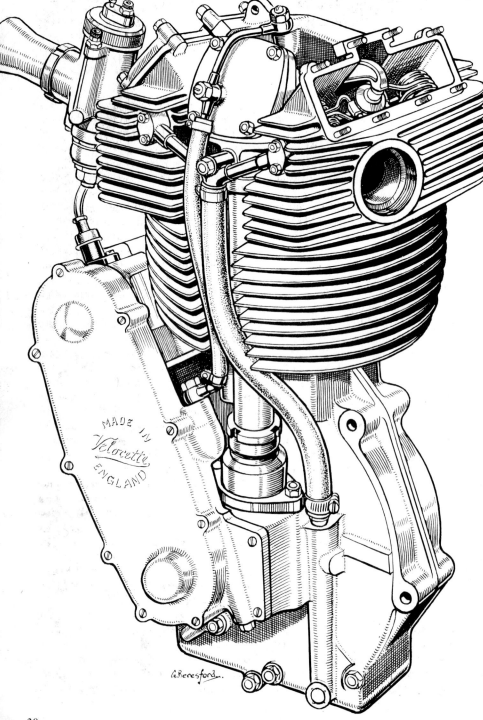

The Velocette works 350 cc engine of 1937, showing eccentrically pivoted exhaust-valve rocker and hairpin return springs. Following Harold Willis' tragic death from meningitis, the design stagnated after the war and was soon out-stripped by Norton

In his first year in the works Norton team (1938) Harold Daniell scores the first of his three Senior TT victories on one of Joe Craig's double-knocker Nortons. Daniell finished second to Georg Meier (BMW) in that year's European 500 cc championship

bevel drive (although the top and bottom bevels were connected by a splined shaft, not tongued couplings) and a separate oil feed to the cambox. The three-speed gearbox had direct foot control (not ratchet type) and the whole lot was housed in a new cradle frame rather than the earlier diamond frame. A 350 cc version (71 × 88 mm) was introduced in 1928.

But in spite of Tim Hunt's 500 cc European championship in Barcelona in 1929, Bennett's initial success was not consolidated until 1931, when Hunt not only took the title again (at Montlhéry, France) but also spearheaded a Norton one-two-three in the Senior TT and a one-two in the Junior. The reason for the marked upswing was that Joe Craig had taken charge of racing development and had collaborated with Arthur Carroll in a rehash of the original design.

From then on, Norton's classic successes reached unprecedented heights. Joe Craig's wizardry as a development engineer became such a byword that the team had the pick of the finest riders in the game. Up to and including 1938, not a year passed without a TT victory and often a one-two or a one-two-three. Stanley Woods did the Junior-Senior double in 1932 and 1933, Jimmie Guthrie in 1934. Similarly, Norton riders were European 350 or 500 cc champions (sometimes both) until 1938, when they were relegated to second place by Ted Mellors (350 Velocette) and George Meier (500 BMW).

During much of that time, the technical improvements were unobtrusively effective rather than outwardly spectacular: in 1932 aluminium-bronze cylinder heads and ingenious snubber springs to provide progressive damping on the girder forks; in 1933 bi-metal heads and barrels; in 1934 hairpin valve springs. But in 1936 there was a more obvious change when rear springing was introduced. It was a relatively crude plunger layout, with both load and recoil springs but no damping. Yet it overshadowed a more subtle move – a well-guarded experiment with twin-camshaft valve operation, which was tried in practising but not raced.

In 1937 the double-knocker engine was given the go-ahead and a progressive series of bore increases (with corresponding stroke shortenings) was initiated to make room for bigger valves and raise peak revs for the same mean piston speed. The following year the girder fork was ditched in favour of a telescopic fork (which was also undamped initially), while conical wheel hubs and

brake ventilation were also introduced.

By then, however, the blown multis from Germany and Italy had the legs of the big Norton (as did Velocette and DKW in the 350 cc class) and even the most heroic riding failed to stem the tide. Joe Craig's development work was not entirely exhausted, however, although it needed the postwar ban on supercharging to set the BMWs and Gileras back and let the Nortons flourish for a few more years.

Enter the multis

Strangely enough, it was neither BMW nor Gilera who first heralded Norton's downfall by posing the warning of impending multi-cylinder superiority. The message came, in the mid-1930s, from two entirely unconnected vee-twins – the 50-degree Swedish Husqvarna and the 120-degree Moto Guzzi. Although they were as different in design as a couple of vee-twins could be, both exploited the attractive compromise offered by that engine type: brisker performance, smoother running and a compact installation just as slim as a single.

Although much the less imaginative in design, the Husqvarna was first to ruffle the Nortons and many of its victories fell to home-bred stars Ragnar Sunnqvist and Gunnar Kalen. At Saxtorp in 1933 Kalen won the European 500 cc championship and, in the 350 cc event, R. Jonsson was beaten only by Simpson and Guthrie on works Nortons.

The following year, when the titles were up for grabs at Assen, Husqvarna had to be content with third place in the 500 cc race by a local rider A. van der Pluym. But that unexciting result conveys nothing of the team's

impact on the classic scene that year. Earlier in the season their dominance of the Swedish TT had been even more emphatic than usual, for engineer Folke Mannerstedt had boosted acceleration and braking during the winter by slashing dry weight from 347 lb to 274 lb, largely through switching to light alloy for the cylinders, heads, connecting rods, tanks and cone hubs.

On the Isle of Man – where their very arrival was heroic following a dockside catastrophe at Gothenburg, when a broken sling deposited the lorryload of TT bikes upside down on the quayside – the Huskies soon proved they had the legs of the works Nortons, if not their roadholding, the five-hundred clocking 118 mph.

In the Junior race, despite a persistent misfire and lurid slides on an oil-soaked rear tyre, Ernie Nott finished third to Guthrie and Simpson. A few days later on the bigger Husky, Stanley Woods would have split Guthrie and Simpson in the wet and misty Senior race had his tank not run dry only eight miles from the finish, after he had made the fastest lap (80·49 mph).

For the rest of the season, Sunnqvist and Kalen harried the winners of the remaining 500 cc grands prix, while in the 350 cc class Nott was overshadowed only by Simpson. But if proof of Husqvarna's straight-line speed was required, it came spectacularly in 1935, when Sunnqvist beat Karl Gall's works supercharged BMW on the very fast Avus banked track in Berlin.

That performance – along with Woods' victory in the Swedish 500 cc Grand Prix, S. Edlund's third successive win in the Swedish TT (a different event) and Sunnqvist's persistent harrying of the works Nortons elsewhere – augured well for the

Husqvarna's long-stroke vee-twin engine has a conventional 50-degree cylinder angle, with the steeply downdraught inlet tracts crossed over in the middle. Note the slotted magneto mounting for chain adjustment, also the junction boxes for carburettor cables

Swedish team's future. Alas, as their best riders retired or switched camps they found no comparable replacements and their efforts quickly faded. But in their few years on the classic scene they had shown that the single was vulnerable to superior design – and they had done it with a very straight-forward layout.

From its birth in 1931 to its death in 1936, the Husqvarna followed convention not only in its cylinder angle, but also in its long-stroke dimensions (65 × 75 mm), pushrod valve operation and porting arrangement (exhausts front and rear, inlets sandwiched between the heads). Hairpin springs were used from the start but the most striking feature of the original engine was the carburettor layout, with vertical intakes necessitating a frame with two splayed top tubes instead of the fashionable single tube.

With the 1934 change from cast iron to aluminium for the cylinders and heads, the compression ratio was increased from 7·3:1 to 9·5:1. The crankcase was stiffened, the valve gear enclosed, the guides lubricated and the carburettors, although still steeply downdraught, were swung to right and left to suit a single top tube, and provided with intake shields. Unfortunately, the frame never matched the performance of the engine. If only the Husky had handled better, and if only the team had had strength in depth, they might have been the first to topple Norton from their perch.

As it was, that honour fell to the 120-degree Moto Guzzi – an altogether more enterprising interpretation of the vee-twin theme – in the 1935 Senior TT. By that time, Joe Craig's unflinching faith in the single-cylinder engine and unsprung frame seemed more than amply justified by results. So Stanley Woods' sensational last-lap beating of Jimmie Guthrie, with race and lap records, shook the very foundations of classic racing. For not only was Woods' Moto Guzzi a twin – it was rear-sprung too.

Yet it was essentially no more than a logical extension of a 250 cc single that was already highly successful – indeed, Woods himself had won the Lightweight TT on one only two days earlier. For that single had its cylinder horizontal in traditional Moto Guzzi fashion, and the vee-twin simply had the second cylinder squeezed in beneath the saddle.

The twin was conceived in 1933, with a rigid frame. Like the single, it had an outside flywheel. But, unlike any other vee-twin, it did not have a common crankpin for both connecting rods. Instead, there were two separate crank assemblies – one each side of the centre main bearing – with the crankpins spaced at 120 degrees. Thus both pistons were at top dead centre together and the firing intervals were even.

Since each crankpin was formed integrally with both its fully balanced crank webs, the big-end bearings, although of caged roller type, had to be split diametrically – a high-precision technique typical of Italian engineering. The bevel-driven cams actuated the valves through Z-shape rockers and closure was by hairpin springs. To make the most of the natural airflow, the cylinder finning was radial at the front, circumferential at the rear. Each cylinder barrel and head was secured by four long studs (a practice by no means universal at the time) and the magneto was set between the two cylinder bases. As always, the four-speed gearbox was integral with the crank-case.

On a compression ratio of 8·5:1, the original engine put out 44 bhp at 7,000 rpm for a top speed of about 106 mph. By 1935, however, peak revs had risen to 7,500 rpm and top speed to 112 mph. More important, though, the rear wheel had been sprung. And, in keeping with Moto Guzzi's flair for originality and sound engineering, the design was way ahead of the cruder layouts with which most factories groped their way into the era of rear springing.

While more conservative marques started off with plunger-type layouts, Moto Guzzi went straight to a pivoted fork. Furthermore, to prevent the left and right arms from de-flecting independently and twisting the wheel, the fork was triangulated. And, to keep the centre of gravity as low as possible, both the triangulation and the horizontal spring boxes were below, not above, pivot height. Damping was by variable friction, with a remote control lever alongside the tank.

Woods' early showing in the Spanish Grand Prix (he was robbed of victory at Montjuich Park by a puncture) gave a foretaste of the 500 cc Moto Guzzi's imminent threat to Norton's TT supremacy. And for several years after the war that elegant vee-twin – and the 250 cc single from which it sprang – were still winning classic grands prix.

Courage

By the late 1930s, the blown 250 cc DKW split-single two-strokes were so superior to the best four-strokes that even Moto Guzzi put a blower on their ohc single, using a large gas reservoir above the cylinder to marry the steady delivery to the pulsating demand and leaving the rider to adjust to the consequent lag in throttle response.

In that harshly competitive climate, it needed courage as well as engineering flair to sustain a serious grand prix challenge with an unblown single-cylinder four-stroke.

Neither of those qualities was lacking at the small Benelli factory in Pesaro, on Italy's Adriatic coast. And although they tacked a supercharger on the left-hand end of the crankshaft in 1940 (when classic racing was already in abeyance) it was in unblown form that their bright-red, high-revving, double-knocker lightweight achieved its greatest prewar renown.

Established in the early 1930s, the basic layout was conventional enough, with an upright cylinder, a long train of gears serving the cams, magneto and oil pump, and chain drive to a separate four-speed gearbox. Right from the start, though, there was ample scope to raise peak revs in the pursuit of power, for the typically Italian use of an outside flywheel allowed the designers to make the crankcase really compact and robust and the crankshaft stiff and well supported.

By 1938, progressive development had led to a carburettor size of $1\frac{5}{32}$ in (larger than many a works three-fifty at the time) so that the engine breathed freely enough to peak at 8,400 rpm – where its 30 bhp matched the DKW's power – and romp up to 9,000 (115 mph) in favourable circumstances, albeit with phenomenal reliability. The penalty for such high tuning, however, was a lack of useful urge below 6,000 rpm, so that the clutch came in for plenty of slipping. And, since the clutch then ran in an oilbath chaincase, a long warm-up period was necessary before each race to get the oil thin enough to banish clutch drag.

At the same time, the machine had acquired an oil cooler in the scavenge line and friction-damped rear springing that combined a pivoted fork with plunger boxes. That was the state of the Benelli when Emilio Soprani won the Italian 250 cc Grand Prix at Monza, with both lap and race speeds faster than Ted Mellors achieved in winning the 350 cc race on a works Velocette.

Quick to spot the chance to fulfil his long-standing ambition to win a TT, Mellors arranged to give the Benelli its Isle of Man debut the following year. In atrocious

The combination that dented Joe Craig's faith in single cylinders and unspring frames – Stanley Woods wins the 1935 Senior TT by four seconds on the Moto Guzzi rear-sprung, 120-degree vee-twin. A tankside lever adjusts the rear friction damping

weather, he won handsomely. The blown Moto Guzzis of Stanley Woods and Omobono Tenni may have had an edge in top speed but they were not yet 100 per cent reliable, while the wet weather played havoc with Ewald Kluge's DKW plugs. Mellors' engine never missed a beat and his victory (by a massive 3 minutes 45 seconds from Kluge) gave him equal third place with Nello Pagani (Moto Guzzi) in the European championship.

Integral blowers

Fascinating though they undoubtedly were, the supercharged singles of the early and mid-1930s were essentially rather ungainly conversions of established models, with the compressor tacked on wherever space could be found, lots of assorted plumbing and the inevitable large gas reservoir. If the full benefits of forced induction were to be obtained, the blower had to be an integral part of the engine and there should be at least two cylinders, preferably more.

First to grasp the idea – certainly the first to exploit it successfully in road racing – were BMW. Originally, from 1930 to 1933,

Worm's-eye view of the double-knocker engine BMW introduced in 1935 and with which Georg Meier won the European 500 cc championship three years later. Mounted on the front of the crankcase, the Zoller eccentric-vane compressor is fed by a large carburettor at the top right and delivers mixture at 15 psi through long induction pipes under the cylinders to the rear-facing inlet ports

they built a Zoller eccentric-vane compressor on to the top of the gearbox and drove it (at half engine speed) from the tail of the magneto shaft. Power of the flat-twin engine went up to a more-than-competitive 55 bhp, but in other respects the machine was far less advanced, with hand gear change, push-rod valve operation and a trailing-link fork with leaf springing.

Prospects were enormously enhanced in 1935 by the introduction of wholesale improvements, including a new engine (66×72 mm) with double overhead camshafts and left-side foot change. Strangely for a double-knocker layout, the valves were operated by short rockers. This was because the bevel drive went straight to the exhaust shaft on the right and the inlet shaft on the left, and the other camshafts were geared directly to them. Hence the cams were much too close together to operate the valves directly.

The supercharger was switched to the front of the crankcase, a move that brought several advantages. Driven directly from the nose of the crankshaft, it ran at engine speed to deliver a boost of no less than 15 psi. Sweeping under the cylinders to the rear-facing inlet ports, the long induction pipes had ample capacity. And the direct air cooling of the whole system kept charge heating in check, so minimising any drop in density.

By way of a bonus, the new blower position improved weight distribution. And although the rear wheel remained unsprung

for a while, new ground was broken at the front with the first-ever hydraulically damped telescopic fork.

It needed only the addition of rear springing (plunger type) in 1936 to put BMW as firmly on the map in classic racing as they already were in world speed records. With 68 bhp at 8,000 rpm and a weight of only 302 lb, the power/weight ratio of the road racer was more than a match for any rivals, as was the top speed of 140 mph.

A string of Continental victories by Karl Gall and Otto Ley preceded some sterling performances by Jock West, who finished sixth in the 1937 Senior TT, then won the Ulster GP, on the ultra-fast Clady circuit, two months later. The following year West improved to fifth in the TT before repeating his Ulster victory, while Germany's new star George Meier wrenched the European 500 cc championship from Norton's grasp.

In 1939 Meier made TT history as the first foreigner to win the Senior race, which he did at the record speed of 89·38 mph, ably backed up by West in second place. BMW's fame in classic racing had reached a pinnacle and Meier seemed unbeatable.

Brief invincibility

Seldom can such impressive invincibility have been so short-lived. At Saxtorp and Sachsenring, Dorino Serafini's blown Gilera four showed such incredible speed and acceleration in winning the Swedish and German GPs that Meier and most of the BMWs pranged trying to hold him and the German team had no option but to withdraw from the Ulster, the last prewar grand prix. There, Serafini easily brushed aside Freddie Frith's masterly effort on the un-blown Norton, to win the world's fastest pre-war road race at 97·85 mph (lap record, 100·03), so clinching the European 500 cc championship and relegating Meier to second place.

In engineering terms the Gilera's supremacy was inevitable, for a blown four has a greater power potential than a blown twin. Even so, the suddenness of Serafini's success came as a surprise to many because Gilera had previously concentrated more on world records than road racing. Piero Taruffi had fought a long battle with BMW's Ernst Henne for the 500 cc flying-kilometre record, which Henne eventually captured with 174 mph to Taruffi's 170·37. But Taruffi put the classic hour record beyond grasp with a spectacular performance on the Brescia-Bergamo autostrada in the spring of 1939.

Riding his fully enclosed machine back and forth along a stretch only 28 miles long, he not only had to stop and be humped round at each end but coasted two miles to the fourth turn with a dry tank. In spite of all this time wasting, he packed no fewer

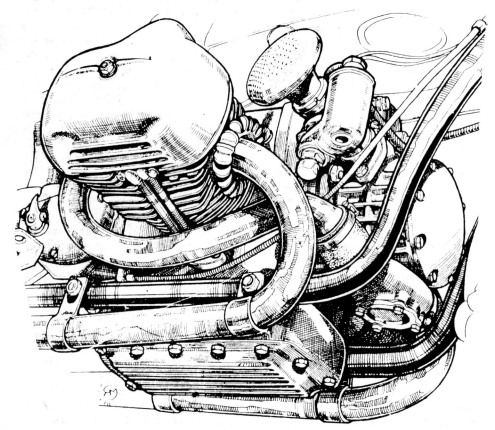

Top-dog five-hundred at the outbreak of war, the blown Gilera four had the radiator between the front down tubes and the oil cooler beneath the seat. A Roots-type blower above the crankcase fed the inlet ports through a large inter-cooler. The water impeller is above inlet camshaft. Note the adjustable friction damping for the rear springing

than 127 miles into the hour, which compares extremely well with Mike Hailwood's non-stop, flat-out 144·83 miles round the smooth Daytons oval 25 years later on a 500 cc MV Agusta four.

Original ancestor of Gilera's 500 cc double-knocker four was the 1934 Rondine (Italian for swallow). Its 52 × 58 mm water-cooled cylinder block was inclined forward 40 degrees and fed, via a heavily finned manifold, by a Roots-type blower with a meshing pair of three-lobe rotors on top of the crankcase. The blower, four-speed transmission and both camshafts were all driven from the middle of the crankshaft. Both the unsprung frame and the girder fork were made from steel pressings, the front part of the frame forming a cowl for the radiator and fairing the rider's legs into the bargain.

With 60 bhp at 8,500 rpm, the Rondine was competitive enough to win its very first race, the 1935 Tripoli GP, where Taruffi beat the formidable Moto Guzzi 120-degree twins. Far from resting on their laurels,

however, Rondine immediately ditched the original frame for a duplex-tubular structure with friction-damped pivoted rear springing – and Taruffi obliged by winning the Rondine's second race, the Pescara GP.

At the end of the year the makers (CNA in Rome) sold the design to Gilera (in Arcore, near Monza) and Taruffi then enlisted the talents of Giordano Aldrighetti to design the all-enveloping shell, with tail fin, used to boost speed for the world-record programme.

It was 1937 before Gilera got down to a serious bid in classic racing. And the machine, which rocketed Serafini to the top two years later, was basically the same as Taruffi's Pescara winner, although developed in detail – with wide duplex frame, pivoted rear springing and pressed-steel girder fork; water-cooled, four-abreast engine inclined steeply forward; impeller driven from inlet camshaft; Roots-type blower; dry-sump oiling with ribbed tank; 8:1 compression. But peak power was up to 85 bhp and top speed to 145 mph. There was, at the time, no one to pick the bones out of that!

Dynamo or blower!

Alas, British factories were tardy making up their minds to court road-racing success through supercharged multis. First to take

the plunge were AJS. Indeed, although the Velocette Roarer showed much more promise some years later, nobody in Britain but AJS actually got a blown multi to a grand-prix start grid. It was a 50-degree vee-four of 495 cc (50 × 63 mm) and it was born in most peculiar circumstances – for it was first displayed on the factory's stand at the 1935 London Show, equipped with lights, tools, pillion seat, number plates and silencers, and listed at £89 5s (£89.25). It was, the makers claimed, a dual-purpose machine and the only clue to the hairier side of its character was the makers' offer to substitute a compressor for the front-mounted dynamo should the customer so desire.

There can have been few who would have invested in that degree of compexity for a bread-and-butter roadster. The separate cast-iron cylinders and heads were bolted to the crankcase by 16 full-length studs, like a pair of vee-twins side by side. At each side a single carburettor fed a T-shaped manifold in the old-fashioned way, so that the exhausts faced front and rear.

Supported in no fewer than five ball and roller bearings, the hollow crankshaft had its pins spaced at 180 degrees. And to obviate the need to offset the cylinders each crankpin carried one plain and one forked conrod. Each cylinder had its own overhead camshaft, and a 2:1 reduction gearing in the

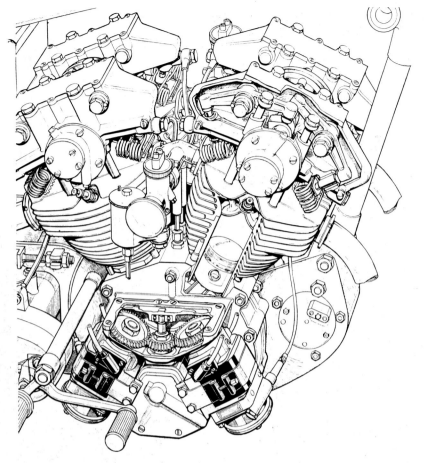

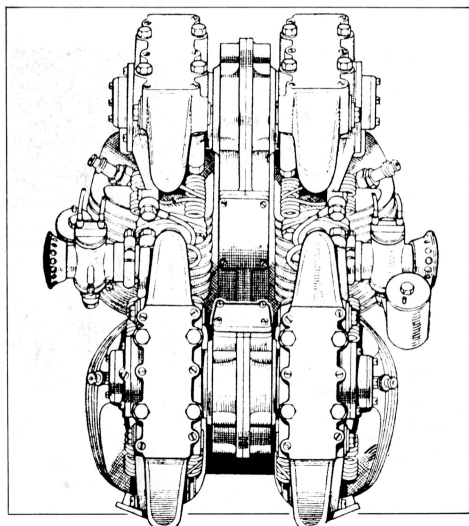

Left: *original version of the AJS vee-four with dynamo mounted in the front engine plates. Separate bevel-driven magnetos served the front and rear cylinders. Valve rockers were in duralumin, with eccentric pivots for clearance adjustment. Note the overlapping hairpin valve springs*

Below: *separate carburettors fed the right- and left-hand cylinders of the AJS vee-four. A long chain in a cast-aluminium case between the cylinders drove all four camshafts from half-speed gearing in the middle of the crankshaft*

Opposite, top: *a masterpiece of plumbing – 1936 version of the blown AJS vee-four with all exhausts facing forward. Just discernible between the exhaust bends is the induction pipe that sweeps from the bottom of the supercharger up and over the central cam drive to the rear-facing inlet ports*

Opposite, below: *George Rowley and the AJS blown four at the apex of Ramsey hairpin in the 1936 Senior TT*

middle of the crankshaft served the long chain drive, which was housed in an aluminium casting.

From the driving sprocket (which thus ran backward) the chain went up to the rear camshaft sprocket, down under an idler sprocket (adjustable for initial assembly) then up to the front cam sprocket and back down to the driving sprocket. The front (slack) run was tensioned by a Weller spring-loaded steel blade.

Tongued couplings on both sides of the top sprockets drove the right and left camshafts. Eccentrically pivoted for clearance adjustment, I-shape duralumin rockers actuated the valves through short, cylindrical tappets; valve closure was by overlapping hairpin springs. Each cambox was pressure fed from a crankcase gallery and scavenged by its own small pump.

Nor was that the end of the engine's complexity, for a cluster of bevel gears in the right-hand crankcase half drove the main oil pumps and a pair of BTH twin-spark racing magnetos – one serving the front cylinders, the other the rear. Compression ratio was $7.9:1$ and the dynamo (or blower) was housed in the front engine plates. Yet for all the engine's novelty it fitted into the standard unsprung frame of the 500 cc ohc single with only a slight alteration to the seat tube.

It was in racing trim, and looking much different, that the AJS vee-four was next exposed to the public gaze the following spring. After bench tests in the Woolwich factory and track tests in a TT frame (still unsprung) at Brooklands and Donington, many modifications had been incorporated.

A Zoller compressor replaced the dynamo and was driven at half engine speed by a chain enclosed in a forward extension of the oilbath primary chaincase. The clutch, however, was brought outside the case to run dry and cooler. Light alloy was now used for the cylinders and heads and the compression ratio had been lowered in deference to the supercharging. The rear heads had been

The 1939 version of the AJS blown four-cylinder engine, with water cooling, rear-facing exhausts and pannier oil tank. Maximum power was about 80 bhp

reversed so that all exhausts faced forward. A massive Amal carburettor on the left fed the blower at the top, while the outlet from the bottom swept up and over the cam chaincase, with branches to the four rear-facing inlet ports.

Plumbing galore

The AJS was a masterpiece of plumbing, looked extremely businesslike and proved fast in a straight line. But unspecified mechanical troubles eliminated both Harold Daniell and George Rowley from the 1936 Senior TT and development rather than racing occupied the factory throughout the following year.

When the vee-four reappeared, for the 1938 Senior TT, it had acquired rear springing in the interest of better handling, with a triangulated fork pivoted on the seat tube and spring boxes oscillating on vertical guide rods at the back of a sub-frame. The front brake had grown to 8 in diameter in a wide light-alloy hub. Partly to let the engine be moved back for lighter steering and partly to get a freer airflow over the rear cylinders, the separate oil tank was ditched and a compartment provided in the petrol tank.

Also discarded was the oilbath chaincase, in favour of a guard.

On the engine side, as distinct from handling, compression was raised to 7:1, boost pressure regulated at 5 to 6 psi and the induction plumbing simplified and reduced in diameter. Instead of a positive oil feed to the blower, two per cent of oil was mixed with the petrol, two-stroke fashion. Engine lubrication was revised, too, while the cam boxes were reduced in size and conventional threaded tappet adjustment was substituted for the eccentric arrangement.

Bob Foster's retirement with engine trouble in the second lap seemed a poor reward for so much development and AJS then faced the choice of shelving the vee-four altogether or rehashing it in a big way. To their credit they took the second course and the 1939 version was scarcely recognisable from its predecessors.

For a start it was water cooled to overcome cylinder distortion, circulation being first by thermosiphon then by an impeller on the left-hand end of the crankshaft. The linered aluminium cylinders were made in two blocks, front and rear, and all four exhausts faced backward so that the pipes were comparatively straight. The valve springs were fully enclosed.

A new duplex frame was fitted and although the rear springing was similar in

principle, it was considerably cleaned up in detail with the spring boxes built into the frame. Cable operation isolated the rear brake from suspension movement; the front brake had sprouted a small air scoop and two large snubber springs damped the front fork action. Fuel capacity was increased to six gallons and a separate oil tank was re-instated, on the right-hand side behind the gearbox.

A try-out in the North-West 200 showed plenty of speed until Bob Foster was foiled by a blown head gasket. So the radiator was deepened for the TT and both machines survived the seven laps, although Walter Rusk's 11th place and Foster's 13th hardly set the race alight.

There was a different story in the Ulster GP two months later, by which time the engines were churning out 80 bhp and the bikes were clocking 135 mph, albeit weaving alarmingly. Foster went out with his engine burning oil but Rusk set a fearsome pace from the start. His was the first ton lap in classic racing (precisely 100 mph) and he was leading the field when the right-hand lower fork link broke on lap four and rendered the bike uncontrollable, even by so wild an Irishman.

Serafini's subsequent lap record was only marginally faster (by 0·03 mph in fact) and it was clear that further development in AJS navigation and improved penetration would

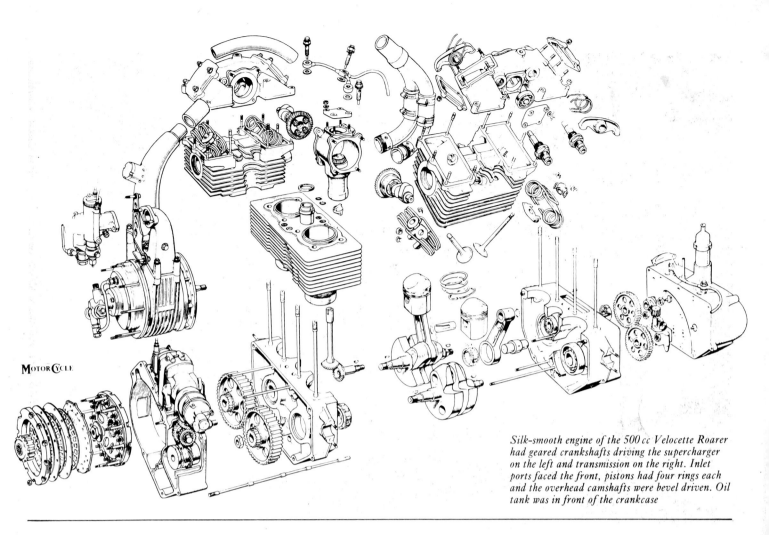

Silk-smooth engine of the 500 cc Velocette Roarer had geared crankshafts driving the supercharger on the left and transmission on the right. Inlet ports faced the front, pistons had four rings each and the overhead camshafts were bevel driven. Oil tank was in front of the crankcase

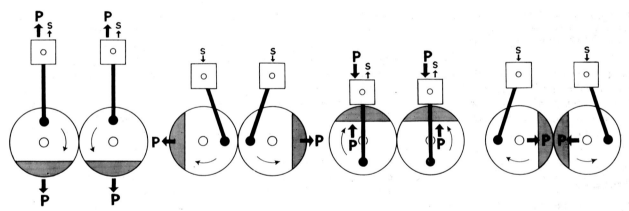

have given Rusk the chance to tackle Serafini on level terms had the war not intervened.

Sophisticated Velo

Altogether more homogeneous and sophisticated was the Velocette Roarer – only a twin, it is true, and none too light, but one with every indication of having a higher speed/power ratio than any of its rivals. When first track tested, for example – in practice for the 1939 Senior TT – it was putting out the same power as the factory's 500 cc single (38 bhp on the Velocette dynamometer). Yet its much smoother engine contours, especially the rounded oil tank on the crankcase nose, gave it an extra 6 mph – 130 mph – and that was faster than the works Nortons for

which, as mentioned earlier, 50 bhp was claimed.

Georg Meier's dominance of the 1938 European 500 cc championship and Jock West's two consecutive Ulster victories had convinced Harold Willis that the unblown single, for all its easier handling, was a spent force. He wanted the extra power that supercharging could give and he wanted tip-top handling too. What is more, he saw no point, with the extra power, in persisting with exposed chain transmission which, as often as not, sprayed a thin film of oil on one side of the rear tyre.

So Willis' first priority in laying out the Roarer in the 1938–39 winter was enclosed shaft drive, *à la* BMW. What he disliked about the German twin, though, was the

How the Velocette Roarer's geared cranks achieved near-perfect smoothness. At top and bottom dead centres the heavy counterweights entirely cancelled the pistons' primary inertia forces. At midstroke the horizontal forces from the counterweights neutralised one another. Only the secondary forces were unbalanced

Velocette's chief mechanic Tommy Mutton works on The Roarer engine in 1939. Note the long induction tract from supercharger to the forward-facing inlet ports

vulnerability of the cylinder heads and its occasional skittishness. Popular opinion attributed that to torque reaction from the longitudinal crankshaft but Willis poohpoohed the idea, blaming gyroscopic precession instead – the tendency for the crankshaft to yaw when tilted suddenly by bumps.

Either way, he solved both his problems by standing the cylinders side by side and gearing the two crankshafts together in opposite rotation. The right-hand shaft drove the transmission, the other the sixblade Centric compressor and magneto. Simply by using a 100 per cent balance factor* in each crank assembly, he completely cancelled the primary inertia forces at top and bottom dead centres, while the consequent horizontal forces at midstroke neutralised one another within the specially stiffened crankcase.

As in the BMW, each piston had a fourth ring to help dissipate the extra heat. To keep down crankcase width, the big-end eyes of the connecting rods were devoid of bearing sleeves. Otherwise, proven KTT practice was followed wherever possible and each cylinder had a bevel-driven overhead camshaft.

Water cooling was envisaged initially, so

* In all engines, the rotating mass of the big-end assembly (including the lower part of the connecting rod) is completely counterweighted in the crankshaft. The balance factor is the percentage of the reciprocating mass (piston assembly and upper part of connecting rod) that is also counterweighted. This additional counterweighting, while reducing the effect of the primary inertia forces at tdc and bdc, introduces an unbalanced horizontal force at midstroke.

the exhaust ports faced rearward, with straight pipes saving a mite of power, and the inlet manifolding swept over the engine to the forward-facing inlet ports. When a drawing board switch to direct air cooling was made before building began, the porting layout was retained and aluminium side scoops were added to channel air to the exhausts.

Centre of gravity of the engine was commendably low, the crankshafts being well below wheel-spindle height. The difference in centre heights was spanned by putting the gearbox output shaft above the input and using the large-diameter narrow gears possible with an engine-speed input.

Building was finished by the spring and when Woods tried it in the Isle of Man (it was never intended to race it in the 1939 Senior) he was delighted with its superb handling, silk-smooth running and uncommonly broad spread of power – from 2,000 to 7,000 rpm against 4,500 to 6,700 for the single. Considering the engine's modest initial state of tune (only 4 psi boost and a $\frac{15}{16}$ in carburettor) there seemed ample scope for really competitive performance.

Willis was always sceptical of bhp claims. He reckoned the Gilera got its 140 mph from no more than 50 genuine bhp. Be that as it may, he geared the Roarer for 145 mph at 7,000 rpm (3·737:1 in top) and set himself the task of getting enough power to reach the target.

Following his tragic death in Birmingham during the TT period, the job landed in the lap of his assistant, Charles Udall. By driving the blower from a separate source, Udall was able to ring the changes on boost pressure, compression ratio, carburettor

size and valve timing. Within two months boost was up to 13 psi, compression down to 7·5:1, carburettor size up to $1\frac{1}{16}$ in and valve timing lengthened. Sixty-two bhp at the gearbox, less eight to drive the blower, meant a net 54 bhp. Considering the Roarer's performance on the original 38 bhp, and considering there was a whole winter ahead for further development, it is a fair bet that the war robbed Stanley Woods of an odds-on chance of becoming 1940 European 500 cc champion.

Gathering dust

Many another blown racer gathered dust in the years of strife while its creators dreamed of European glory, come the peace, never suspecting that supercharging would be outlawed. Most of these machines were Italian, the simplest being 250 cc singles by Moto Guzzi and Benelli.

The Moto Guzzi, built initially for a successful assault on world records, had already had two or three years' development as a grand-prix machine. By then it was pushing out 38 bhp at 7,800 rpm and reaching a speed of 125 mph. The Benelli was a more recent adaptation of the phenomenal unblown featherweight, with a heavily finned compressor outboard of the flywheel case. The gas reservoir behind the cylinder head was even more liberally finned and the exhaust pipe was plain, not megaphoned. Peak power was variously quoted as 35 or 45 bhp at 8,600 to 9,000 rpm and top speed was similar to the Moto Guzzi's.

Much more exciting, though, were a brace of blown 250 cc fours, one from Benelli, the other from Gilera. So many cylinders for so small a total displacement was even more surprising then than when Honda followed suit 20 years later. Like Moto Guzzi's blown single, the Benelli four was conceived as a record breaker but was equally intended to put an end to DKW's grand-prix supremacy. Indeed, the compact water-cooled engine was housed in the same frame as was used for the singles.

With the 42 × 45 mm steel-sleeved, light-alloy cylinder block leaning forward at 15 degrees, the engine had a primary chaincase on the left and a train of gears on the right serving the double overhead camshafts, oil pump and water impeller. The compressor was driven at half engine speed from the clutch and the generously finned, cylindrical inlet trunk served as an intercooler. Maximum power was said to be 52 bhp at 10,000 rpm, giving a speed of 140–145 mph in grand-prix trim and 155 mph when streamlined for record bids.

Above: not suspecting that supercharging would be banned when classic racing resumed, Benelli tacked a supercharger on their high-revving 250 cc single in 1940. The exhaust lost its megaphone and peak power went up from 30 bhp to 35 or more

Right: driven at half engine speed from the clutch, the compressor on the tiny Benelli four was installed on top of the gearbox. The cylindrical inlet manifold was heavily finned for intercooling. The primary drive was by enclosed chain, and the magneto was in front of the cylinder block

Little was heard outside Italy of Gilera's experimental 250 cc blown four, but from a published Italian drawing it seems to have borne a much stronger external resemblance to the postwar 500 and 350 cc world beaters than did Serafini's 1939 water-cooled job. It was air cooled, with the cylinder block inclined forward at 30 degrees and the transmission and accessories taking their drive from the middle of the crankshaft.

The blower seems to have been built on to the front of the crankcase and wet sump, with an intercooler feeding inlet ports at the front of the head. Both front and rear forks were steel pressings, the rear controlled by torsion bars.

At the top of the capacity scale (500 cc) there was a blown four from Bianchi and a three from Moto Guzzi. The Bianchi looked anything but sleek – a clumsy bike with upright air-cooled cylinders (52×58 mm), bevel driven twin camshafts, the blower chain-driven from the clutch on the left, a pressed-steel girder fork and plunger rear springing.

In complete contrast, the Moto Guzzi was technically novel in several respects and looked every inch a racer. The three-throw (120-degree) crankshaft was supported in four bearings, while the air-cooled cylinders (59×60 mm) were inclined forward 45 degrees, their double overhead camshafts driven by a long chain in a triangular case on the right. Gears drove the supercharger and, beneath it, the gearbox started a new trend in having five speeds.

Part-tubular, part-pressed, the frame had similar suspension to its stablemates (girder front fork, triangulated rear, friction damped), and soon the front brake acquired two leading shoes, another fresh trend. With 80 bhp at 8,000 rpm, the blown three from the lakeside factory at Mandello del Lario would have taken a lot of catching in the title chase.

Finally, supercharging was spreading in Germany too, where NSU decided to abandon the Walter Moore singles, even though Otto Steinbach and Heiner Fleischmann had finished second and third respectively to Freddie Frith's Norton in the 1936 European 350 cc championship at the Sachsenring.

A cumbersome double-knocker parallel twin in an unsprung frame, the new blown three-fifty made its debut in Fleischmann's hands two years later, again at the Sachsenring. But its speed potential was severely hampered by its inadequate cornering clearance and Fleischmann soon pulled out. By the following season it had acquired plunger-type rear springing and an eight-gallon pistol-grip tank. Although it showed

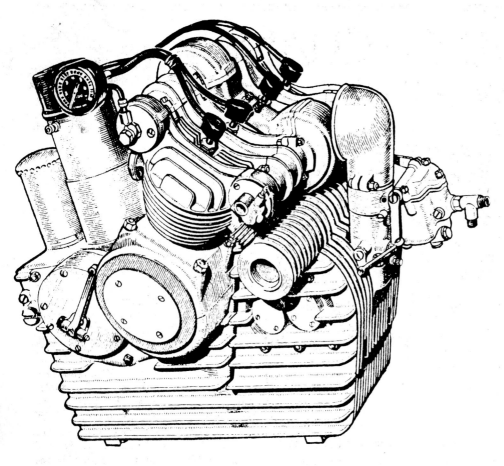

competitive speed, it was far too heavy and none too reliable.

Strangely, a British Centric blower was fitted, which was chain driven from the clutch, and fed the cylinders separately at 5 to 10 psi. Valve operation was rather complex, with separate bevel drives to inlet and exhaust, and couplings connecting the left- and right-hand shafts – a system inherited by the first version of that postwar worldbeater, the 250 cc NSU Rennmax twin.

In German national races shortly after the war – where blowing was allowed prior to Germany's readmission to the FIM in 1951 – the bugs were ironed out of the three-fifty and the cylinder dimensions increased from 56 × 70·5 mm to 63 × 80 mm to provide a five-hundred with 80 bhp at 8,500 rpm. On this Fleischmann proved a match for Meier and the blown BMW.

Once Germany was back in the fold and the bikes were no longer eligible for road racing, NSU extracted the last bit of glory from them by going for world records. In 1951 Wilhelm Herz boosted the 350 and 500 cc speeds to 172 and 180 mph respectively on an autobahn. Five years later, with full enclosure and the engines tuned to 75 and 110 bhp on methanol, he went to Utah and averaged speeds of 189 and 211 mph respectively.

Nowadays supercharging is mostly confined to drag racing. And technically fascinating though that sport is, it is my guess that the aborted 1940 classic road-racing scene would have made it seem like a village fair by comparison.

Above: *from this Italian drawing, Gilera's 250 cc blown four (rather than Serafini's 1939 blown five-hundred) seems to have inspired the factory's highly successful postwar fours. The camshafts and transmission are centrally driven, the front-mounted blower appears to have twin rotors, and the exhausts face rearward*

Below: *one of the most promising blown five-hundreds to be outlawed by the postwar supercharging ban – the 1940 rear-sprung three-cylinder Moto Guzzi. Triangular case houses chain for the double overhead camshafts. Gear-driven blower is above the five-speed gearbox. Power output was 80 bhp at 8,000 rpm*

WIND OF CHANGE
PREWAR TWO-STROKES

INCREASING success in harnessing the natural gas resonances has given the two-stroke engine a virtual monopoly of classic racing since 1968, despite its great thirst and lingering propensity for sudden and expensive mechanical tantrums. Notwithstanding its unhappy toll of riders abruptly cast off without the option, no manufacturer from Honda's pull-out in 1967 until their return to classic racing in 1979 has been able to resist the overriding attraction of maximum engine power from minimum weight.

In the light of that situation, it seems incredible that the story of the prewar grand-prix two-stroke is a one-make monologue from Zschopau, in Saxony, where DKW patiently developed their lightweight dominance – and whence, indeed, the postwar two-stroke boom got its initial impetus in the form of MZ's fundamental development work.

Before the war, the art of exploiting natural resonances was largely confined to musical instruments. Consequently most race engineers saw the two-stroke's symmetrical port timing as an insuperable barrier to competitive power – the inlet phase too brief, the late exhaust closure too wasteful of fresh gas. During the time of the European championships (long after Scott's TT heyday) nobody but DKW accepted the challenge – or saw so early the significance of the loophole in the regulations that allowed supercharging.

From the factory's track debut in 1925, every racing DKW was supercharged to make the most of the short inlet phase. Initially, there was a single working cylinder – upright and water cooled, with a deflector-top piston and twin-plug head – and a finned charging cylinder beneath the crankcase. Since the charging piston moved in opposition to the working one, it increased the engine's displacement considerably for induction, then similarly boosted crankcase compression.

Although that model had power and speed enough to dominate the 175 cc championship on various circuits for about five years (although not the 250 cc title chase), its peak power stuck at about 70 bhp/litre (for both versions) as a result of the limitations of its symmetrical port timing without today's powerful offsetting pressure waves to limit loss of fresh charge, both back through the carburettor and into the exhaust.

The first German to win a TT, Ewald Kluge (DKW) dominates the 1938 Lightweight

Splitting the single

In 1931 Ing Zoller produced a solution to the problem by adopting the split-single layout. In this there were two cylinder bores in tandem (in the same casting) topped by a single combustion chamber with the plug slightly to the front. The two exhaust ports were in the rear bore, the transfer ports in the front.

The secret of the scheme was the connecting rod arrangement. The main rod, which was attached to the exhaust piston, had a boss on the front of its big-end eye. And to that boss was hinged a shorter rod, attached to the transfer piston.

The effect was that the exhaust piston had a permanent lead over the transfer piston, so that the exhaust ports not only opened before the transfers in the usual way but closed before them on the upstroke, too, hence reducing the escape of fresh gas to the exhaust and allowing more complete cylinder filling.

This layout was unchanged throughout a whole series of split-singles; only the induction system was altered from time to time. At first, to obviate blowback through the carburettor, an automatic reed valve was fitted in the head of the large-bore charging cylinder, which had a capacity of 452 cc and jutted from the front of the crankcase. Actuated by a separate connecting rod, the charging piston breathed through two carburettors on its inward stroke, then closed

the valve and pumped its charge through the transfer ports to the working cylinders.

Sure enough, power went up by nearly 50 per cent, with noise to match, and Walfried Winkler and Arthur Geiss took first and third places in the 1934 European 250 cc championship at Assen, split by Les Archer on a works New Imperial. The following year megaphone exhausts were introduced and from then on the raucous sound of TT Deeks plummeting flat out down Bray Hill was annually heard on the English coast, 60 miles across the sea!

On his TT debut in 1935 Geiss finished a creditable seventh, then won the European championship in Ulster. In 1936 the Lightweight TT was as good as won for Stanley Woods when his engine jibbed on the last lap after he had raised the record to 76·20 mph. Geiss lasted the distance and improved to third. Later on, Ewald Kluge finished second to Tyrell Smith (Excelsior) in the championship race at the Sachsenring.

In 1937 Ernie Thomas duplicated Geiss' third place in the TT and Kluge ran third in the championship at Berne, Switzerland. Although the split-single was clearly on its way, the engineers well knew why the results were not better. The reed valve had caused another bottleneck in the pursuit of power. Twenty-five bhp at 4,000 to 4,700 rpm showed remarkable efficiency but all attempts to push up the peak revs for more power resulted in reed failure.

Reed out

So the reed valve was scrapped in favour of a cylindrical rotary valve, fed by a carburettor at each end. At the same time the charging cylinder was switched to a vertical position at the front, its piston driven by a train of gears which then continued up to the rotor. For good measure the rear wheel was sprung.

Within two years of its birth in 1936 the engine was delivering 30 bhp at 6,000 to 7,000 rpm and judged ripe for the TT. Ripe indeed! Kluge left the field nowhere, shattered lap and race records and – despite the heaviest fuel load in the race and an extra pit stop – finished with more than 11 minutes in hand. In those days championship races in general and the TT in particular were long enough to penalise machines with a heavy thirst. But there was no squealing from DKW. They were happy to pay the price of their speed (in weight as well as thirst) and Kluge went on to spear-

Above: an early DKW – the supercharged single that dominated the European 175 cc championship in the late 1920s. Firing cylinder is water cooled, with two plugs; finned charging cylinder is under the crankcase. Note the microscopic front brake

Below: six variants of the DKW split single. In the five with side-by-side cylinder bores, the hinged con-rod arrangement gives the exhaust piston a permanent lead over the transfer piston. In the opposed-piston layout, the same effect is achieved by coupling the two crankshafts out of phase.

Split single engines (two working pistons and a compressor) were made in 175 and 250 cc. Larger sizes comprised two split singles side by side with a 180-degree crankshaft. In this case the compressor piston had a double action, serving left- and right-hand crank chambers alternately.

The essential differences between the various layouts shown here lies in the induction systems. These are: (1) reed valve to charging cylinder; (2) rotary valve to charging cylinder; (3) conventional piston valve to crankcase (compressor at bottom); (4) piston valve to crankcase (compressor at front); (5) eccentric-vane compressor to crankcase; (6) eccentric-vane compressor to reservoir surrounding transfer ports

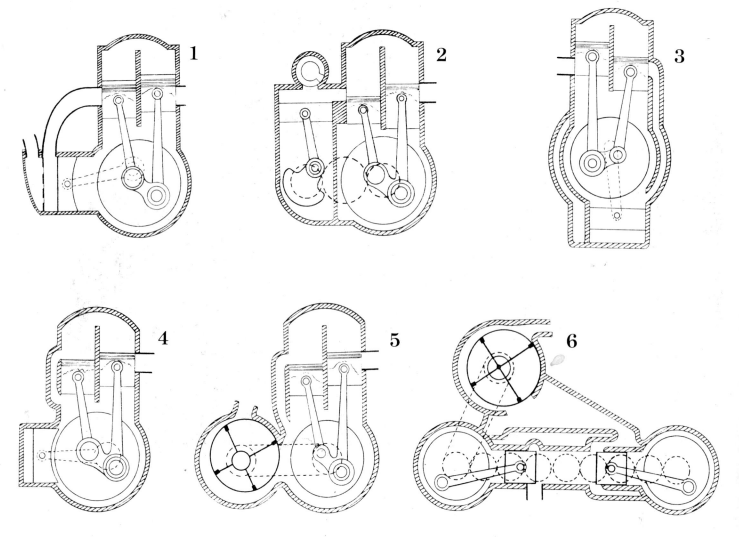

head a DKW one-two-three in the European 250 cc championship, the first to be determined on an overall points basis.

Although Kluge's bike proved much less amphibious than Ted Mellors' winning Benelli in the aquatic 1939 TT, he again headed a factory one-two in the 250 cc championship, while Heiner Fleischmann edged Mellors (Velocette) out of the 350 cc championship on a split-twin. This was virtually a pair of split-singles side by side with a 180-degree crankshaft.

Like many of the catalogue racers (with which DKW reaped extra glory) it had rear-facing carburettors, with the inlet ports controlled by the skirts of the exhaust pistons, and a charging cylinder at the bottom in which a double-acting piston served the left and right crankcases alternately. A variant of this layout had the charging piston at the front (not the bottom) as in the reed-valve engine.

But even while they were hammering the nails so firmly in the lid of the lightweight four-stroke coffin, DKW were laughing up their sleeve. In a lighthearted speech at the 1938 TT prize-giving, team manager Meurer hinted at secret developments when

Above: *Ewald Kluge and his DKW 250 cc split-single at Union Mills during his winning ride in the 1938 Lightweight TT. Note the left-facing carburettor feeding one end of the cylindrical rotary valve on top of the vertical charging cylinder*

Below: *Walfried Winkler with a 1938 DKW 350 cc split-twin. Carburettors are between the exhaust pipes, with induction controlled by the rear-piston skirts. The underslung charging cylinder has a double action, serving the left- and right-hand crank chambers on alternate strokes*

he predicted that the next works two-fifty would be considerably faster than Kluge's rotary-valve job that had made such mincemeat of the opposition.

A further 10 bhp

In the new engine, supercharging was no longer by a large-diameter piston but by a Zoller eccentric-vane compressor built on to the front of the crankcase. Chain driven at engine speed, it breathed through a pair of carburettors and fed the crankcase, which thus served as a gas reservoir. Used only in training sessions before war broke out, the engine gave 40 bhp to its predecessor's 30, so amply justifying Meurer's confidence. Moreover, it was doubled up into a four-piston split-twin with the object of consolidating the factory's newly-won 350 cc championship.

Nor was even that the last word from the DKW technicians, for they next refined the split-single principle in a way that enabled them easily to alter the exhaust piston's lead. This they did by swinging the two cylinder bores out to opposite sides of the combustion chamber, so that the pistons worked crown-to-crown in a double-length cylinder with a small crankcase at each end. Since the crankshafts were connected by a train of gears, it was a simple matter to remesh these to experiment with various exhaust leads.

Chain driven from the exhaust crankshaft, the compressor fed a gas reservoir surrounding a ring of transfer ports in one end of the cylinder. A ring of exhaust ports was formed in the other end, so that the gas had the so-called uniflow motion – in at one end of the cylinder, out at the other. Just how feasible an engine of such awkward shape would have been is arguable but there is no disputing the large port areas available for quite modest port heights – to the obvious benefit of torque.

Today's racing two-strokes spin two or three times as fast as the prewar Deeks. Although the ban on blowing that brought that about is technically fair, it has also led to a comparatively dull uniformity in engine layout. More diversity of design came out of that one German factory in the 1930s than all the postwar two-stroke stables have contributed in any comparable period.

Top: *close-up of a 350 cc split-twin engine, showing carburettor positions and high-tension leads from the flywheel magneto*

Left: *last of the works DKW 250 cc split-single engines to use a piston-type compressor (in front of the working cylinder). The compressor breathes through a gear-driven rotary valve (fed by a carburettor at each end) and pumps its charge into the front bore of the split cylinder. The compressor is air cooled, the working cylinder is water cooled*

REARGUARD ACTION
POSTWAR FOUR-STROKES

STARVED of their beloved sport for a seemingly eternal seven or eight years, the prewar stars were as keen to get back on the track as the new young hopefuls were to prove their prowess. But the response of the factories to the FIM's virtual reprieve for unblown singles varied enormously, from heroic at best to pathetic at worst.

Most of the heroism came from Italy. Benelli dusted off Ted Mellors' 1939 TT-winning two-fifty, lowered the compression just enough to suit the pink-prone fuel of the time, pushed peak revs up still farther and entrusted the bike to their dynamic new star, Dario Ambrosini. A lone hand, he immediately started showing his megaphone to some of Britain's best three-fifties in minor races, although his impact on the world championship was delayed by a spill in the first lap of the 1949 TT. A year later he not only won the TT spectacularly but went on to bring both the individual and manufacturers' titles to the tiny Pesaro factory. The following year, 1951, promised a repeat performance as Ambrosini amassed world-title points galore, even though over-jetting in hot weather took 500 rpm off peak revs and cost him another TT by a few seconds. Sadly, he was killed instantly during the French GP meeting at Albi, when scorching heat melted the tar and he skidded into a telegraph pole during training. What further lightweight glory Benelli might have earned can only be guessed at, for the team was much too small to shrug off such a tragic loss.

Moto Guzzi, too, lost no time adapting their old 250 cc racers to the low-octane fuel, switching from girder to leading-link front forks (teles were not good enough for Giulio Carcano) and regaining the lightweight supremacy they had lost to the blown DKWs before the war. By 1952 they had won their third world championship within four years, manufacturers' titles as well as individual, and they had the confidence to stretch their five-speed engine/gearbox unit, in two stages, to 350 cc.

It is an old truism that you get a livelier three-fifty by scaling up a good two-fifty than by scaling down a good five-hundred. Moto Guzzi proved it emphatically by pushing Norton off their 350 cc perch straight away and dominating the class for their remaining five years in classic racing. Nor was that all, for they cheekily stretched that all-conquering three-fifty into a highly competitive 500 cc single, which was fast (150 mph), agile and extraordinarily light.

Bob McIntyre at Ballaugh Bridge on a Bianchi twin in the 1961 Junior TT

Alas for Britain, Velocette were the first to die in that early postwar scramble. Harold Willis, the only engineer who could have kept their 350 cc singles in the hunt, proved irreplaceable. His inspiration sorely missed, the factory made few changes and the most notable of those was far from successful. This was a rehash of the double-knocker layout; in theory it should have boosted performance. In practice both Freddie Frith and Bob Foster usually preferred the greater tractability of the old, single-knocker engine.

By the time Foster (1947) and Frith (1948 and 1949) had won the first three postwar Junior TTs and shared the first two world 350 cc championships (Frith 1949, Foster 1950), Joe Craig's Nortons had more than made up the leeway in raceworthiness. What was more, Harold Daniell's evergreen craftsmanship, in consolidating his 1938 Senior TT victory for Norton with repeats in 1947 and 1949, was soon backed up by a flood of eager new talent, notably Geoff Duke, Artie Bell, Reg Armstrong and Ray Amm.

The combination of all that riding ability with the vastly improved handling of the duplex featherbed frame and Craig's unrelenting engine development kept Norton in the vanguard of the title hunt until Moto Guzzi took over in the 350 cc class, with their much better single-cylinder layout, and Gilera added decent handling to the superior speed of their four in the 500 cc class.

Following a change of management, Norton withdrew from classic racing at the end of 1954, but not before Joe Craig had seen the writing on the wall. Scheduled for 1955 but never raced was a horizontal single with external flywheel and integral five-speed gearbox in a large-diameter spine frame. But it is doubtful whether it would have disturbed Moto Guzzi for (copy though it was) it was nothing like so low or light and the cylinder finning was circumferential, not radial (although that could easily have been changed).

Also laid out, but never even built, was a water-cooled 500 cc Norton double-knocker four in a featherbed frame. But, since the sump was too wide to slot between the bottom frame tubes, the machine's centre of gravity would have been too high to match the handling of the singles.

That theory, by the way, was proved in 1961, when Norton development engineer Doug Hele produced a racing version of the pushrod 500 cc Dominator parallel-twin engine as a possible and less costly successor to the catalogue Manx model. So successful was Doug's engine tuning that the Domiracer matched Manx performance and Tom Phillis turned the first 100 mph TT lap with a pushrod engine. But the crankcase was again too wide to slot between the bottom rails and the consequent raising of the centre of gravity meant that the Domiracer never handled quite as well as the Manx.

The other outstanding big single in the early postwar period was the so-called Boy Racer, the 350 cc AJS 7R. First marketed in 1948, it got off to a quiet start as a fairly unblushing copy of the Mark 8 KTT Velo, from which it took its 74 ×81 mm cylinder dimensions, single ohc, eccentric rocker spindles and magnesium-alloy cone hubs. It differed from the KTT, however, in having a telescopic (not girder) front fork, coil springs (not air) as the rear springing medium, and chain drive (not bevel gears) for the camshaft. It was also noticeably lighter, thanks to a welded frame, aluminium tanks and magnesium engine castings.

An experimental three-valver (two exhausts) designed in 1952 by Ike Hatch, who had laid out the four-valve Excelsior Mechanical Marvel engine before the war, showed promise when New Zealander Rod Coleman won the 1954 Junior TT, so curtailing a five-year Norton monopoly. Within a month an improved version (the 7R3B) was giving more power (some 39 bhp to

Left: *Benelli's lone star Dario Ambrosini, world 250 cc champion in 1950*

Centre: *Freddie Frith winning the 1949 Junior TT on a works double-knocker KTT Velocette. He went on to become world 350 cc champion*

40 bhp at 8,000 rpm), but the factory quit official racing at the end of the year and the 7R continued only as a two-valve catalogue racer, developed to a wonderful pitch by Jack Williams, who, despite a shoestring budget, pushed the power up from 37 bhp at 7,500 rpm to nearly 42 bhp at 7,800, meanwhile cutting the weight from 310 lb to 285 lb.

Testing the winners

It was in the early 1950s that I first became involved in the fascinating ritual of testing the TT winners for *Motor Cycle* – the next best thing to full-time professional racing. With an eye to the future, I had just switched from occasional to full-time journalism but had managed to persuade the editor that the odd freelance outing in the Isle of Man and elsewhere was essential to my sanity. The happy result was that team managers quite confidently trusted their precious machines to my care, while the editor realised that a racing man's assessment of them was more authentic than that of a non-racing journalist, who might be too overwhelmed by the excellence of racing standards in general to form an objective judgement of any machine in particular. For the sake of privacy, these tests were usually conducted during dinner time on race day, when most folk were eating, or at five or six o'clock the following morning, while they were snoring. And, except when mountain mist forced us lower down, we used the highest and remotest part of the course.

My first test was of the Gambalunghino Moto Guzzi on which Fergus Anderson had just won his first TT (the 1952 Lightweight 250 cc) at the record speed of 83·82 mph. Indeed, in that first year following Ambrosini's tragic death, Gambalunghinos had made a clean sweep of the race, with Enrico Lorenzetti second, Syd Lawton third and world champion Bruno Ruffo pushing the lap record to 84·82 mph before slowing on the final lap, seemingly on team orders.

A few surprises awaited me at the Italians' Douglas Bay Hotel headquarters that Wednesday evening, even before I cocked a leg over the bike. The handlebar was only 18 in wide, with no more than 6 in separating the clutch and front-brake nipples, yet there

In 1953 Norton translated Eric Oliver's stream-lined kneeler concept from sidecar to solo for Ray Amm. It never caught on for road racing, although Amm stretched the hour record to 134 miles on the Montlhéry banked oval

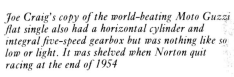

Joe Craig's copy of the world-beating Moto Guzzi flat single also had a horizontal cylinder and integral five-speed gearbox but was nothing like so low or light. It was shelved when Norton quit racing at the end of 1954

Envisaged but never built – the water-cooled 500 cc Norton four. With the duplex-loop featherbed frame shown, the wide engine would have been too high to match the superb handling of the single

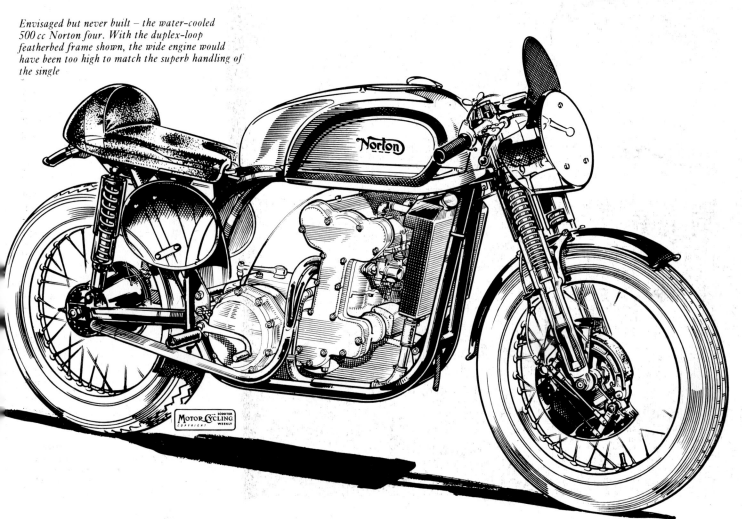

Above: *following his first TT victory, in the 1952 Lightweight 250 cc race, Fergus Anderson (second from left) compares notes with the author during a test of the winning Moto Guzzi Gambalunghino. Studying the Dellorto concentric carburettor is C. R. B. Smith, an Amal representative. Extreme left is Harry Louis, then editor of Motor Cycle*

Right: *one of the few frames that was designed rather than just happened. Bob McIntyre's home-made frame for his AJS 7R eliminated vibration and gave extra cornering clearance by enabling footrests and exhaust to be tucked farther in. After his death it was raced by Jack Findlay on a Matchless G50*

was no steering damper. With the course as diabolically bumpy as it was then and the bike good for 115 mph, that said a great deal for the steering and suspension.

There was evidence of some aerodynamic thinking in the shape of the four-gallon tank, which extended forward round the steering head to blend with the front number plate and was profiled to match the rider's forearms. Accustomed as I was to gearing my bikes for 7,000 rpm and hearing the dreaded valve float at 7,500 rpm or thereabouts, the 10,000 rpm calibration on the tachometer dial struck me as well-nigh astronomical. Five speeds, too, were a

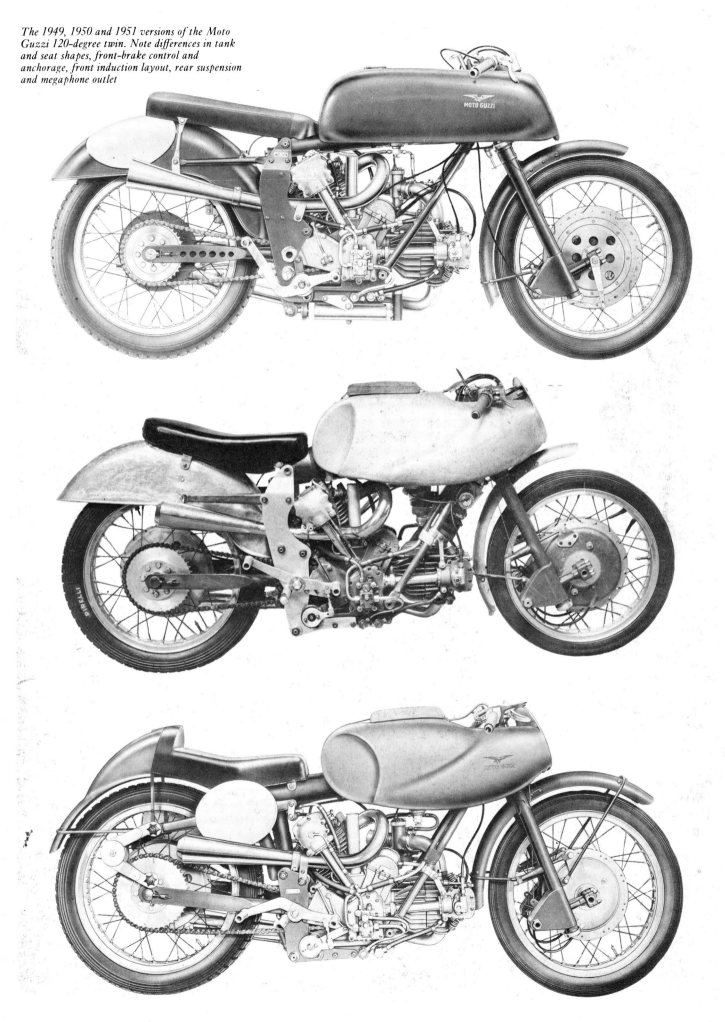

The 1949, 1950 and 1951 versions of the Moto Guzzi 120-degree twin. Note differences in tank and seat shapes, front–brake control and anchorage, front induction layout, rear suspension and megaphone outlet

Last of the works 350 cc Norton engines (1954) has a two-piece crankshaft with outside flywheel and rubber-block shock absorber. Oil pump has three chambers: one for delivery, two for scavenge. Crankcase breathes through a pair of non-return valves. Flat piston crown matches cylinder head segments for squish at tdc. The cams are driven by bevels and five spur gears, the fuel pump by the inlet camshaft. Exhaust valve is sodium filled, and its guide is oil cooled

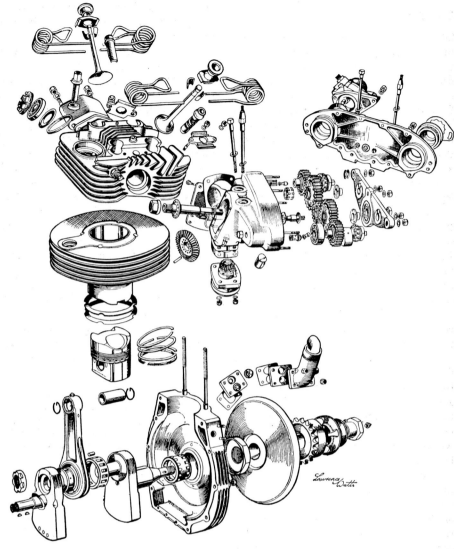

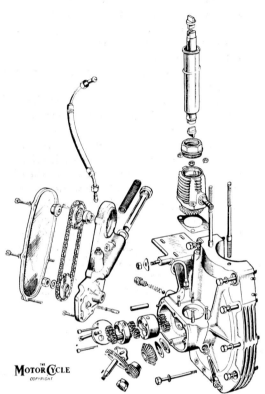

THE MOTOR CYCLE COPYRIGHT

novelty I could hardly wait to try, as was the concentric float chamber on the steeply downdraught Dellorto carburettor, designed to ensure a consistent fuel level in the jet regardless of braking, acceleration and cornering effects.

Making my way up the Snaefell road to our rendezvous, I found the engine delightfully tractable on one-third throttle up to 3,200 rpm. From there to 5,000 "megaphonitis"* played havoc with the power un-

* The purpose of a megaphone on an exhaust pipe is to accentuate the negative pressure wave reflected back to the port at the time of the following valve overlap – exhaust closing, inlet opening. This depression increases the pressure differential across the valves, so helping to get the fresh charge moving into the cylinder (hence the term "free supercharging").

With a fixed pipe length, however, the arrival of the depression corresponds with valve overlap only over a narrow rpm range – and pipe length is calculated to produce the effect at peak-torque rpm. At substantially lower speeds, a positive pressure wave arrives at the exhaust port during overlap, so hindering induction and causing irregular running – "megaphonitis".

less the engine was eased through the period by delicate throttle juggling. That was no criticism of the engine, however, for no rider would be that low in the rev band during a race. Indeed, Fergus Anderson's advice for starting and pulling away from really slow bottom-gear corners was to use full throttle and slip the metal-to-metal clutch for as long as necessary to keep the revs between 7,000 and 8,000 rpm.

"The clutch is indestructible," he assured me, and so it proved – even under the brutal treatment of turning round in the narrow road at the Guthrie Memorial and doing a virtual standing start up the steep gradient. Those alternate steel and bronze plates, running in oil, were a revelation after the dry clutches, with inserted friction pads, that were then common on catalogue racers.

As with most successful racing machines, the Gambalunghino was a sheer delight to ride from every point of view. Thanks to the small, stiff crankcase and large-diameter outside flywheel, the single-ohc engine was turbine-smooth. It was surprisingly eager, too, so that one had to catch it early when changing up: at 7,500 rpm from bottom to second, 7,800 rpm for the next two changes and 8,000 rpm from fourth to top.

"Eight-five won't break it," said Fergus. Indeed, that was where it gave its 27 bhp and it happily spun faster downhill. The gear change was short, light and quick to a degree that had taken a lot of work to match on my Mark 8 KTT Velos. Not surprisingly for a bike weighing only 257 lb, the single-leading-shoe brakes, in which an internal scissors action equalised cable pressure on the front shoes to give a floating-shoe effect, were amply powerful. Nor did I experience any judder, although the absence of a pivoted front-brake anchorage tended to extend the leading-link fork and so resist nose dipping.

Above all, however, none of the vicious bumps on the Mountain Mile seemed to get past the suspension and the steering remained rock-steady as well as light. What is more, despite Fergus Anderson's several extra inches in height, the riding position and control layout suited me fine, proving an old conviction of mine that there is less difference between the ideal layouts for different statures than there is between good and bad layouts. A simple example: if a rider has to lift his foot from the rest to change up or down or to apply the rear brake, then he or the designer is a trifle short of grey matter.

Comparison

Of the three TT machines I tried the following year, one held an extra interest for me. It was the works Norton on which Ray Amm had won the Junior race at the record speed of 90·52 mph (including a record lap at 91·82 mph). In the same race, I brought home the first standard Manx Norton (a two-year-old long-stroke owned by Barnsley dealer Tom Garner) and I was keen to draw a comparison.

That year, the AJS "Boy Racers" had the legs of Tom's Norton by 8 to 10 mph and it was only the lovely flip-flop handling of the featherbed frame that enabled me to scratch back some time and finish as high as 12th at 83·62 mph. But my real interest was to discover how the latest Joe Craig special compared with the rather sluggish old catalogue 40M Manx model.

In a nutshell, there was simply no comparison in any department: engine, brakes, suspension, steering, even noise. Amm's riding position was superbly comfortable, especially the forward setting of the backrest on the seat. Outstandingly light and smooth, the controls could not have been better positioned, except that the gear pedal was a trifle too high – something with which Amm agreed, although he had not bothered to adjust it!

The exhaust note was much less raucous than a standard machine, thanks to the reverse cone on the megaphone. The effect of that, and the cleaner carburation that resulted from the novel, weir-type float chamber, was to make the engine extremely tractable once it was through its full-throttle "trumpeting" speed of 5,000 rpm. And its smoothness, throughout the normal rev range, was uncanny.

As for power, the almost-square (75·9 × 77 mm) engine seemed like a five-hundred. Joe told me its 37 bhp came at 7,700 rpm (equivalent to 120 mph in top gear) but I believe the works riders frequently saw 8,000 rpm on the revmeter. Certainly I had no difficulty in getting 7,700 rpm on open roads in the early morning and could undoubtedly have got more under racing conditions. To my surprise, Joe propounded the theory that one should change up at peak torque (7,200–7,300 rpm in this case) rather than peak power. That has never made racing sense to me and I suspect he was simply trying to make doubly sure I did not over-rev his precious engine. I was impressed by the fact that, however rapidly I dabbed the pedal, it was impossible to fling through the next gear into a false neutral, as sometimes happened with the standard Norton gearbox. No doubt the camplate had been lightened to reduce its inertia, and the indexing mechanism carefully set up.

The suspension was far more sensitive than standard, as I expected from the manual

check I made before starting up. When I pumped the back of the bike down by hand, the resistance was initially soft with a progressive build-up. When I released it, there was no lively bouncing: the recoil was stiffly damped to the sound of protesting hydraulic fluid being forced through tiny orifices. On the bumpy Mountain Mile that translated into an uncannily steady ride, with no pitching and the wheels seemingly glued to the road.

Good as the Manx steering was by the standards of other catalogue racers, it was impossible not to envy Ray the greater precision of the works bike and the absence of snaking on bumpy bends. Even allowing for the superior front suspension, that clearly reflected the difference in the rear subframe, which was welded to the main frame on the works machines (a very stiff arrangement) but only bolted to it on the production models.

That year, we Manx riders had been plagued by fracture of rear-strut piston rods regardless of make. Some struts even

First Moto Guzzi experiment in stretching their successful 250 cc engine to 350 cc. On the low-slung 320 cc prototype, Fergus Anderson rounds Creg-ny-Baa in 1953 Junior TT. He finished third and went on to win the world championship

fractured during warm-up, pinpointing the natural vibration frequency of the bolted-on subframe as the culprit. Later in the week I was robbed of sixth place in the Senior when a fractured rod at the apex of Sarah's Cottage brought me down on the sixth lap and promoted Peter Davey from seventh spot.

The following year, the factory welded the subframe on the Manx models as well as on the works specials. As a result, Manx steering benefited from the elimination of subframe flexure, while piston-rod fracture was cured by the raising of the subframe's natural frequency.

My final impression of Amm's Junior winner concerned the braking: whereas it was a matter of luck whether the production-line Manx twin-leading-shoe front brake was powerfully smooth or lethally harsh (a locked front wheel unseated me at Greeba during 1954 TT practice after I had ignored the warning signs on several previous applications), Amm's works brake combined light control pressure with great power and utter smoothness. It was possible to squeal the tyre controllably, and any steering bias because of the one-sided torque anchorage was virtually undetectable. Naturally, the usefulness of the single-leading-shoe rear brake was limited by forward weight transfer,

but the control leverage was such that a good deal of feel was obtained without locking the wheel.

That 1953 layout was not the end of development for the works Nortons, however. In the year or more before they pulled out, the stroke was shortened to 78·4 mm for the five-hundred (90 mm bore) and to 73 mm for the three-fifty (78 mm bore) and the connecting-rod was shortened in proportion as an additional means of cutting engine height. To maintain the necessary flywheel inertia with the shorter rod, the traditional pair of internal flywheels was abandoned in favour of an Italian-style external flywheel of 9 in diameter. The crankshaft itself was a two-piece forging in KE805 steel, with the hollow crankpin formed integrally with the drive-side web, bobweight and mainshaft, on which was mounted a four-vane rubber transmission shock absorber. Depth of cylinder finning was increased, although the height of the crankcase mouth left room for only six fins on the 350 cc barrel and eight on the larger one. Squish bands in the combustion chamber gave compression ratios of 10·4:1 (500 cc) and 10·8:1 (350 cc), while carburettor sizes were $1\frac{13}{32}$ in and $1\frac{3}{16}$ in respectively with 20 degrees downdraught.

An unusual but logical feature was oil cooling of the exhaust-valve guide: cambox oil drained through a spiral groove round the outside of the guide, to take away heat transferred from the valve head to the stem

by the sodium splashing about inside; it then passed through a small radiator on its way to the bottom bevel housing for scavenging.

Unfortunately for Norton, Joe Craig's tentative shift towards Moto Guzzi single-cylinder design features was too late and too slow, and it was left to the Italian team, under Giulio Carcano's brilliant guidance, to show the imagination necessary to exploit the single's fundamental advantages of light weight, low centre of gravity and tiny frontal area, which more than compensated for the extra engine power of the multis.

Scaling up

It was late in 1952 that Fergus Anderson realised the 250 cc Gambalunghino's potential in the larger classes. In June that year, his own Lightweight TT victory was Moto Guzzi's seventh in the class and, by the end of the season, Enrico Lorenzetti had clinched the factory's third world 250 cc championship in four years. Anderson was convinced that the Gambalunghino chassis could handle plenty more power. What was more, increasing the cylinder size meant adding little weight to the bike's 264 lb, thus giving it a very competitive power/weight ratio.

Tentatively, engine capacity was boosted to 320 cc by boring the cylinder from 68 to 72 mm and moving the crankpin closer to the edge of the crank webs, so stretching the stroke from 68 to 80 mm. That pushed peak power up from 28·5 bhp at 8,400 rpm to

31 bhp at 7,700 rpm and the results surprised even Anderson: clocking 130 mph in top gear, he won the 350 cc German Grand Prix at Hockenheim (then an ultra-fast loop) and chased the works Nortons of Ray Amm and Ken Kavanagh home in the Junior TT. It needed no more encouragement for Carcano to go ahead with a full-size engine (75 × 79 mm), which gave 33·5 bhp at 7,500 rpm and much better torque. Anderson finished the 1953 season as world 350 cc champion.

Almost inevitably, such quick-fire results brought teething troubles. Big-end life was short in the new engine while cylinder distortion gave rise to heavy oil consumption. For 1954, therefore, the cylinder liner was thickened and the piston redesigned (with a full skirt), two moves that restored oil consumption to normal. Big-end stamina was achieved by ditching the one-piece crankshaft, with its split crowded-roller bearing, in favour of a three-piece shaft with the caged-roller bearing necessary for such duty. The net result was that Anderson retained his title.

Nevertheless, wholesale modifications were made for 1955: cylinder dimensions went very much oversquare (80 × 69·5 mm) with carburettor and valve sizes increased to match. Construction was altered, too, the light-alloy bore being hard-chromed (with an etched finish) instead of sleeved, and the piston clearance being greatly reduced to suit. Twin camshafts were adopted, as was battery-powered dual ignition, with two 10 mm plugs fired simultaneously by separate coils and contact breakers.

Supplementing these engine changes, which lifted power to 35 bhp at 7,800 rpm, was a multi-tube space-frame designed to support a full "dustbin" fairing, and a new position for the tank. This was changed to a cylindrical shape slung transversely just above the engine. A pump, driven by the inlet camshaft, lifted fuel to the carburettor and a padded dummy tank served as a chest support for the rider.

That was the bike Bill Lomas rode to his first world championship and, only a few hours after his record-breaking Junior TT victory, I got my eager hands on it for a test. By the time I had finished with it, I was convinced that that bike was everything a racing machine should be. So comprehensive were its virtues that it was difficult to single out any one as being the most significant, but nothing was more impressive than the near-perfect steering and handling.

Many years later, after he had switched to successful yacht design, Carcano told me that particular frame was Moto Guzzi's best. The small-diameter tubes provided really firm support for the fairing; the width across the tubes gave ample lateral stiffness; and the enormous effective diameter of the structure ensured great torsional stiffness.

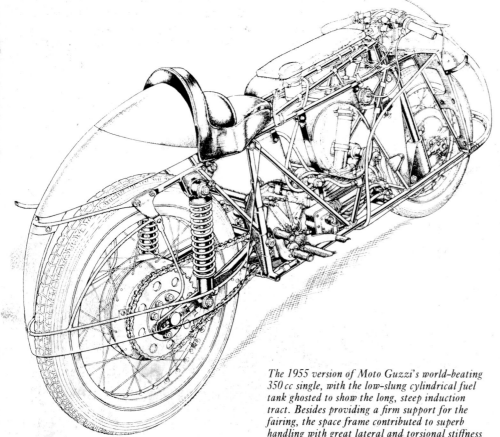

The 1955 version of Moto Guzzi's world-beating 350 cc single, with the low-slung cylindrical fuel tank ghosted to show the long, steep induction tract. Besides providing a firm support for the fairing, the space frame contributed to superb handling with great lateral and torsional stiffness

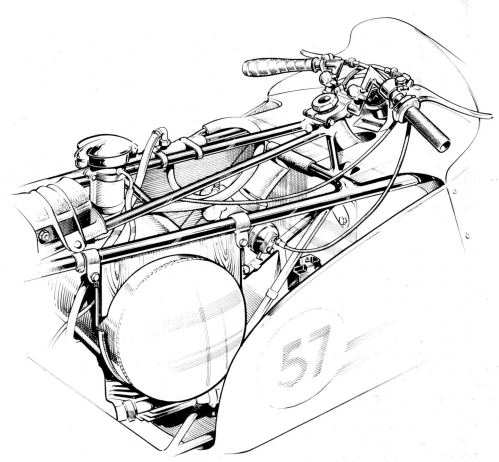

Close-up of Moto Guzzi's low-slung fuel tank, extended filler and some of the plumbing in the pump feed to the carburettor

New dimension

Certainly, those theories were borne out on the road. Even allowing for the bike's lightness and exceptionally low centre of gravity, I was amazed at the ease and confidence with which I could flick it from lock to lock at any speed. And it was not until I heard something vibrating up front that I realised the friction-type steering damper had slackened right off! For me, that Moto Guzzi added a new dimension to the concept of steering, although Australian Ken Kavanagh brought me down to earth a little by saying that no rider's education was complete until he had taken that streamliner flat-out and airborne past the Highlander.

As usual, the exhaust resonances went wild just below 5,000 rpm on a wide-open throttle. But progressive grip twisting took the engine cleanly through the period, and that was the technique employed by the team riders when pulling out of slow corners. One of the engine's most uncanny features was its turbine-smoothness at all revs. Considering the theoretical impossibility of balancing a reciprocating single, that engine made nonsense of the textbooks. It was helped, of course, by the fact that the 9 in-diameter external flywheel had most of its weight concentrated in the rim. Flywheel

A Moto Guzzi mechanic obliges with a helpful shove as the author sets out in blustery rain on a test run on Ken Kavanagh's 1956 Junior TT-winning Moto Guzzi single. The fuel tank had not been replenished since the beginning of the seven-lap (264-mile) race

inertia and the machine's light weight combined to produce the slight lurch characteristic of Moto Guzzi singles when changing up, but every change was fast and light. The top two changes (third/fourth, fourth/fifth) were made without declutching, and the relatively wide spacing of second and third was noticeable only when changing down.

Calculation showed that maximum speeds in the gears were 57, 73, 104, 121 and 132

mph, but even the last of those speeds was wholly deceptive because of the cosy shelter provided by the little cockpit and the uncannily absorbent suspension. From rest to flat out the Moto Guzzi accelerated at a rate that utterly belied its modest power, impressive confirmation of the virtues of light weight at the lower end of the speed range and low drag at the upper end.

Flywheel inertia (reinforced by the low

After sampling Bill Lomas' 1955 Junior TT-winning Moto Guzzi flat single, the author tries Bob McIntyre's second-place Manx Norton (1954 Model). The home cobbled fairing boosted top speed but overheated the engine and brakes

drag) was again evident when the throttle was snapped shut at top speed, for engine braking was less than expected. Not that there was the slightest cause for alarm, for light control pressure produced smooth, straight and incredibly powerful braking from the duplex front and single rear drums, another bonus of light weight.

For comparison I had persuaded Bob McIntyre to bring along the second-place Norton on which he had startled everyone by leading Bill Lomas for the first four laps, until the Norton engine and brakes went sick. It was not a works bike, just a year-old standard Manx, home-tuned in Glasgow and dressed in a blunt, flat-sided dustbin fairing (also a d-i-y job) that enabled Mac to gear up one tooth on the engine sprocket (five per cent) and still get 7,500 rpm in top. For seven flat-out laps, however, that hastily cobbled fairing had robbed Mac's engine and brakes of most of their customary cooling air. The results were obvious: compression was so poor that the Norton could easily be wheeled in bottom gear, and the engine rattled ominously as it struggled up to an apologetic 115 mph. Similarly, the brakes had clearly suffered from overheating. Those

defects apart, my general impressions of Mac's streamlined Manx were similar to those I had just formed on Lomas' wonderful Moto Guzzi, except that gusty side winds plucked much more strongly at the high, flat sides of the Norton fairing than at the Moto Guzzi's low curved flanks.

Electrifying talent

If that comparison showed that sound ideas are best carried out with proper engineering facilities and know-how, it also convinced me that McIntyre's race performance that day was one of the most brilliant in TT history. Indeed, with his subsequent Isle of Man rides – notably on works Gilera and Honda fours but also on private singles – it stamped McIntyre as arguably the greatest-ever master of the TT course. Here was a rider whose tremendous natural talent, strength, courage and determination were galvanised into supreme achievement by his recognition of those $37\frac{3}{4}$ tortuous, bumpy miles as the greatest challenge in grand-prix racing. Lesser events meant little to McIntyre, but his stupendous response to the TT's unique challenge ensured that, equally mounted, he could and did take half a minute or more a lap out of the likes of

For 1956, the 350 cc Moto Guzzi single acquired this sleeker fairing, while the rear subframe was stiffened by a triangulated cluster of short tubes

acceleration and enabled the overall gearing to be raised a little, lifting top speed to 135 mph at 7,600 rpm.

The eventual outcome was a repeat world 350 cc championship for Bill Lomas, although it was Ken Kavanagh who escaped valve-gear trouble to win the Junior TT in foul weather and whose bike I collected from the Douglas Bay Hotel that afternoon. It was no secret that the Moto Guzzis had no need to refuel in seven laps. Even so, I could scarcely believe my eyes as Carcano drained Ken's tank for an accurate check of consumption before tipping the fuel back in for my test. In 264 non-stop miles, lapping in the low-90s, Ken had used little more than four gallons – an average of 60–65 mpg! Nor was that at all unusual: a similar check after Bill Lomas won the German Grand Prix at Solitude a few weeks later gave 62 mpg. A comparable modern two-stroke gulps fuel at three or four times that rate.

Weather conditions for my ride were just as foul as they had been for the race (for all its privileges, a journalist's life is no bed of roses), but I found the steering, suspension and engine smoothness as impeccable as ever and the gear ratios better spaced than in 1955. The improved fairing shape was evident in an even smaller curb on speed when the throttle was snapped back and Kavanagh told me that this had caused him to revise his cornering technique completely compared with the way he used to ride the unfaired factory Nortons. Enter a bend too fast on a naked Norton, he said, and you could escape disaster by shutting the throttle, for the bike would lose speed immediately. The same action on the streamliner would be quite ineffective, however, so it was imperative never to tackle a corner too fast; trying to shed speed by grabbing those potent brakes with the machine banked to the limit was unthinkable. In strong winds, too, it paid to seek the sheltered side of the road (if any) and to anticipate the inevitable swerve at breaks in the shelter.

Discontent

With the last four world 350 cc championships in the bag, many a race engineer would have been content. But not Giulio Carcano: the faster Gilera and MV fours were yapping at his heels and the three-cylinder DKW two-stroke was showing an embarrassing turn of acceleration from low and medium speeds. More to the point, however, Carcano was convinced that the extra top-end performance he had obtained in 1956 had cost him too much in terms of bottom-end punch. Putting his convictions to the test with a practice session on the twisty Modena circuit, he found that the 1954 long-stroke single-knocker lapped faster, simply because of its better acceleration out of slow corners.

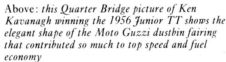

Above: *this Quarter Bridge picture of Ken Kavanagh winning the 1956 Junior TT shows the elegant shape of the Moto Guzzi dustbin fairing that contributed so much to top speed and fuel economy*

mere world champions. In all its years the TT has never known a more electrifying talent.

For 1956 the most noticeable improvements to the Moto Guzzi singles were an even sleeker fairing and considerable stiffening of the rear subframe by a cluster of short triangulated tubes. Equally significant but less obvious, 30 lb was slashed from the already low weight and the cam form was modified to give substantially more torque and a mite more power. Spacing of the five speeds was improved while the extra torque, lower weight and reduced drag boosted

So the twin targets for 1957 were even more low-speed torque and less weight. After two years, the oversquare cylinder dimensions gave way to the old 75×79 mm bore and stroke, although the carburettor size remained 37 mm and the valve diameters (39 mm inlet, 33 mm exhaust) were not reduced quite to their earlier dimensions. Magneto ignition was reinstated, with only one plug (still 10 mm) – dual ignition had given a slight gain in low-down power and might have been retained if a suitable twin-spark magneto had been available, but the extra weight and bulk of the battery, two coils and two contact breakers was not thought worthwhile. Anyway, dual ignition called for appreciably less spark advance; and if one plug should foul (the 10 mm size was then a trifle sensitive) the timing was much too late for the surviving one.

These alterations produced the required boost in torque and a power bonus, too, pushing the peak up to 38 bhp at 7,800–8,000 rpm. In spite of the pioneering use of single helical springs for the valves, these remained under control right up to 8,400 rpm.

As to weight, the absence of the customary inner valve springs and the tiny plug size were just two of many contributions, most of them insignificant on their own, towards a further 30 lb reduction. Wherever possible (nuts, banjo unions, oil-pump body), aluminium was substituted for steel or cast iron. Except for the cylinder and head, aluminium gave way to the even lighter magnesium for the engine castings. Studs were waisted, gears perforated. And, since less weight requires less braking power, one front brake was shed.

The overall result was that the 350 cc Moto Guzzi, in Continental trim (with small tank and 2·50 in-section tyres), weighed a mere 216 lb; the fatter tyres (2·75 in front, 3·00 in rear) and extra tankage necessary for 264 non-stop miles made it a bit heavier in TT trim. The net result in achievement was the fifth world individual 350 cc title on the trot, by Australian Keith Campbell. In the Junior TT, however, he was beaten into second place by the invincible Bob McIntyre on a four-cylinder Gilera, who thus made his initial contribution to that factory's double world manufacturers' championship.

When I collected Campbell's bike for test a few hours after the race, the 30 lb weight reduction was immediately noticeable, both in handling and acceleration. At 140 mph, its top speed was probably 5 mph down on the Gilera (surely no more, since Moto Guzzi's 50-year-old tester Alano Montanari made the fastest 350 cc lap at Monza that year, in a race won by Bob McIntyre), but the Moto Guzzi scored in being fast everywhere, not just on the straights. It could be

Now used by top-flight skiers and bob-sleigh teams, the Moto Guzzi wind tunnel near Lake Como permitted full-scale tests of machines and riders. A large ring of lights facing him indicated wind drag to the rider and so enabled him to determine the fastest riding position

braked later and cornered faster (as Campbell showed a few weeks later when beating McIntyre in the Dutch TT on the very twisty Assen circuit). I certainly found no shortage of stopping power as a result of the switch to a single front brake – just a bit less harshness and even better wheel adhesion by virtue of the lower unsprung weight.

Starting was tricky. The carburettor had to be flooded but the combination of a horizontal mixing chamber and the unusually steep inlet tract put too much emphasis on luck if the mixture reaching the cylinder was not to be too wet for a clean pick-up. Below 5,000 rpm the engine still did not relish full throttle and Campbell told me he slipped the clutch at the ultra-slow Governor's Bridge and Ramsey hairpins, but used the progressive-throttle technique where the revs fell no lower than 4,000 rpm.

Ultra-light weight increases the difficulty of achieving perfect suspension because it reduces the ratio of sprung to unsprung weight. Yet Campbell's machine was as impressive as earlier Moto Guzzis on the mountain stretch I used for my tests. Keith said that he gave the steering damper a precautionary tweak only on the notoriously rough sections such as Bray Hill, Union Mills and Glen Vine.

Stunned

The riders were not alone in loving that 1957 model, for it was as easy to service as it was

to ride. With the previous year's valve-gear vulnerability beaten, it needed almost no maintenance and the high torque did away with the necessity to change the internal gear ratios for different circuits.

Unknown to the team, however, or even to Carcano, their days of joy and well-deserved achievement were soon to end. The Moto Guzzi, Gilera and FB Mondial managements had come to a joint agreement to quit grand-prix racing. At Modena, final round of the Italian championships, Carcano was stunned to learn of the decision, not from the management but from a third party.

Gone like a dream were those enthralling inter-make contests between engineering cunning and brute power in the 350 cc class. Gone, too, was the secret prospect of a similar contest in the 500 cc championship. For Carcano had built a big, four-valve single that weighed no more than the double-knocker three-fifty but would have produced a lot more power. Its smallish valves were set at a narrow angle to give a compact combustion chamber. And to combine high peak revs with easy maintenance, short pushrods were chosen. By the time the bad news broke, that engine was ready for bench testing. Alas, it never ran.

Britain first

The first multi to win a world championship was not the howling Gilera four, or even a BMW sidecar outfit, but the AJS Porcupine twin on which Les Graham took the very first 500 cc title in 1949. Unhappily, that success proved to be something of a flash in the pan. In retrospect, the rather ungainly double-knocker parallel twin can only be seen as the design that was caught on the hop, both by the ban on blowing and by a lamentable lack of continuity in its development.

Strangely, the Porcupine was Joe Craig's idea, dreamed up while he briefly worked at the AMC factory in Plumstead during the war. Mindful of the overwhelming power superiority that supercharging had bestowed on the BMWs and Gileras just before the war, and inspired by Velocette's courageous acceptance of the Continental challenge with the Roarer, Joe made blowing the cornerstone of his AJS design. That accounts for the vacant cradle on top of the integral four-speed gearbox (intended for a gear-driven Roots-type blower); the prone position of the cylinders to catch as much cooling air as possible for the heads; the peculiar pattern of the deep finning to promote air circulation; and the unusual layout of the original inlet ports.

Instead of approaching the valves from the cylinder-wall side (ie, from the top since the cylinders were horizontal), the ports came to the valves from the other side, beneath the inlet cambox – a common arrangement in vee-formation car racing engines. The chief purpose of this layout was to get a much straighter gas path into the cylinders and minimise the amount of

fresh gas blown past the exhaust valves during overlap. But there was a bonus as the long sweep of the inlet tracts, forward over the cambox and back to the valves, increased the gas capacity, so helping to damp down pressure fluctuations.

Right from the start, spike finning was used on the one-piece cylinder head but the separate barrels were originally intended to have continuous helical finning, to "screw" away the air between them and so prevent it from remaining undisturbed. When it came to casting, however, the foundry decreed that helical finning was impossible, so the fins had to be chopped into several sections, like turbine blades.

Other concessions to supercharging were sodium cooling for the exhaust valves; the overwide 90 degree angle between the valve stems (copied from other blown engines); the high speed of the clutch (0·7 times engine speed) to cope with the expected high torque; its ventilation (the enclosed clutches on the blown BMWs were known to resent abuse); and the heavy emphasis on robustness.

Machined from a single steel forging, the backward-rotating crankshaft had a large plain bearing in the middle as well as a massive roller bearing at each end. Split

plain bearings were also used in the big ends of the forged aluminium-alloy connecting rods. The full-skirt pistons were forged, too, as were the hollow camshafts, each supported in five roller bearings. Benelli-style, the camshafts were driven by a train of eight gears running on roller bearings stabilised by an outrigger plate. A ninth gear took the drive up to the oil pump and magneto on top of the magnesium-alloy crankcase. On the left a pair of $\frac{5}{8}$ in-wide straight-cut gears drove the clutch for the four-speed Burman-AJS gearbox, in which the free pinions as well as the shafts ran on roller bearings.

That, then, was to be AJS's blown challenger for postwar honours – but it was outdated by the FIM ban even before it was completed. Worse still, Joe Craig left to re-join Norton and Phil Irving – who, although not responsible for the design, had done a lot of the detail work – went back to Vincent. Hurriedly, someone else at Plumstead re-hashed the cylinder head with conventional inlet porting and a higher compression ratio and the Porcupine started its track career with 40 bhp at 7,600 rpm.

Ted Frend got it off to a good start in 1947 by winning the Dunholme 100-mile Grand Prix in Lincolnshire. But further staff problems followed and the engine was never

The 1950 version of the 500 cc AJS Porcupine twin engine. Cylinder barrels have second-stage (radial) finning; heads retain original spike fins. The one-piece crankshaft has a plain middle bearing. Gears on far side of crankcase drive magneto and oil pump

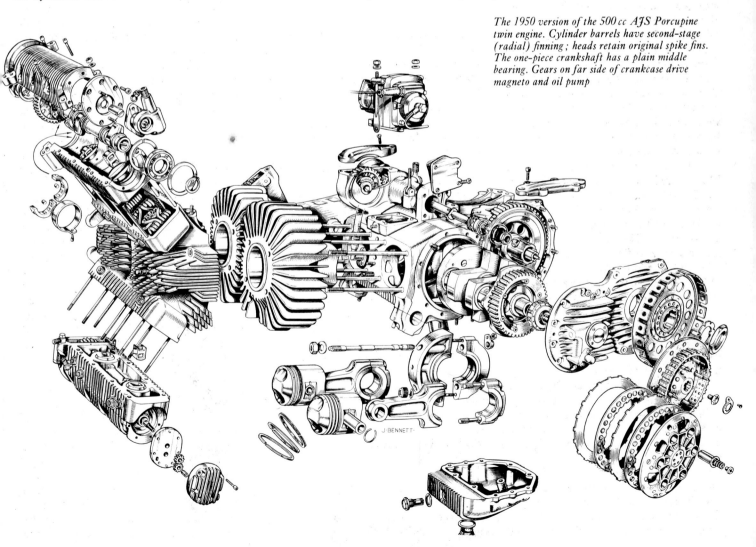

free from carburation troubles, in spite of changes in the inlet-pipe layout. Nor was the handling ever in the top grade, since the frame's potential was masked by the makers' obstinate refusal to ditch their own suspension struts for proprietary units.

Prospects perked up when Matt Wright, a prewar New Imperial wizard, left Vincent to apply his touch to the Porcupine, and it was under his influence that it was made sufficiently competitive for Les Graham to don the first world 500 cc crown. It was only cruel misfortune that year (1949) that robbed him of an even more popular achievement in British eyes – a Senior TT victory – when the magneto shaft sheared two miles from the chequered flag.

During Matt Wright's stay several modifications were made. They included revised barrel castings, first with Moto Guzzi-style radial finning, then ordinary circumferential finning when the cylinders were swivelled up 45 degrees; chain drive for the magneto to cure shaft failure; and wet-sump oiling instead of dry. Peak power was stepped up by stages from the original 40 bhp to 55 by the mid-1950s. But at all levels it was produced at about 7,600 rpm whereas – with twin overhead camshafts and a stroke of only 68·5 mm (bore 68 mm) – the engine should have peaked around 9,000 rpm.

Notwithstanding spasmodic successes for a few years following Les Graham's championship, the Porcupine never really

On the previous year's version of the AJS Porcupine twin, Bill Lomas swings into Parliament Square, Ramsey, in the 1952 Senior TT. He finished fifth. Note the fat rear-suspension struts (AJS "jampots") – the cause of much controversy between factory and riders

recovered from the attempted transition from the comparatively low-revving, high-boost machine it was originally intended to be, to the high-revver, with much wilder valve timing, that the postwar formula demanded.

Going for revs

Even while that rev-shy British twin was tantalising the factory's development engineers, their counterparts at NSU, in Germany, were ushering in the era of the high-revving multi in the most spectacular way with their 250 cc Rennmax twin.

In returning to the tracks, the factory's underlying aim was worldwide prestige through racing successes. "Even if we had been making domestic appliances," the brilliant Dr Walter Froede commented later, "it would still have made sense to race motor cycles . . . successfully. We were marketing a comprehensive range of high-class two-wheelers – mopeds, scooters and motor cycles. We wanted to make the name NSU a household word." Lesser spirits would have jibbed at such a confident assumption of success, but not NSU. They knew they had the engineering brains to develop competitive machines; with those they could command world-class riders. That made for an unbeatable combination. The results – three world titles for Werner Haas and one for Rupert Hollaus, all within two years – amply justified NSU's self-confidence. Yet the phenomenal Rennmax and its stablemate, the 125 cc Rennfox single, both grew and blossomed from the seeds of failure.

That fortuitous failure was a four-abreast

five-hundred, designed by Albert Roder to contest the big class of the world championships once Germany was readmitted to the FIM in 1951. At 53 bhp, its initial power was promising enough. But its short-term prospects were clouded by so many problems – with carburation, valve gear, lubrication and cooling – that it was soon abandoned, and NSU's postwar track debut was made with borrowed 125 cc Lambretta two-strokes!

A desperate need for more power was soon obvious, so a special crankcase was made for one cylinder of the 500 cc four and the resulting unit was substituted for one of the two-stroke engines. Within a few weeks, that hybrid machine was beating the formidable DKW two-strokes, which had a cylindrical rotary inlet valve across the back of the crankcase.

NSU were quick to take the hint. At the end of 1951 Albert Roder was given the job of developing the 125 cc single while Walter Froede created the Rennmax by grafting a pair of the five-hundred's cylinders on to the crankcase of a 250 cc sports twin he had previously laid out but which had been shelved for policy reasons.

In its original form, the Rennmax retained the 54 × 54 mm cylinder dimensions of the sportster, its pressed-up crankshaft with three main bearings and (optimistically, considering its high-revving potential) enclosed chain primary drive to the integral four-speed gearbox. From the prewar blown three-fifty it inherited separate splayed bevel drives to the inlet and exhaust camshafts (the overlapping hairpin valve springs were exposed). Since Roder's one-two-five had suffered a lot of magneto trouble in the early stages, ignition was by battery and coil.

By the following spring the engine was already giving a competitive 27 bhp at 9,000 rpm in preliminary bench tests. During the season, development boosted this to 31 bhp at 10,400 rpm. Although unreliable gear indexing occasionally let the engine scream briefly up to 15,000 rpm, the valve gear remained happily free from trouble. Impressive performances at Hockenheim, Nürburgring and Avus (in Berlin) were spectacularly capped at Monza in September. In the Italian Grand Prix, Werner Haas scared the pants off the Moto Guzzi team by finishing only inches behind world champion Enrico Lorenzetti and beating Fergus Anderson into third place.

For 1953, gears took over the primary drive, while the duplex-loop frame and telescopic front fork were superseded by a pressed-steel beam frame and leading-link fork, such as the one-two-five had from the start. Also, the first step was taken to gain speed by reducing drag, with a neat steering-head cowl extended rearward to fit snugly around the rider's forearms. Throughout the season Haas dominated the classics on his way to the championship. Indeed, he was

A rare picture – the 53 bhp engine of the 500 cc NSU four designed by Albert Roder for Germany's readmission to classic racing in 1951. After its abandonment, individual cylinders were built into the world-beating Rennfox single and Rennmax twin

relegated to second place only twice, by Anderson in the TT (where Haas was a newcomer) and by Lorenzetti in the Italian GP, where the Moto Guzzi's more extensive dolphin fairing gave it a sufficient edge for a 3·3-second winning advantage.

Cockpit

Following that TT I had my first chance to ride a Rennmax – a practice machine, since Haas' race bike had been shipped out of the Island immediately after the event. The initial impact was uncanny. For the first time, I had the strange sensation of being cooped up in a small cockpit, so effectively did the fairing keep the wind from buffeting me. And for the first time I not only saw five-figure calibrations on the revmeter dial but was obliged to keep the needle in that rarefied sector to do the engine justice.

Bill Lomas, who had been involved as a rider in the bike's early development, gave me the run-down. I would have to use race-weary batteries, he apologised; the fuel level in the left-hand carburettor was a shade on the high side; and the clutch and gear change were not so featherlight as on the race bike. A trifle short of perfection those shortcomings may have made the training model but they detracted not a bit from my enjoyment.

To bring the engine to life, the traditional

run-and-bump was simply a waste of energy – it was enough just to walk the machine in bottom gear and drop the clutch. At low revs, the left-side mixture richness tended to aggravate the engine's trumpeting. But thanks to the 3 ft-long shallow-taper megaphones this was not very pronounced and cleared at 4,000 rpm. From there upward, the engine's gluttony for revs was accentuated by the alternate firing of the cylinders.

The 1953 version of the 250 cc NSU Rennmax engine, with the pressed-up crankshaft assembly of a shelved sports twin, four speeds, square

To an ear accustomed to the beat of a single, the sharply soaring pitch of the exhaust seemed almost limitless and 10,000 rpm sounded more like 20,000. I snicked into second gear at 9,000 rpm and made the other two changes at 10,000 rpm. If that was a sub-standard gear change, I could only marvel at the Germans' perfectionism.

The dreaded mist on the mountain forced me to stay below Windy Corner, where the

cylinders, battery ignition and the splayed camshaft drives inherited from the prewar blown three-fifty

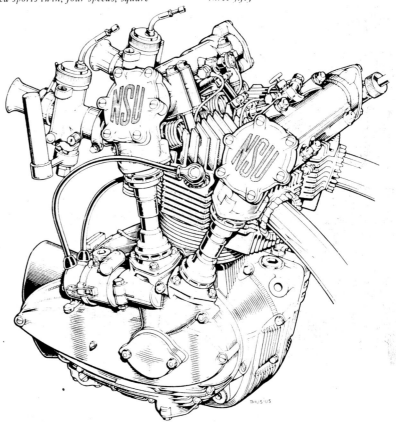

roads were less deserted and so more caution was required. Even so, the Rennmax eagerly romped up to 10,000 rpm in top – not far short of 120 mph – while the need to temper my enthusiasm for much of the time revealed the engine's extraordinary tractability. Surging power was on tap all the way from 4,000 to 10,400 rpm.

On the debit side a slight high-frequency tremor (typical of secondary engine vibration) could be felt through the footrests. And the bike showed a slight inclination to snake when speed was killed harshly. Both single-leading-shoe brakes were immensely potent, although I would have welcomed less leverage at the rear to prevent the wheel from locking so readily.

Front and rear, the suspension had the hallmark of unobtrusiveness under all conditions, while the taut handling and steering amply justified the change in frame and fork design. Although only half the season had been run, it was clear that nothing short of catastrophe could rob Haas of the championship and his continued superiority for the remainder of the season came as no surprise.

Fundamentals

True to their engineering instincts, NSU resisted the temptation to be dazzled by their quickfire successes. After all, the Rennmax at that stage was still part sportster, part racer – part prewar, part postwar. The bottom half, with its pressed-up three-bearing crankshaft and four-speed transmission, clearly limited the potential of the top half. The complex camshaft drive was unnecessarily weighty and generated too much friction, while the exposed valve stems – necessitating a tightish fit for the cam followers to prevent oil leakage – were anachronistic by German standards.

Dr Froede got down to racing fundamentals: first, coaxing the maximum weight of air into the cylinders in a given period of time (130 per cent breathing efficiency was measured on an airflow meter, while peak revs climbed steadily from 10,400 to 11,500 rpm); second, burning each charge as efficiently as possible; third, minimising loss of power through friction, flexure, distortion and pumping; fourth, cutting air drag still further.

The bottom half of the engine was entirely recast, as was the top, and even the cylinders in between were flattened from 54×54 mm to $55 \cdot 9 \times 50 \cdot 8$ mm to suit bigger valves and ports and keep piston friction in check. Supported in four massive roller bearings, the new forged crankshaft was in five pieces: a short central shaft incorporating a spur gear; a 5in-diameter inner flywheel disc each side with integral crankpin; and finally the two outer discs with integral mainshafts. For the utmost rigidity and narrowness (10 in overall), the five parts

The author's first ride on an NSU Rennmax twin, after the 1953 Lightweight 250 cc TT. Five-figure rpm rates were then a novelty. Leading-link front suspension had superseded the telescopic fork

were united by Hirth couplings, in which the four pairs of mating faces were radially serrated and clamped together by three differentially threaded bolts.

Because of loose bearings, magnesium was abandoned in favour of aluminium for the four-part crankcase, which housed a compact six-speed, all-indirect gear cluster, running in needle bearings. Above the crankshaft, and driven by the central spur gear, was a jackshaft that distributed the drive to the ventilated clutch and valve gear on the left and the ignition on the right.

Four separate stubby camshafts were used, joined left-to-right by tongued couplings and supported in a total of eight roller bearings. A single vertical bevel shaft drove the inlet camshafts and from there a train of three spur gears took the drive forward to the exhausts. Pivoted fingers transferred cam motion to the valve stems; to preclude float the valves were accelerated fiercely to only quarter-lift (2 mm), leaving the springs that much more time to arrest and reverse the motion.

The size of the Amal GP carburettors was increased progressively from 22 to 28 mm; the inlet valves grew to $1\frac{9}{16}$ in diameter and the exhausts were sodium cooled. After experiments ranging from 8:1 to 11:1, compression ratio settled down to 9·8:1. The forged pistons had full skirts and Al-Fin bonded construction was used for the separate cylinders. To ease big-end

stresses and tame the secondary vibration, 10 mm was added to the connecting rod length. The rods had stiffening webs at both ends, with caged-roller bearings at the bottom and fully-floating bronze bushes at the top. Strangely, oil for the big-end bearings was squirted into annular channels in the inner faces of the middle flywheel discs and flung outward centrifugally. Another unusual feature for a grand prix engine was the use of centrifugal ignition advance up to 5,000 rpm. There was a separate contact set for each cylinder and a pair of six-volt batteries, wired in parallel, lasted five hours.

If the 1953 Rennmax had stunned the opposition, the 1954 version utterly demoralised them. By the time of the TT peak power was up to 33 bhp at 11,000 rpm and a sleek dolphin fairing, with a peak over the front wheel, boosted top speed to 125 mph. It was there, in the Isle of Man, that the Rennmax gave its most haughty demonstration of superiority. With the sun glinting on their polished aluminium fairings, Werner Haas, Rupert Hollaus and Reg Armstrong left the field for dead and circled in line astern from start to finish. Haas' race and lap records bettered Fergus Anderson's 1953 figures by an unprecedented 6 mph. Yet, although he averaged over 90 mph, Haas' fuel consumption was a modest 42 mph – not up to subsequent Moto Guzzi standards but well above average.

Opposite, lower: tucked down behind the slender fairing, with its projecting beak, the author squeezes 123 mph out of "Happy" Müller's 250 cc NSU Rennmax twin the day after the 1954 Ulster Grand Prix

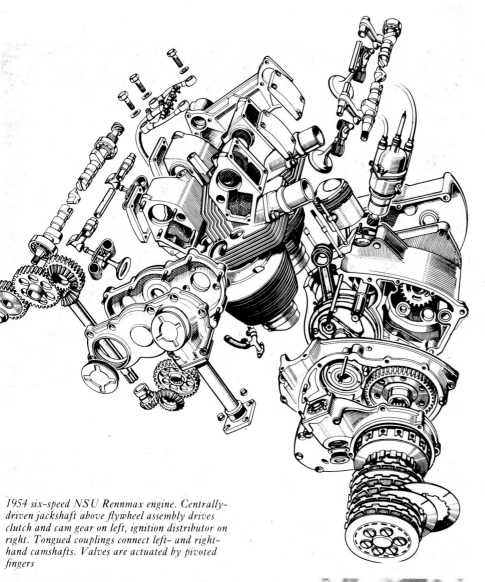

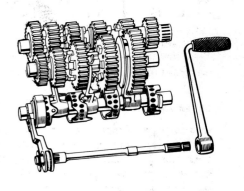

1954 six-speed NSU Rennmax engine. Centrally-driven jackshaft above flywheel assembly drives clutch and cam gear on left, ignition distributor on right. Tongued couplings connect left- and right-hand camshafts. Valves are actuated by pivoted fingers

Postponement

Bad weather for the rest of TT week delayed my promised test until the day after the following week's Ulster Grand Prix – a postponement I welcomed since I was still nursing four cracked ribs and a dislocated shoulder from my Norton practice prang at Greeba. My test bike was the one "Happy" Müller had ridden into third place the previous day and we selected a deserted stretch of the notoriously bumpy seven-mile Clady straight that was such a bike-killing part of the old Ulster course.

Even for my brief ride, the mechanic insisted on preheating the 20-grade castor oil to 90 degrees C (running temperature was 60 degrees), although I was spared the engine heating, with hot-air blower and massive trunking, that was such an awesome part of NSU's pre-race ritual in that year's paddocks.

Starting was again a walking-pace exercise, although out of consideration for my injuries I let the mechanic do the walking while I straddled the bike. On two soft plugs I made a few warming-up runs, building the rpm up to 9,000, and noticed the familiar footrest tremor at the lower end of the rev range. In fairness, though, it would probably have been imperceptible had the rubber inserts not been removed from the rests because of the wet race conditions the previous day.

With the hard plugs in and the needle beyond the 5,000 rpm "tantrum" level, I tucked myself in and made a series of full-bore runs, changing up at 11,000 to 11,500 rpm. The fairing, with its padded arm recesses, seemed "skintight", the handlebar was delightfully narrow and all the controls were perfectly positioned, silky to use. And yes, the gear change was better than on the 1953 practice model – so short, light, quick and dependable as to be a sheer delight.

Eleven-thousand came up repeatedly on the counter-clockwise tacho (123 mph) and I might have got a shade more if I had been wearing leathers. But my strongest impression was the absolute deceptiveness of the speed. Not a trace of wind roar or eddying disturbed the peace behind that low curved screen. There was, however, an occasional tendency to snake slightly at top speed – an inevitable effect of the gusty wind on the fairing's large flat sides.

Unfortunately there was no scope for cornering, save for a broadside each time I did a U-turn in the road and fed in the clutch at 5,000 rpm or more (tread compounds were not so grippy those days). But the bumps, although not Clady's worst, showed that the suspension (tailored to individual riders) suited me as well as it did

Müller. There was neither jarring nor pitching – ample vindication of pivoted rear and leading-link front forks. The brakes, still of single-leading-shoe pattern, could hardly have been bettered for their combination of power, smoothness and controllability.

Before the season was out, Dr Froede had pushed peak power up to 39 bhp at 11,500 rpm, and still with that incredible flexibility all the way from 5,000. What is more, he had extended the front of the fairing to encompass the wheel. With the raised gearing that these developments made possible, it was no wonder the Rennmax was timed at 135 mph at Hockenheim – way ahead of anything else in its class.

But by the end of the year the pay-off in prestige was wearing thin. So overwhelming and so utterly predictable had NSU's classic racing achievements become that the German press no longer considered them newsworthy. Only failure to achieve the impossible would have rated the headlines of old. So NSU pulled out and left the struggle for 250 cc supremacy to less inspired designs – until Honda enlivened the scene seven years later.

High-revving fours

The first torch-bearer for the high-revving multi in the 500 cc class was the Gilera four (there was a 350 cc version, too, but the

Moto Guzzi flat single robbed that of much of the glory that would otherwise have come its way). As early as 1950, and again in 1952, Gilera's Umberto Masetti had speed enough (130 mph rising to 140 mph) to win the world 500 cc championship. Yet the handling was primitive and it was not until Geoff Duke joined them from Norton in 1953 that Gilera established the all-round dominance that made them unassailable on the tracks for the next five years. For Duke brought them more than an exquisite riding talent. He brought, too, a genius for liaising with development chief Piero Taruffi. As a result, the riding position, suspension and braking were rapidly improved while the centre of gravity and overall height were lowered. The weight tended to creep up rather than down over the years (bigger brakes, stiffer frame, streamlining) but the engine wizards piled on power, so that progress was made in speed as well as controllability.

The general contours of the engine, along with its air cooling, wet sump and more up-right stance, suggest that its design inherited more from the wartime blown two-fifty than from Serafini's 1939 world beater. Incidentally, that forward lean, even at only 30 degrees, precluded the use of down-draught induction. Indeed, it was difficult if not impossible to avoid updraught. By contrast, the Moto Guzzi flat singles benefited both in torque and economy from up to 33 degrees of downdraught. But the restric-

The similarity of the early Gilera and MV fours reflects Pietro Remor's influence on both. This 1949 Gilera has two 28 mm carburettors with long trumpets, central plugs, pressed-steel front and rear forks with friction damping but torsion bars only at the rear

tion on cylinder filling that lack of down-draught imposes is less critical in smaller cylinders, because port areas are relatively much larger.

Originally, there were only two carburettors, with long trumpets and a choke size of 28 mm. The frame was part tubular, part pressed, with torsion bars controlling the pivoted rear fork, and friction damping for both that and the girder front fork. At about 290 lb, weight was comparable to that of the rival singles, while engine power (in 1949) was 50 bhp at 8,500 rpm.

Soon the choke size of the carburettors was increased to 30 mm – helping to add 2 bhp and 500 rpm to the power peak – while the torsion bars gave way to horizontal spring boxes under the saddle, actuated by levers sprouting up from the fork pivot, although friction damping was retained. Bolder modifications were made in 1951, when each cylinder was given an independent carburettor and the suspension took on a more conventional look, with a telescopic fork at the front and a pair of hydraulically damped spring struts at the rear.

The following year Gilera obtained a further 3 bhp and 1,000 rpm and dipped an exploratory toe in the waters of wind cheating with rudimentary fairings round the steering head and sump. In the sidecar class, a massive U-shape brace was clamped to the front-fork sliders in a vain bid to help Ercole Frigerio try to topple Eric Oliver and his Norton-Watsonian outfit off the world perch.

However, all previous developments seemed piecemeal compared with the pace of progress once Duke was on the payroll. Taking on a Norton look here and there, the bike shed a bit of height while acquiring a fatter rear tyre (4·00 × 17 in) for more traction and high-speed cornering grip, a high-back seat and a twin-leading-shoe front brake – and Geoff added his first Gilera world championship to the three he had already won on Nortons.

There was no slackening of effort during the following winter. Trivial though it seemed, a mere 0·8 mm was added to the stroke, bringing it to 58·8 mm (bore 52 mm) so as to obtain the 6 or 7 cc by which the capacity previously fell short of the class limit. The valve angle was widened and the exhaust stems filled with sodium. And while these and other engine changes pushed peak power up to 65 bhp at 10,400 rpm, the one-gallon sump was narrowed to get the exhaust pipes closer in, the gear cluster acquired a fifth speed and a dustbin fairing was designed for use on the fastest circuits. There, top speed reached 150 mph and Duke retained his firm hold on the title.

Frustrations

Up to that time, though, Geoff had been

In a bid to halt Eric Oliver's run of world sidecar championships, Gilera stiffened the telescopic front fork of Ercole Frigerio's machine with a massive U-shape brace in 1952

frustrated in his ambition to win the Senior TT for Gilera (he had done it twice for Norton). In 1953 a power slide at Quarter Bridge had put him out while he was leading Ray Amm's works Norton at half-distance. The following year he was second to Amm after a controversial decision had stopped the race midway because of appalling weather when Duke had stopped to refuel and Amm had not.

But everything clicked for Geoff and Gilera in the 1955 Senior. With his machine wearing only a steering-head fairing, he outclassed the field so emphatically that only his team mate Reg Armstrong could finish within two minutes of him. Briefly, Duke was even credited with the glory of the first 100 mph lap – until it was realised that the timekeeping was too coarse to be certain. A lap time of 22 minutes 38·4 seconds was required for the magic ton – and the time-keepers, working only to the nearest whole second, gave Geoff 22 minutes 39 seconds (99·97 mph) since he had not broken 22 minutes 38 seconds! A few months later, however, there was the consolation of his third world title on the trot.

Although the race shop sustained its efforts, there was a major setback in 1956. The FIM suspended Duke for the first six months of the year for having supported a privateers' strike against paltry starting money in the previous year's Dutch TT and, during his absence from the tracks, John Surtees piled up points for MV Agusta.

Back in action for the Belgian GP, Duke showed every bit of his old superiority. But a piston disintegrated while he was leading handsomely towards the finish, and Surtees took over for another eight points. By the time Geoff opened his score by winning the Italian GP at Monza it was too late. That was the last classic race of the year and Surtees' first world championship was already secure.

Meanwhile, with the help of megaphone

To minimise front fork twisting on the Gilera fours in 1956, the upper and lower yokes were braced by a welded-in sheet-steel box

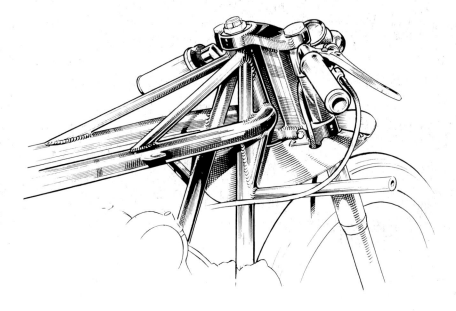

In a class of his own in the 1957 eight-lap Golden Jubilee Senior TT, Bob McIntyre tames the fully streamlined Gilera four and cracks in the first four ton-laps in Island history

exhausts, the engine had reached a new peak of 70 bhp at 10,500 rpm. The rear subframe had been stiffened by triangulation, while the upper and lower yokes of the front fork had been braced by a welded-in sheet-steel box to prevent twisting. Finally, a bit of curvature had been put into the previously flat sides of the dustbin fairing to reduce the bike's susceptibility to side winds.

Off the hook

For Duke, though, there was another false start to the season when a lurid slide at Imola put him out of action just before the TT. But Gilera were let off the hook when Geoff, with a shrewd eye for talent, recommended Bob McIntyre as his replacement.

Warming up with a convincing win in the Junior TT despite riding a whole lap on three cylinders before stopping to change a plug, the Scot went on to score one of the most magnificent of all Senior TT victories. With extra pannier tanks in the fairing sides and with the race stretched to eight laps (302 miles) as a Golden Jubilee gesture, Mac cracked in the first four ton laps ever and more than wiped out Surtees' 2½-minute

starting advantage before easing the pace in response to Geoff's signals.

A neck injury at Assen detuned the Scot for the season's later races and the factory steered their home-grown protégé Libero Liberati to the 500 cc championship. But only just – in the decisive round at Monza Mac trounced him in the 350 cc race before a bilious attack (an effect of the neck injury) prevented him starting on the five-hundred. In the end Gilera's tally of world championships for 1957 was three – Liberati's title and both manufacturers' awards.

For the record

The big Gilera had a built-up crankshaft with six roller main bearings and roller big ends too. Between the middle main bearings was the driving gear for clutch and camshafts. The four cylinders were separate, the heads in left and right pairs and the cam covers full width. The valves were inclined at 100 degrees to one another, with the 10 mm plugs plumb in the middle, but recessed and firing through narrow slots. Sparks were supplied by a Lucas rotating-magnet magneto (which relieved the armature windings of centrifugal stresses) and each pair of carburettors was inclined inward to clear the rider's knees. For quick engine removal, the lower left frame tube was detachable.

The precise specification was tailored from circuit to circuit – carburettor size ranged from 25 to 28 mm and tank size up to 32 litres (7 gallons). There was a choice of fairings, too, also of front-brake diameter (210 or 250 mm).

Had it not been for the agreed withdrawal from racing, the Gillies would not have been caught for a long time, and probably not by any machine of similar type. In all-out speed, only the Moto Guzzi vee-eight was faster, but any serious challenge might well have come from a much simpler machine with a quicker steering response and a design philosophy that recognised the futility of ever-increasing weight and bulk eating into a power surplus.

Be that as it may, Gilera decided to quit the limelight with a flourish. On the sickening bumps of Monza's concrete oval in the November they set their sights on the world hour records. With a third wheel hitched to one of the five-hundreds, Albino Milani logged 116 miles for the sidecar record. But when his brother Alfredo could only scratch at Ray Amm's four-year-old Norton record with 134 miles, Bob McIntyre again came to the rescue. Deliberately choosing the three-fifty, he jammed the throttles wide and fought the bouncing bike until the tank ran dry. Fortunately, the hour was up and the record stood at 141·37 miles – the first time it had ever fallen to a three-fifty.

MV take over

As it turned out, the Gilera's immediate successor at the top of the 500 cc heap (and the 350 cc category) *was* a machine of similar type – the MV Agusta four. This came about quite simply because there was then no other serious contender, and its remarkable similarity to the Gilera reflected the fact that Ing Pietro Remor had a big hand in both designs. Externally, indeed, the only noticeable difference by that time (1958) was that MV had long switched their plugs from a central to a side position.

As originally conceived, the MV four was even more off-beat than the Gilera. Among the many common features were the partial use of pressings in the frame and girder fork; torsion-bar rear springing; friction damping at both ends; two carburettors; central plugs; a 90-degree valve angle and 30-degree engine lean; four speeds and plain exhaust pipes (soon to grow megas). But the MV differed from the Gilera not only in its slightly different cylinder dimensions (54 × 54 mm) but also in more obvious features. There was torsion-bar springing of the front fork, too, and shaft final drive was on the left, with the rear fork doubled up in the form of a pivoted parallelogram to suit the action of the universal joints.

Since the crankshaft was set across the frame in the usual way, the drive from the gear-driven clutch was turned through 90 degrees by a pair of bevel gears so that the two gearbox shafts lay fore-and-aft, making the power unit a bit longer than it might otherwise have been. With 50 bhp at 9,000 rpm, that first MV five-hundred was fast for its day but distinctly awkward.

The first move to make the machine competitive came late in 1950, when Les Graham joined the Gallarate team. Friction-damped torsion bars were scrapped in favour of a telescopic front fork and a pair of proprietary hydraulic struts at the rear. Four carburettors were fitted and the plugs moved sideways in the cylinder heads. But the following season Graham found the handling still poor, gear indexing uncertain and speed inadequate. So big changes were put in hand for 1952.

Shaft drive was dispensed with and so, therefore, was the need for a double rear fork. Instead of a one-piece block, four

First of the MV Agusta fours, before the switch from central to side plugs and from plain to megaphone exhausts. Only two carburettors were fitted. Torsion-bar springing and friction damping were used at both ends. Layout of left-side shaft drive dictated pivoted-parallelogram rear fork

Pioneer of the rear-wheel drift, John Surtees shows winning form on his 350 cc MV Agusta four at Francorchamps in the 1957 Belgian GP

separate cylinder barrels were used, with a bore and stroke of 53 × 56·4 mm, while compression was stepped up to 11:1. The exhaust pipes were siamesed, and the gear cluster acquired a fifth speed, while a rather clumsy looking Earles-type pivoted front fork was adopted.

With 60 bhp at 10,500 rpm then on tap, Les Graham fared better in 1952. His second place in the Senior TT split the works Nortons of Reg Armstrong and Ray Amm. In the Ulster GP he set a lap record before the rear mudguard stripped the tyre tread off on Clady's vicious bumps. Then he rounded the season off with emphatic victories at Monza and Montjuich Park, Barcelona, despite one plug lead dangling for nearly half the latter race.

Prospects looked bright for a keen Gilera-MV struggle the following year, with Duke and Graham as the respective stars. But tragedy intervened in the second lap of the Senior TT. Les was killed when his MV became unmanageable at the foot of Bray Hill, while he was second to Duke, and only a day after he had won the 125 cc race on a double-knocker MV single.

It was during that ill-starred year that the 350 cc (47·5 × 49 mm) version of the four made its debut, with 35 bhp at 11,000 rpm – hardly adequate for what was virtually a scaled-down five-hundred.

Although development ticked over during the next year or two – with the frame and fork modified to trim overall height, and various degrees of streamlining introduced for different sorts of circuit – it was not until 1956 that MV really found a sense of direction again. Their salvation was the signing of John Surtees, a formidable rider and the answer to the development engineers' prayers. With Geoff Duke smarting under the FIM suspension, John lost no time in giving MV the first of their many Senior TT wins and world 500 cc championships.

Inevitably, with the Gilera team at its invincible best in 1957, even John's stoutest efforts were overshadowed. But 1958 heralded his phenomenal string of 350/500 cc classic doubles and world championships, a trend continued almost unbroken by Gary Hocking, Mike Hailwood and Giacomo Agostini until first Honda then Yamaha proved too much for MV.

Getting the drift

One of John's first achievements was to

Monza test of a 500 cc MV Agusta four, September 1958. Left to right: Vic Willoughby, Tarquinio Provini (world 250 cc champion), Arturo Magni (chief mechanic) and Nello Pagani (team manager)

pioneer a new cornering style to suit the MV four. In this there were two elements, first, hanging his body well inside the bike to keep the bike itself that much more upright and so prevent the wide engine from grounding; second, the use of a controlled rear-wheel drift. I was intrigued as much by this new departure as by the prospect of sampling the MV's power and speed when I stayed on at Monza after the 1958 Italian GP to ride John's spare 65-bhp five-hundred, on which Remo Venturi had finished second to him two days earlier.

"Monza's not the best place to try it," said Surtees with a sadistic grin. "Too smooth, too easy. You'd learn a lot more on the Nürburgring or the Isle of Man." I was not worried. For me Monza was infinitely better than nothing. "When the pressure is off, it's easier to ride than a single," John continued. "It's so much more tractable." (By then the engine was even more undersquare at 52×58 mm and pulled cleanly from 4,500 rpm upward.) "Indeed, at Francorchamps two months ago I often held top gear all the way from the Burnenville downhill sweep to La Source, the hairpin just before the pits – about two-thirds of the lap.

"But it's a different story when you're scratching. The greater weight and higher centre of gravity call for much more physical

Streets ahead of the opposition, John Surtees holds top gear on his 500 cc MV Agusta four for much of the Francorchamps lap in the 1958 Belgian GP. With Gilera no longer competing, that year marked the start of MV's long supremacy in the biggest solo category

effort to get from lock to lock. And because the steering response is more sluggish you can't flop it around in fast bends to pass slower riders. Line is more critical – you take aim at the start of a fast bend and then you're committed. What's more, you need a more sensitive throttle hand if the rear wheel is not to break away, especially if a bend is bumpy."

John led me round for a few slow laps (slow for him anyway) then left me on my own. With full throttle extending the front fork and pushing the needle rapidly round to 10,500 in every gear, the MV's acceleration was breathtaking, deceptively so because of the smoothness of the engine and the width of the track. Without the backrest on the seat, that bike would have been un-rideable. It is one thing to listen to a rapid succession of upward gear changes when watching a grand prix, quite another to experience the sustained thrust in the pants that makes that quickfire tap dance necessary.

Ten-five came up in top – 145 mph. Again the spaciousness of Monza and the calm of the cockpit made it deceptive, except when the six-row start grid flashed under the wheels like a smudge of white chalk, or the trees closed in from the sides where the track suddenly narrowed a quarter-mile farther on, heading for the Grande Curve. Another sharp reminder of the speed came whenever I sat up in top gear and changed down. First my cheeks beat a tattoo on my teeth, then the wind tweaked my ankle smartly as I swivelled my toes round to the

underside of the gear pedal for that honey of a change.

Naturally, the MV was nothing like so effortless to handle as those Moto Guzzi singles. Although Surtees and his illustrious successors clearly mastered it, Giulio Carcano was unquestionably right in arguing that light weight and a low centre of gravity give any rider much more confidence in exploring the limit of cornering speed.

Lacking Surtees' confidence, I was inhibited by the pitching induced by the undulations round the Grande Curve and by the steering flutter caused by the shorter bumps on the apex of Vialone. I could see what John meant about learning more on trickier circuits.

John's theory on hanging in was easy to understand – elementary mechanics, as illustrated also by a sidecar outfit cornering with the chair and passenger airborne on the inside. But I queried his claim to drift, as other riders disputed it, too. "Any really fast men who claim not to drift," John countered, "are simply drifting and don't know it.

"It just isn't true that if you can accelerate through a bend you're going too slowly in the first place. By feeding the power in with the bike cranked over, you tighten the bike's cornering radius and get through faster than you would without drift – it's what car racers call oversteer. Indeed, if you close the throttle in a curve the bike immediately runs wide. It's second nature now for me to tweak the grip with the same hand movement that releases the front brake as I crank into a bend."

Above: *during his last season with MV, Mike Hailwood dominates the 1965 Dutch GP on the way to his fourth consecutive world 500 cc title*

Right: *with the fairing showing signs of his second-lap spill, Gary Hocking takes the 286 cc MV twin to victory in the 1960 French 350 cc GP at Clermont Ferrand. Despite a 10 bhp deficiency the bored-out two-fifty was a match for the full-size four on give-and-take circuits*

I decided to give the idea a tentative try-out on the two second-gear Lesmo Curves and on the second-and-third-gear Vedano Curve. Without question, the MV was steadier and faster through those curves under power and – though I was not going at John's speed – I was pleased to find the road come up and caress my right boot.

John's reign as MV superstar lasted until 1960 and during that period there was much more progress in handling as a result of his suggestions than there was in engine performance. Indeed, when Geoff Duke dusted off the old Gileras in 1963 and substituted dolphin fairings for the outlawed dustbins, his riders (John Hartle and Phil Read) showed how little MV performance had improved in six years by finishing second in the Senior and Junior TTs and the Dutch and Belgian GPs.

Even so, early in Surtees' time, MV built a six-abreast five-hundred, expecting that Moto Guzzi's water-cooled vee-eight, with its enormous power and speed, would soon be the bike to beat. But MV were nothing like so adept at miniaturisation as Honda subsequently proved to be. The six was wide and cumbersome, which meant it was little more than a straight-line tool.

Enlightenment dawns

There was a brief sign in 1960, however, that MV had cottoned on to the futility of worshipping engine power if it brought its own handicap of bulk, weight and a high centre of gravity. They bored out one of their all-conquering 250 cc twins from 53 to 57 mm (stroke 56 mm), so increasing the capacity to 286 cc – and Gary Hocking won the 350 cc class of the French GP at Clermont Ferrand in spite of a second-lap spill on a damp hairpin bend.

What that bike lost in being 10 bhp down on the full 350 cc four it recouped in being lower, considerably slimmer and 60 lb lighter, and Surtees supported Hocking's

With three cylinders and 12 valves, Giacomo Agostini's 350 cc MV in 1966 was the Italian factory's answer to the Honda four. But he was beaten by Mike Hailwood both here (in the French GP at Clermont Ferrand) and in the world championship

view that it was a match for the four on give-and-take circuits. But that sign of enlightenment was premature and it was not until 1965, the last year of Mike Hailwood's four-year reign as MV superstar, that the factory made a worthwhile attempt to trim weight and width and obtain their power in a more sophisticated way.

This was a belated response to Honda's three-year-old takeover in the 350 cc class. Following the explosive impact of their 250 cc fours on the 1961 world championship, Honda had scaled them up to 285 cc early in 1962 and to full size later in the year, and Jim Redman had already romped comfortably to three of his four successive 350 cc titles.

It had taken a long time for the obvious lessons to sink in at Gallarate – first, that a scaled-up two-fifty will always beat a scaled-down five-hundred; second, that the Japanese threat would not recede for being ignored; third, that the two-valve head had had its day.

Mike's new bike, then, was a three-fifty (Honda had yet to launch their 500 cc challenge, so the big MV four was still

sitting pretty). To reduce width (by 5 in overall) it had only three cylinders (56 × 47 mm), while to boost power it had paired valves and peaked at 12,500 rpm – 1,500 more than the original four. Even so, it was no match for the Honda four and Redman gained his fourth 350 cc title, while Hailwood matched that tally in the 500 cc class.

The situation was complicated in 1966 by four factors – Hailwood switched to the Honda camp on rumours of an up-to-date five-hundred; Agostini took over Mike's job at MV, so giving the factory the enormous incentive of trying to steer an Italian rider, rather than a foreigner, to a world title; Honda's preparation of their new four failed to match up to their immaculate reputation; and they made a strategic blunder in choosing the faithful Redman (then in the twilight of his career) rather than Hailwood to spearhead the 500 cc effort.

Had Hailwood ridden the big Honda on its winning debut at Hockenheim, he would have beaten Ago for the 500 cc championship in spite of his mechanical breakdown at Monza when the title hung in the balance. But Redman's Hockenheim points were wasted (except in the manufacturers' championship) when he broke an arm at Francorchamps a few meetings later.

As it was, Agostini and MV rose to the challenge magnificently. Monza erupted when the big Honda clanked to a halt and an

Italian assumed the 500 cc mantle for the first time in nine years. And throughout the year the Gallarate boffins took the scaling-up lesson to heart, boosting the capacity of their three first to 420 cc then to 489 cc (62 × 54 mm) to provide Ago with a much more competitive five-hundred than any of his foreign predecessors at MV had had.

The Italian worthily retained his title in 1967. Then, once Honda pulled out of classic racing altogether at the end of the year, Ago and MV were virtually unchallenged in both 350 and 500 cc classes for an incredible five years in succession. Once again there seemed little incentive to get back to the drawing board and both machines finished up as seven-speeders – the big one pushing out 78 bhp at 11,600 rpm and weighing 320 lb, the other 60 bhp at 12,800 rpm and 308 lb.

Back to four

But the incentive came eventually, from Yamaha, and again it came first in the 350 cc class as the two-strokes spread their influence further up the capacity scale. On the less-demanding Continental circuits, the overbored 250 cc Yamaha twins were already making life hard for Ago in 1971 and MV built another four-cylinder engine (still with paired valves). With a bore and stroke of 54 × 38 mm, the new engine gave 10 per cent more power (66 bhp at 14,000 rpm).

Above: *final version of MV's 500 cc four, with 16 valves, front-mounted magneto, long slim oil sump and cooler in fairing nose*

Right: *seen here winning at Assen in 1973, Phil Read brings MV the last but one of their world 500 cc titles. Note the disc front brakes*

Yet the bike was no wider than the three and only 9 or 10 lb heavier.

At the Salzburgring and Imola early in 1972 the new four gave a good account of itself. But in the Isle of Man it was shipped home after practice because the TT course so blunted the challenge of the air-cooled Yamahas that Ago's well-tried three was in no danger of being beaten.

It was duly superseded by the four, however, for the Italian to retain his 350 cc title in 1973. At the same time it was scaled up by stages to 500 cc to meet the serious challenge from Jarno Saarinen's 80 bhp Yamaha four. That challenge ended abruptly in mid-season when the Finn was killed at Monza and the 500 cc title went to Phil Read, who had joined Ago in the MV team.

It was, indeed, Agostini's annoyance at not having the pick of the five-hundreds that prompted his move to Yamaha in 1974, when he won the 350 cc championship, although Read retained the big one for MV. That was to prove their last classic title. The two-stroke steamroller moved on. Agostini rubbed salt in the MV wound by regaining his 500 cc crown on a Yamaha four, while his team mate Johnny Cecotto topped the three-fifties on a twin. MV pulled out at the end of 1975.

Carcano's complex eight

In the mid-1950s the rumour of a Moto Guzzi water-cooled vee-eight, even in the 500 cc class, was too fantastic for the critics to take seriously. Mindful of the extraordinary variety of engine layouts that had come from Giulio Carcano's drawing board

– singles, twins, threes and fours – they conceded there might be some substance in the hints of an experimental eight in the lakeside race shop. But although all Carcano's machines except the shaft-drive four had been highly successful, the consensus among the pundits was that, this time, he had tried to be different once too often.

On the contrary, Carcano's choice of the most complex engine layout in classic racing history, at a time when his singles were proving the merits of the simple approach, was typical of his foresight and complete open-mindedness. Indeed, within a year of its track debut, the vee-eight had the legs of the all-conquering Gilera four and was generally regarded as the only bike with a chance of dethroning it.

The Moto Guzzi 350 cc single was only just clinching the second of its five consecutive world championships when thoughts of a multi with more than four cylinders first stirred in Carcano's mind. Watching practice for the 1954 Italian GP at various places on the Monza circuit, he became convinced that the time would come when – on the ultra-fast circuits at least – his five-hundreds and three-fifties would need more power than could be squeezed from a single cylinder. At the same time, he was as conscious as ever of the folly of paying for power with excessive weight and bulk, to the detriment of acceleration, braking, speed, climb and handling.

Dustbins were already in vogue by then and Carcano realised that the minimum width of such a fairing was dictated by the FIM requirement of a total of 40 degrees of steering lock (20 degrees each side). This minimum fairing width he calculated to be

50 cm (19·7 in), which agreed well with the limit set by the breadth of the rider's shoulders and pelvis. The problem, therefore, was to devise the most powerful engine within that compass. As it turned out, the vee-eight engine measured 46 cm (18·1 in) across and the fairing 49 cm (19·3 in) – only 3 cm (1·2 in) wider than the shell for the 350 cc flat single.

In making his choice of engine, Carcano rejected the shaft-drive four because its longitudinal crankshaft lengthened the wheelbase and impaired handling, while the engine-speed clutch spoiled the gear change. (That four had been designed for minimum engine width before fairings came into use.) Four cylinders abreast would have seemed like a copy of Gilera and MV; anyway, those factories had a considerable lead in development.

For all its complexity and power, the engine of the 500 cc Moto Guzzi vee-eight was only 18·1 in wide – 1·2 in narrower than the fairing. The front suspension struts shown here have two-rate springs

Six or eight cylinders abreast? No, the long crankshaft would have suffered from torsional vibrations; and the engine would have been too wide, especially if streamlining were banned entirely. A vee-six was ruled out because of inherently poor balance. All of which left the 90-degree vee-eight as a virtually automatic choice.

Its crankshaft was short and stiff. Depending on crank layout, its balance was good at worst, perfect at best. Engine width was no problem with a 50 cm-wide fairing and would not be excessive if the FIM outlawed streamlining. Total valve area was large enough for tip-top breathing at ultra-high revs, while the small exhaust valve heads would run cool and compression could be high. On the other hand, internal friction would be high (especially in view of the high rpm) and water cooling would be necessary because of the masking of the rear cylinders. But on balance Carcano felt he was on to a winner.

Incredibly, considering the very idea of going for power had not crystallised in Carcano's mind until September 1954, the Moto Guzzi vee-eight was bench-tested and

The two-stroke threat that forced MV to scale-up Agostini's 16-valve engine from 350 to 500 cc – Jarno Saarinen wins the 1973 French GP on his 80 bhp Yamaha four

Above: *in the Belgian 500 cc GP in 1956, Bill Lomas heels the Moto Guzzi eight into La Source hairpin ahead of Reg Armstrong (Gilera, 26), Umberto Masetti (MV Agusta, 52) and Walter Zeller (BMW, 2)*
Right: *despite a couple of unscheduled stops and finishing "on 6½ cylinders," Dickie Dale brought this Moto Guzzi vee-eight home fourth in the 1957 Senior TT. The front shock absorbers are externally mounted to facilitate experimental changes*

track-tested (at Monza) the following spring – a mere six months from drawing board to race track.

Two-plane crank

In the intense development phase that followed, various frames were tried (all of them having the five litres of engine oil in the large-diameter top tube to save weight and space) while the front shock absorbers were mounted externally, rather than inside the fork stanchions, to simplify experimental changes. But the most major change was a complete rehash of the crankshaft layout, necessitated by persistent cracking of the main-bearing webs.

Originally, a single-plane crankshaft was chosen for convenience. With its cranks spaced at 180 degrees (as in an ordinary straight four), this gave perfect primary balance, although the secondary forces from the front and rear banks combined in a high-

frequency fore-and-aft vibration. Carcano decided to risk this because the two-up, two-down crank arrangement enabled him to use a fairly shallow one-piece crankcase, into which the shaft and connecting rods could be assembled from the drive side.

Unfortunately, the unbalanced secondary forces were too much for the main bearing webs and he had to switch to the more usual two-plane shaft (cranks at 90 degrees) to

obtain perfect secondary balance as well as primary – even though the four groups of rods necessitated a deeper crankcase, which had to be split for assembly from below.

On Easter Monday 1956, following two practice appearances the previous season, the vee-eight made its race debut in the Gold Cup meeting at Imola, where Ken Kavanagh did ten laps before encountering trouble. Yet it was only three months later, in the

German GP on the demanding Solitude circuit, that an enthralling scrap between Bill Lomas on the eight and Geoff Duke on the Gilera four left no doubt that the new Moto Guzzi was already competitive.

"We'll beat the Gilera"

Way ahead of the pack, they passed and re-passed one another for 25 minutes until first the Gilera packed up with ignition failure and then the Moto Guzzi – left with a handsome lead – followed suit after spewing hot water over Lomas' right thigh.

Afterwards, he commented: "With more development, we'll have the beating of the Gilera. There's nothing to choose between them for handling. In top speed, I had a slight edge but the Gilera's five speeds gave Geoff an advantage on the long climb. I had only four of the six gears in the Moto Guzzi box – that was ample at Francorchamps the previous week and we hadn't had time to fit the extra cogs. The wider spacing of my four ratios was also a slight handicap when braking on the engine from top speed, while the high bottom ratio necessitated clutch slip on three slow corners – a hazardous technique with so much surging torque.

"Occasionally I tried outbraking Geoff. I got by all right – and on the flat single I might have got away with it. But the eight's higher centre of gravity accentuated the forward weight transfer, which left the rear wheel so light that it was difficult to prevent it from locking. While I was busy keeping the bike under control Geoff repassed on the inside."

These difficulties were not expected to arise in the Italian GP on the faster Monza circuit and in preliminary tests Lomas covered the full race distance non-stop at race-winning speed. Hopes of victory were high. But in the earlier 350 cc race, while chasing Libero Liberati's leading Gilera, he pushed his luck too hard on the second Lesmo turn and broke his left arm at 90 mph . . .

Confidence in the eight's future was re-inforced from the very start of the 1957 season. For a trade stunt in the spring, the factory sent a bike to Rome where, on the Appian Way, Lomas broke the world standing-start record for 10 km at an average of 151 mph (on normal fuel). Significantly, the engine was finally revving at 12,200 rpm: 175 mph – a speed that would still have been competitive 20 years later. And at Imola, just before the TT, Dickie Dale won the prestigious Gold Cup Race.

For the Senior TT he used five speeds but, even so, found it necessary to slip the clutch at Governor's Bridge and Ramsey. His fourth place, incidentally, was much more creditable than it seemed, for he stopped at Sulby with a sulky engine, subsequently spent a minute working on it in the pits and finished, as he said, "on 6½ cylinders."

Two views of the Moto Guzzi vee-eight power unit. The left-side view shows the ventilated clutch and the distributors on the ends of the inlet cam-shafts. Between the distributors are the original two large float chambers. Prominent in the right-side view is the large cam-drive case, with water impeller on the side and oil pump beneath. The eight carburettors are interlaced and controlled from a single, cable-operated arm. The massive lug at back of crankcase is the rear-fork pivot

With the fairing removed, the 1956 version of the 500 cc Moto Guzzi vee-eight shows its compact layout and form-fitting tank. Ignition distributors are on the ends of the inlet camshafts – and between them are the two float bowls originally used. Front suspension struts are mounted externally for quick experimental changes. The rear fork pivots in a crankcase lug. Note the oil filler in top front of frame spine

The details

In detail, the engine showed the sort of ingenuity expected from Carcano. Both patterns of crankshaft were machined from solid forgings in nickel-chrome steel and the crank webs were full discs, so that the necessary inertia was obtained without a heavy end flywheel which would have given rise to torsional oscillations. Counter-weighting was effected by dovetailing heavy-metal inserts into the discs, so avoiding holes and changes of section. There were five roller main bearings of which the middle three, like the big ends, had to be split because of the crankshaft's one-piece construction. For big-end lubrication, two of the intermediate main bearings were used as oil distributors – oil spilling from them was caught in annular grooves in adjacent crank-web faces, whence it was centrifuged through drillings to the crankpins, NSU Rennmax fashion.

The crankcase – which incorporated the rear fork pivot as well as the lower halves of the cylinder blocks and housed the gear cluster too – was in magnesium. The cylinder heads, incorporating the upper halves of the blocks, were in Y-alloy, with the wet liners screwed in and corrugated on the outside to improve heat transfer. Bore and stroke were 44 × 41 mm (499 cc) and one of the engine's

most impressive aspects was the interlacing of the eight 20 mm Dellorto carburettors, which were controlled by a single cable and two cross-shafts, and initially fed by only two float chambers, one at each side.

As in the earlier straight four, the valves seated directly in the aluminium heads (no inserts). Since the stems were so slender, it was decided not to groove them for collet retention. Instead, the tops of the stems were enlarged to retain the collets, and this meant the aluminium-bronze guides had to be split for assembly.

Only six gears were needed to drive the four camshafts, since the idler was large enough to drive the inlet shafts direct from the crankshaft pinion. The cam followers were inverted buckets surrounding duplex coil springs, the inner of which kept the split guides in place. Ignition was by battery and coil, with the distributors on the ends of the inlet camshafts.

Primary drive reduction to the ventilated clutch was almost 3:1. To prevent all possibility of slip, without weakening the crankshaft, the shallow taper uniting the drive pinion with the shaft was triangular in section, with radiused corners. Although the gearbox crossed the drive over from left to right, top gear was direct, with the final drive sprocket on the same axis as the input from the clutch. This arrangement was similar to that in the postwar British Vincent big twins, although since the Moto Guzzi primary drive was by gears rather than chain, the engine ran backwards. Common Italian practice was followed in lubricating the gears by splash from the big ends. At peak revs the gear-type pump circulated castor-base oil at the rate of 22 gallons per hour.

From its initial 64 bhp at 12,000 rpm in prototype form, the engine was quickly

developed to give 72 bhp (at the rear wheel) in 1957 and – with new carburettors having individual float chambers – was putting out 80 bhp by the time the management dropped their "withdrawal" bombshell on the race shop. At 320 lb, the bike may have weighed a good deal more than the 500 cc flat single but it was in the same bracket as the rival fours and considerably more powerful.

In retrospect, Carcano's "horses-for-courses" plan for 1958 – fielding the flat single for give-and-take circuits and the vee-eight for ultra-fast ones – seems like a sure-fire recipe for invincibility. Especially as a 350 cc version of the eight, built but never raced, gave 48 to 52 bhp (compared with 45 for the same-size Gilera four), and an appreciably lighter model with only the front cylinder block of the big engine (stretched from 250 to 350 cc) produced 48 bhp. There was never any substitute for genius and it was a great privilege to meet it, along with great personal charm, in Giulio Carcano.

The wrong approach

In the late 1950s, 48 bhp from a three-fifty was a highly competitive power output, provided the weight was low, the frontal area small and the handling good enough for the rider fully to exploit the power. And 48 bhp (at 10,600 rpm) was eventually on tap in Bianchi's 350 cc double-knocker parallel twin, which was laid out by Lino Tonti in 1958 but kept on ice until the factory re-entered racing two years later. But that Bianchi – albeit an overbored two-fifty – was a classic example of over emphasis on the engine. Predominantly an engine man, Tonti let his ingenuity run riot to such an extent that the bike finished up much too tall, which probably accounted for its being rather difficult to handle on bumpy bends. Had it been appreciably more compact and controllable, its power and tractability (the engine was raceworthy from 5,000 rpm) must have brought it better results than Bob McIntyre's second at Assen and third at Sachsenring, and Alan Shepherd's fourth at Monza, all in 1961.

Fast as the Bianchi was – 140 mph and 125 mph on the extremes of overall gearing (for Hockenheim and San Remo) – the Gilera and MV fours had gone as quickly some years earlier. Indeed the Moto Guzzi flat single (admittedly with a dustbin, not dolphin, fairing) had been just about as quick in 1957 with 10 bhp less and 70 lb less weight.

When I called on Tonti early in 1962 to analyse the engine, it was clear where weight and bulk could have been saved. Tonti had an obsession with friction – and since friction absorbs power it is admittedly desirable to reduce it. But the chief sources of engine friction are the pistons, which are virtually large plain bearings.

With their pure rolling motion, ball and roller bearings are practically friction-free. Yet, to save "two-tenths of damn-all" Tonti

incurred the extra weight and bulk of mounting four of the seven gears in the camshaft drive on double bearings running within double bearings! In one case two small needle-roller bearings ran side-by-side in two larger bearings of the same type. In the three other cases two needle bearings ran in the bores of two journal ball bearings.

A similar extravagance with materials was seen in the massive flanged housing for the inner two main bearings and one of the three jackshaft bearings. This housing was not only spigoted and clamped by nine flange bolts to the inner wall of the left crankcase half (each half had two vertical walls) – it was also held by six radial and chordal screws and downward extensions of the inboard four crankcase-mouth studs. Construction of the crankshaft and its central gear was also weighty, while each connecting rod had four stiffening webs – two extending completely round the periphery and two more round the small end. Even the oil filter showed a belt-and-braces approach, with three coaxial gauze sleeves.

Surprisingly in view of all this prodigality, Tonti claimed that the bike weighed only 285 lb dry – albeit 33 per cent more than

the much more successful Moto Guzzi flat singles. If this claim was true, it reflects the compensating virtue of having scaled the bike up from a $55 \times 52 \cdot 5$ mm two-fifty (in which the bulk was even more reprehensible) by increasing the bore size to 65 mm. To be sure, the tubing in the duplex frame was unusually small in diameter, while the tyre sizes were a mere $2 \cdot 75$ and $3 \cdot 00 \times 18$ in front and rear respectively.

Other features of the design, although not adding to bulk or weight, smacked of amateur enthusiasm rather than professional hard-headedness. For example, there was a choice of three primary reduction ratios ($29:51$, $30:50$ or $31:49$) in the gear drive from the half-speed jackshaft to the clutch – surely an unnecessary refinement with chain final drive. Also, the carburettor mouths were partially boxed in by rubber sheeting and the resulting chamber fed with cold air by two ducts from the high-pressure area at the fairing nose, regardless of the nullifying pressure losses in two 3 ft lengths of small-bore corrugated tubing, not to mention the lack of hermetic sealing.

In other respects the engine design was sound and up-to-date, although not inspired.

This Italian ghosted drawing shows how slots in the fairing nose lead air to the front brakes and low-slung radiator on the Moto Guzzi vee-eight

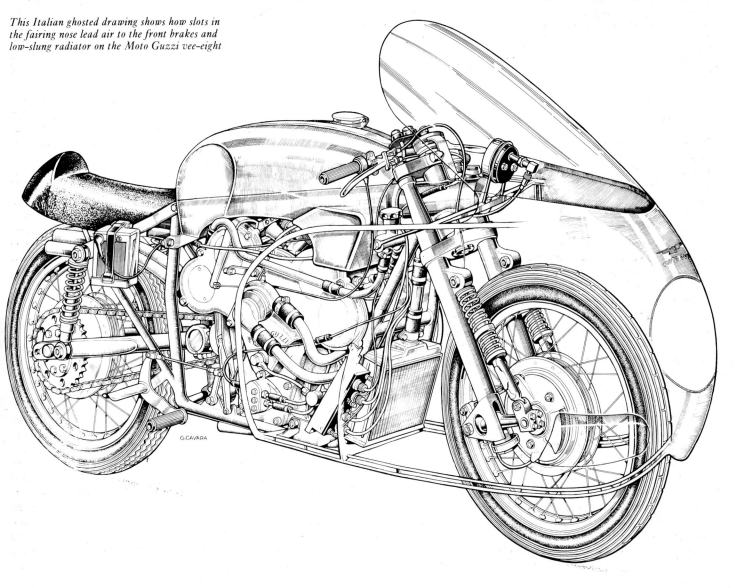

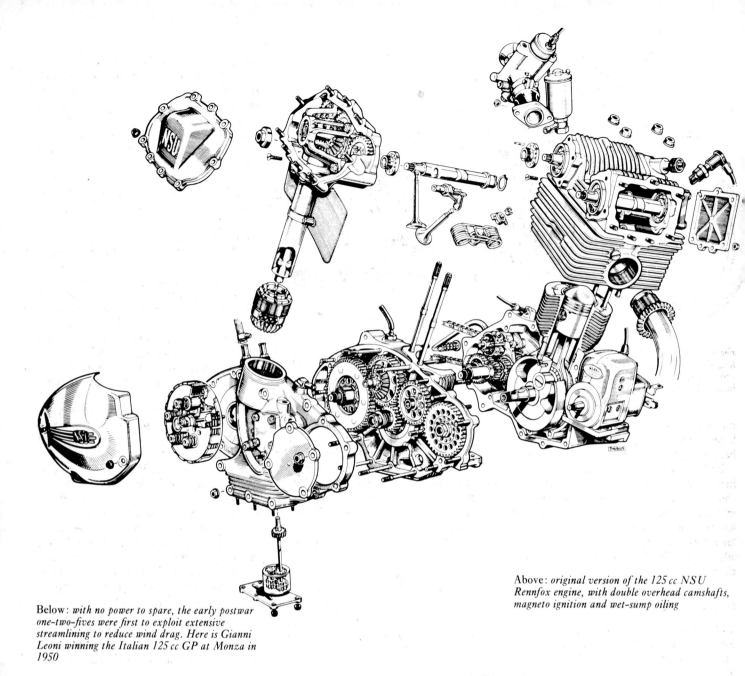

Above: *original version of the 125 cc NSU
Rennfox engine, with double overhead camshafts,
magneto ignition and wet-sump oiling*

Below: *with no power to spare, the early postwar
one-two-fives were first to exploit extensive
streamlining to reduce wind drag. Here is Gianni
Leoni winning the Italian 125 cc GP at Monza in
1950*

The valves seated directly in the high-duty
alloy head, in which the seats had been work-
hardened, while the cams let the valves
down gently. A battery and four sports coils
fired the four 12 mm plugs, two in each head.
Indeed, a good deal of the engine's performance was probably due to dual ignition –
for the high compression ratio (9·8 : 1),
achieved in spite of a wide valve angle (78
degrees), large valves (39 mm inlet, 35 mm
exhaust) and no squish, inevitably involved
humped piston crowns and an "orange-
peel" shape for the combustion space.

Originally, the engine was set to peak at
12,000 rpm but persistent breakage of the
hairpin valve springs led to a reduction to
10,600 rpm and a redesign of the springs. In
case desmodromic valve operation should
prove desirable, the two idler gears connecting the camshafts ran at the same speed
as the shafts and could have been adapted to
carry the closing cams.

There were six speeds in the gearbox but
the power characteristics were so good –

For its second season in 1954, NSU changed the Rennfox engine experimentally to a single overhead camshaft, an oversquare cylinder, battery ignition and dry-sump oiling

tractability from 3,000 rpm and a really broad spread of torque – that the riders were happier with the alternative five speeds.

Enthusiasm exuded from Lino Tonti like sweat from a prize-fighter. And his choice of a twin seemed a logical compromise between a single and a four. If only he had kept his feet more firmly on the ground, his riders might have gained a world title to add to Tino Brambilla's 1961 Italian 350 cc championship.

Italian lightweights

Both before the NSU blitzkrieg of 1953–4, and after it until the Honda takeover in 1961, the 125 cc championship was dominated by high-revving Italian double-knocker singles from FB Mondial and MV Agusta. With few exceptions – such as bevel cam drive on the Mondial and a gear train on the MV – they might almost have come from the same drawing board.

Originally, they had upright cylinders (53 × 56 mm) with the magneto in front, a small outside flywheel, megaphone exhaust, dry sump oiling, girder front fork and four speeds. Ignition later went to twin plugs and battery power, the fork to telescopic; gears multiplied to six or seven. And – because they had less power to waste and were not so much troubled by side winds as were faster machines – they were among the first to adopt streamlining, with comprehensive fairings at the rear as well as the front.

It was much the same story in the 250 cc class after the NSU era (Benelli and Moto Guzzi had been the top dogs before it), except that MV progressed from a single to a parallel twin, while Mondial took the opposite course and changed from a twin to a single. Yet some of the most fascinating

machines in both classes never won a title – the 125 cc Gilera twin, the 250 cc Moto Morini single and the 125 cc desmodromic Ducati singles and twins.

First to dominate the 125 cc class was Mondial, for whom Nello Pagani won in 1949, Bruno Ruffo in 1950 and Carlo Ubbiali in 1951, before Cecil Sandford put MV on top in 1952. Incidentally, the NSU Rennfox single that eclipsed the best Italian efforts for the next two years was by no means just a half of the 250 cc Rennmax twin (page 60).

Developed separately by Albert Roder, it

1956 was the first year lightweights were catered for in the postwar Belgian GP. On the ultra-fast Francorchamps circuit, the extensive front and rear streamlining on world champion Carlo Ubbiali's winning 125 cc MV Agusta (seen here at La Source hairpin) not only boosted top speed but also minimised the benefit rival riders could gain from slipstreaming

started in 1952 with a standard-looking pressed-steel spine frame and leading-link fork. Inclined at 25 degrees, the 54 × 54 mm engine had wet-sump oiling, the magneto in front of the crankcase, a mixture of bevel and spur gears to the twin overhead camshafts and the valves actuated by pivoted fingers.

By 1954, however, it had changed considerably, both in specification and appearance. Cylinder dimensions were 58 × 45 mm and the valve gear had made the unusual switch to a single overhead camshaft, with the bevel drive on the left. In distinct contrast to its Italian rivals, it had an enormous downdraught angle. Oiling was dry sump, ignition by battery. There were six speeds in the gearbox and two leading shoes in the front brake, which had a floating shoeplate to prevent interference with fork action. Streamlining followed Rennmax practice, progressing from a beak to a full dustbin, which boosted top speed to about 115 mph.

In MV's long run of 125 cc championships once NSU were gone, there was a notable hiccough – in 1957, when Mondial benefited from the return of designer Alfonso Drusiani and Provini won the title. By the time Honda dethroned them, the MV tiddlers were pushing out about 20 bhp at 12,500 rpm and topping 120 mph.

MV's two-fifty started, in 1955, simply as a one-two-five bored to the limit (68 mm) for a capacity of 203 cc. What it lost through its 20 per cent sacrifice in capacity it made up in being tiny and weighing only about 15 lb more than its smaller stablemate. It was competitive enough to bring the factory the manufacturers' championship in 1955, although the individual title that year went to "Happy" Müller on a full-size two-fifty.

(That was the catalogued 28 bhp NSU Sportmax single, with the overhead camshaft driven by a pair of long connecting rods.)

For 1956 MV took the hint. They bored and stroked their engine to 72.7×60 mm, so gaining a further 3 bhp and enabling Ubbiali to take the 250 cc title as well as the 125 cc. Mondial put MV's nose out of joint in the 250 cc class as well in 1957, when Cecil Sandford came out top, but Provini restored MV's pride the following year.

Meantime, even while the 125 cc single was being bored out to 203 cc, a 250 cc twin was being developed at Gallarate. This was virtually a brace of 125 cc singles side by side, with the ohc gear train still on the right-hand side. Although power was initially 5 bhp up on the 203 (32 bhp against 27 bhp in 1955), MV were dissatisfied, for the twin was appreciably heavier and the full size version of the single did not lag far behind the twin in development for power.

So the twin was rehashed for 1959, the new engine being distinguished by a five-degree forward lean and wet-sump oiling. Before long, power was up to 37 bhp at 12,500 rpm, top speed to about 135 mph, and Ubbiali regained his crown. It was on the twin again that he kept it in 1960 – his last taste of glory in a long and distinguished career.

By the time Provini put the 125 cc Mondial back at the top in 1957 it had acquired seven speeds, a record at the time, and one of the most elegant front and rear fairings ever seen on a lightweight. Small wonder the factory, like MV, had decided to double-up the engine into a 250 cc parallel twin. Unlike MV, they soon got the sort of power they wanted (35 bhp at 10,000 rpm in 1956). But track performance was hampered by the bike's exorbitant weight (for a two-fifty) of 310 lb and the project was dropped like a hot potato.

To take its place for 1957, Drusiani designed a brand-new, full-size single. Bore and stroke were 75×56.4 mm and bevels were forsaken in the double-knocker drive, which comprised a long train of spur gears. Fed by a 32 mm carburettor, the inlet tract was angled steeply downward. Two plugs were fitted, fired either by a twin-spark magneto or battery and coils. There was a choice of five or seven speeds to suit different circuits, a twin-leading-shoe front brake and, of course, a full dustbin and tail. Many of the cycle parts were virtually the same as on the one-two-five, so that the weight came out at 220 lb – some 90 lb lighter than the abandoned twin. As a result, the inevitable sacrifice in power

First one-two-five with more than one cylinder – the elegant little Gilera twin of the mid-1950s, being warmed up here by Romolo Ferri at Monza

(only 29 bhp at 10,800 rpm was claimed) was more than compensated and Sandford's world title was backed up by Provini's victory in the hotly contested Italian championship.

Fascinating non-winners

Of the fascinating trio of lightweights mentioned earlier which never scaled the championship heights, the pretty little 125 cc double-knocker Gilera ridden by Romolo Ferri in the mid-1950s was the first machine in its class with more than one cylinder. Virtually, the engine comprised the middle two cylinders of one of the fours, scaled down to 40×49.6 mm. Hence the camshaft gear train was sandwiched between the cylinders, not out to one side, and the engine leaned forward 30 degrees, with no induction downdraught whatsoever. A six-speed transmission was used.

Suspension and brake layouts followed current Gilera practice, as did the dustbin –

The 1960 version of the phenomenal 250 cc double-knocker Moto Morini engine with which the lone Tarquinio Provini put the wind up Honda three years later. At this stage, it had six speeds, dry-sump oiling and a long gear train serving the camshafts, oil pump and contact breaker for the twin-plug ignition. Its 35 bhp was eventually increased by 3 bhp

This picture of Provini shows the low build of the double-knocker Morini. The tank was slimmed and dented to allow him to tuck away. The machine won four Italian championships in a row and the 1963 Italian GP at Monza

although this was complemented by a substantial tail. Inclusive of fairings, the bike scaled 210 lb (which gives perspective to Moto Guzzi's achievement in making a three-fifty very little heavier). With 20 bhp at 12,000 rpm, Gilera's tiddler was good for two miles a minute. But those were "single-cylinder" revs, so there is little doubt the peak could have been raised appreciably with safety to give the rival singles something to think about.

Sensational Moto Morini

When Tarquinio Provini brought the lone Moto Morini single home third in the 1960 Lightweight 250 cc TT, behind the MV twins of Gary Hocking and Carlo Ubbiali, there was little hint of the sensation it would cause before its career ended. After all, it had been around for a year or two without getting to the top – and although it had just been specially tailored to the stature of the diminutive Italian fireball, nobody without a desmodromic crystal ball could have foreseen that it would come within an ace of dethroning the haughty Honda fours long after they themselves had trampled on the MV Agustas.

Based vaguely on the Rebello, a catalogue racer then only recently increased from 175 to 250 cc for the Italian national "Gran Premio" formula, Morini's response to the challenge of classic racing made a sensational debut in the 1958 Italian GP at Monza. Emilio Mendogni and Giampiero Zubani crushed the MVs by taking the first two places, ahead of Ubbiali, whose team-mate Provini blew up trying to hold Zubani.

The Moto Morini followed current Italian practice, with a considerably oversquare cylinder (72 × 61 mm) and the inevitable long train of gears serving both camshafts, the contact breaker and the oil pump for the dry sump. A battery and coils fired two plugs, one 12 mm, the other 10 mm. The long induction tract had an appreciable downdraught angle. Primary drive was by gears and a ventilated dry clutch to a six-speed gear cluster. Most of the engine castings were in magnesium, the frame was a duplex loop and the front brake had twin leading shoes. Dustbins were already outlawed and the one-piece dolphin fairing was included in the weight of 238 lb. Most significant, however, with 32 bhp at 10,500 rpm, the prototype showed signs of producing more power at lower revs than rival singles – evidence of the extraordinarily efficient cylinder filling and burning for which Morini later became famous.

The Monza victory was followed by many convincing wins, but the tie-up with Provini in 1960 really honed the bike's competitive edge: the oil was switched to the sump and the frame lowered; the fuel tank was slimmed and shaped to fit the rider's anatomy (even to the extent of a sponge-filled dent in the top for his chin) and a two-piece fairing was made, with a distinct waist and beautifully rounded upper and lower portions.

Within the limits imposed by an upright cylinder, it would have been difficult to get a 250 cc single lower or to tuck the rider more completely out of the airstream. At the same time, the engine wizards had pushed peak power up to 35 bhp at 11,000 rpm and the bike was a match for anything in its class, even as a lone entry. By 1963, 38 bhp was on tap, still at 11,000 rpm, and top speed approached 140 mph. The best bmep (average pressure on the piston throughout a complete cycle) was a remarkable 206 psi at 10,500 rpm. To the delight of all Italians, indeed most Europeans, Provini gave Honda's world champion Jim Redman such a close run in the title chase that the issue was wide open at the year's final grand prix in Japan. The final outcome, a two-point advantage for Jim, owed as much to the Italian's loss of edge, following physical and psychological upsets on the trip, as it did to Redman's thoroughly professional consistency and to Honda's extra efforts for their home round.

Cheeky desmo

Of all the lightweights that failed to win a world title, none did so with more cheek, more irreverence for the champions or more

With broad red-and-white stripes on the extensive streamlining allowed up to the end of 1957, the 125 cc desmodromic Ducati single was as distinctive in appearance as performance

technical excitement than the 125 cc desmodromic Ducati. The brainchild of Ing Fabio Taglioni, a genius of an engineer from Bologna University, it so humiliated the proud MVs in the late 1950s that valve springs might well have died a quick death had not Ducati soon pulled out of classic racing, just before Honda came in with paired valves to give return springs a further lease of life.

The chief problem that inspired Taglioni's design (and Honda's paired valves) was the increasing vulnerability of orthodox valve gear to overrevving. Higher peak revs inevitably meant extended valve timings and a wider overlap period around top dead centre. And larger valves meant less clearance between them during that overlap. Despite the use of double overhead camshafts to slash reciprocating weight, a brief bout of overrevving - whether through a fluffed gear change or neglect of the revmeter during a neck-and-neck scrap - caused the valves to float rather than follow the closing flank of the cam. The tiny clearance was then insufficient and the valves kissed. Meanwhile, higher compression ratios meant less valve-to-piston clearance, and a rising piston could overtake a floating exhaust valve. Either way (or both!) the engine went sick and the race was lost.

Taglioni's solution was to stop relying on springs and to use cams to close the valves (through extra rockers) as well as to open them. The idea first took shape in his mind in 1948, but six years passed before he joined Ducati and had the facilities to build an engine. This he did within a year, making a minimum of alterations to the factory's catalogued double-knocker racer, the Grand Prix. Within a further year, Taglioni's desmo made its sensational race debut at Hedemora, where Degli Antoni not only won the Swedish 125 cc GP but lapped every other finisher in the process.

Up to the end of 1957, when the FIM clamped down on dustbin fairings, the triple-knocker Ducati was as distinctive in appearance as it was technically, with broad red-and-white horizontal stripes running the full length of its very comprehensive front and rear streamlining. By the time it made its TT debut in 1958, though, it looked much like any other Italian lightweight in its new dolphin fairing.

Quart in a pint pot

It rattled the MV camp immediately. Luigi Taveri, Ducati's No 1, showed MV's Carlo Ubbiali his megaphone until the desmo engine packed up. Even then, Ubbiali was chased home by three more desmos, ridden by Romolo Ferri, Dave Chadwick and Sammy Miller.

Miller's bike was subsequently brought up to the top of the Mountain course by Taglioni for my test ride (although the race had been run on the Clypse circuit). For the TT, wheel diameter had been increased from 17 to 18 in and on Miller's model the standard riding position had been "stretched" a bit, too. Even so, it was immediately clear that Ducati relied on dwarfs for their star riders. Although no more than 5 ft 6 in and 140 lb, I felt like a quart trying to squeeze into a pint pot.

Handling was definitely of the finger-tip variety. The degree of cornering effort appropriate to a five-hundred would have spelt disaster on the Ducati. I just clung on ever so lightly, with scarcely a muscle tensed, and heeled this way and that with a delicacy of balance that would have delighted a tightrope walker. Only on flat-out, rippled bends did the wheels hop slightly, as if to prove that the bike weighed only 217 lb.

At that stage of development, the positive valve operation was exploited only for mechanical safety at revs that would otherwise cause valve float; the use of higher valve lifts for more power had yet to come. The revmeter dial was daubed yellow at 12,500, where Taglioni told me the engine gave its 18 bhp, and I took a mischievous

delight in watching the needle swing far into the five-figure band.

The rev-happy engine gave of its best only if all five gears were used to the full; Ferri, indeed, preferred a six-speed transmission. After peaking in the first four gears, I got 12,000 rpm in top - 106 mph. Peak revs in top on the Clypse gearing of 7·67:1 was equivalent to 111 mph and Miller said he got more on the drop to White Bridge. With no possibility of valve float, Taglioni told me, the riders were encouraged to outbrake their rivals into slow corners and get extra stopping power by letting the engine spin up to 15,000–16,000 rpm as they snicked smartly through the gears. I tried it and the effect, in conjunction with the immense power of the dual front brakes, was astonishing, standing the desmo on its nose and rendering the rear brake well-nigh ornamental. That sort of treatment must play havoc with the big-end bearings, I suggested. Taglioni admitted that it shortened their life but assured me that only three big ends had failed in four years of desmo racing.

Soon afterwards, with an extra bhp from increased valve lift, Ducati hammered home their engine superiority in the ultra-fast Belgian and Swedish GPs – with Alberto Gandossi and Ferri beating MV's Provini into third place at Francorchamps, while Gandossi and Taveri did the same to Ubbiali in Sweden. Then came the Monza massacre, when a new, 118 mph desmo twin (with 22·5 bhp at 14,000 rpm and safe to 17,000) joined four of the old singles in lapping MV's only finisher, Enzo Vezzalini, after Ubbiali and Provini had wrecked their engines in the forlorn chase.

MV turned the tables in 1959, largely because of injuries to Ducati's star midget, Bruno Spaggiari. Although Mike Hailwood brought a desmo single home third in the TT behind Provini's MV and Taveri's MZ two-stroke, his bulk put him at a distinct disadvantage on so small a bike.

Ingenious conversion

At the end of the year, I went to Bologna to analyse the single-cylinder engine and was amazed to see how much of it was standard. There was even an undrilled kickstart boss in the left-hand crankcase casting and a vacant space on the mainshaft on the same side, where the roadster version had its generator! The secrets of the desmo's superiority lay in the one-piece cylinder head and cambox. Indeed, the desmo head was a straight replacement, not only for the double-knocker head of the catalogued Grand Prix racer but also for that of the older, single-knocker Formula 3 model.

Converting the Grand Prix head to desmodromic valve operation had not been all that difficult, because the bevel drive from the crankshaft was topped by a train of three spur gears in the cambox, the front and rear of which were mounted on the exhaust and inlet camshafts. In principle, then, all that was necessary was to put a shaft in the middle gear and mount the two valve-closing cams on it. The opening cams actuated the valves through pivoted levers while the closing cams depressed rockers, the outer ends of which lifted flanged collars on the valve stems. To my unaccustomed eyes, those closers looked weird, since the lobe rather than the neutral portion occupied the greater part of the cam circumference.

Differences in the thermal expansion rates of the various components obviously made it impossible for the closing cams to hold the valves precisely on their seats at all engine temperatures without ever overloading the rubbing surfaces. Taglioni solved this problem by designing the cams to close the valves to within only about 0·012 in of their seats, leaving valve inertia and gas pressure within the cylinder to do the rest. At first, very light rocker-return springs were fitted to take up that 0·012 in clearance and so ensure full compression at ultra-low rpm. But they were soon discarded to obviate any danger of damage from a broken spring. As a result, when the engine was turned slowly by hand, compression seemed poor; but at push-starting speeds, however, the valves sealed as well as if they had been closed by conventional springs. I asked Taglioni what happened if a piece of grit got trapped under the inlet-valve seat. "Finito," was the succinct reply. But the risk was so remote that he preferred to accept it, rather than restrict the engine's breathing by fitting an air filter.

Above: *while a Ducati mechanic warms up Sammy Miller's 1958 TT fourth-place triple-knocker one-two-five, Vic Willoughby scribbles some technical notes prior to draping himself round the diminutive desmo. On the left is the great Ing Fabio Taglioni; next to him Fron Purslow, Ducati importer at the time*

Below: *Ducati's first desmodromic engine, the 125 cc triple-camshaft single. Only from the cylinder-head joint upward did it differ from the catalogued double-knocker Grand Prix model*

Above: *this 250 cc Ducati desmodromic parallel-twin is virtually a pair of 125 cc singles with the crankshafts clamped together by Hirth (radially serrated) couplings and the camshafts driven by a train of gears in the middle. A similar method of construction was used for 125 and 350 cc twins*

Below: *photographed at the 1959 TT, Honda's first 125 cc twin looked anything but a potential worldbeater. Note the curved frame spine, pivoted front fork of dubious geometry, high tank, bevel camshaft drive and air deflector on cylinder head*

Because the 10:1 compression ratio brought the piston crown so close to the valves during overlap, the opening and closing points remained the same as in the Grand Prix engine. But the lift of the inlet valve was increased from 7·5 to 8·1 mm, and that of the exhaust valve from 7 to 7·4 mm. These fiercer cams, in conjunction with the slightly higher reciprocating weight of the valve gear and the engine's higher rpm, raised the level of the inertia forces, but this was of little consequence, since those forces could not possibly cause the valves to fling.

Other interesting features included the use of spring-loaded, axial-thrust main bearings to eliminate high-speed vibration; steel for the big-end cage to resist centrifugal distortion; a separate, three-volt coil for each plug, fed by a six-volt battery (the second plug was tucked behind the top bevel box); and an ingenious way of accommodating the fifth and sixth gears. Since there was no room for these between the standard main crankcase halves, they were sandwiched between the back of the clutch and the crankcase wall, in the primary drive compartment.

In the single-cylinder engine (55·25 × 52 mm), desmodromics ultimately gave a 3 bhp power bonus over the double-knocker layout (19 bhp at 12,500 rpm against 16 bhp at 12,000 rpm) besides freedom from valve float. And the six-speed, 125 cc twin (42·5 × 45 mm) built in 1958 gave 22·5 bhp at 14,000 rpm. In that engine, the two flywheel assemblies were clamped to the central take-off gear by Hirth couplings (as in the NSU Rennmax) and the camshafts were driven by a train of spur gears in a case between the cylinders. The compression ratio was 10·2:1 and there was room for only one plug per cylinder.

Initially, the twin's 3·5 bhp advantage was not reflected in higher lap speeds because the power curve was too peaky. It was a pity that factory policy then curtailed Taglioni's involvement in classic racing, because that problem was by no means insoluble. And there was already a brisk demand for desmo twins of 250 and 350 cc, while a 125 cc four was on the stocks.

As with Moto Guzzi a couple of years earlier, a management decision taken on economic grounds stifled the prospect of heightened technical excitement and inter-marque rivalry on the tracks. Nevertheless, Taglioni's was a magnificent achievement and it was commercially justified when a simplified desmodromic layout later formed the backbone of a highly successful range of sporting roadsters.

Eastern promise

Notwithstanding Ducati's withdrawal, the lightweight championships in the late 1950s remained an all-Italian squabble, so the

entry of a team of quaint Honda twins in the 1959 Lightweight 125 cc TT gave rise to amusement rather than concern; after all, Japan's European impact at that time was chiefly in the field of toys and transistor radios. Their motor cycle industry still had the cradle marks on its backside. Indeed, exports to Europe had not begun and we knew of Japanese bikes only from occasional press photographs, showing immaculate copies of British machines, usually scaled down in capacity.

Metaphorically, we TT enthusiasts patted the strangers on the head and hoped they would learn from the Europeans. They learned all right, but from ideas that European engineers had either abandoned or had never dared to exploit: paired valves in the first case and tiny cylinders in the second. Right from the start, Honda's cylinder size (62 cc) was as small as anything seen in Europe (such as the wartime Benelli and Gilera 250 cc blown fours, the postwar Gilera 125 cc twin and the Moto Guzzi 500 cc vee-eight) and they went on to win championships with pots of 25, 41 and 49·5 cc. In the nine years during which the haunting, high-pitched howl from their megaphones captured every racegoer's imagination, Honda won 18 manufacturers' championships and 16 individual titles. They numbered 18 TT victories among their 137 grand-prix triumphs and, in the face of repeated two-stroke challenges, showed incredible speed in technical innovation and development.

Back in 1959, however, nobody could have foreseen such overwhelming supremacy. While the officials in that first oriental TT party went round photographing everything they could point their cameras at, the mechanics tended race machines that looked as old fashioned as they were meticulously prepared. Wheel diameter was larger at the front than the rear, a navigational feature long since discarded in Europe; the spine frame was ungainly and the geometry of the pivoted front fork all wrong; the carburettors had guillotine throttle slides such as our forefathers abandoned in the interest of small-throttle mixture control. Some plugs were in the side of the head (two valves) and others in the middle (four valves), the latter with deflector plates to cool them, since the cylinders were not inclined forward. Left-side bevel gears took the cam drive up to the cylinder head, where a train of spur gears served the separate inlet and exhaust shafts; the magneto was driven by the right-hand end of the inlet shaft. Although lubrication was wet sump, gravity was not trusted to return the oil and a scavenge pump was fitted. Ingeniously, the fairing sides had double walls to minimise internal eddying and deflect air to the cylinders.

True, those little six-speed twins, with 18 bhp at 13,000 rpm, proved to be paragons

A rare picture of an early Honda 125 cc twin, with side plug location denoting two-valve cylinder heads

of reliability, finishing sixth, seventh and eighth for the manufacturers' team prize, but they were hopelessly outpaced by MV, MZ and Ducati singles, and their oriental riders were much too raw for the hurly-burly of TT racing.

Undismayed, Honda came back the following year, but with telescopic forks, same-size wheels, inclined cylinders, a couple of Australian riders (Bob Brown and Tom Phillis) and a trio of 250 cc fours with the camshafts driven by a central gear train. Despite adding ninth and tenth places to a repeat of their sixth, seventh and eigth in the 125 cc race, they missed the manufacturers' prize and Naomi Taniguchi, their fastest finisher in that event, was 5·52 mph slower than Carlo Ubbiali on the winning MV single.

Honda fared better in the 250 cc race, with fourth, fifth and sixth places; but Bob Brown, their best finisher, was all of 4·43 mph slower than Gary Hocking, who won on an MV twin. What is more, for all their dependability (no retirements) the 250 cc fours lacked consistent speed; they would spasmodically lose 1,000 rpm in top gear for no obvious reason.

By fair means and foul, we technical journalists unearthed a few details of their design and development. Each inlet port had a knife-edge dividing wall starting some way upstream of the valve heads. The weight of an individual valve (head diameter about 18 or 19 mm) was a bare 12 grammes, only fractionally more than a $\frac{1}{4}$ oz. Even with cam follower, duplex springs and top collar, the total reciprocating weight of each valve assembly reached only 20 grammes (well under $\frac{3}{4}$ oz). No wonder maximum safe revs were quoted as 17,000 rpm.

Left: *first dry-sump version of the 250 cc Honda four in 1961. Excessive oil temperature and leakage from the tank prevented Bob McIntyre from winning the TT and making the first 100-mph lap in the class*

them both (and completed the first TT treble later in the week with a Senior win on a Norton). Luigi Taveri, the dapper little Swiss star, bumped the 125 cc lap record up to 88·45 mph. And Bob McIntyre, in one of the most sensational rides in TT history, made nonsense of all previous 250 cc records with a lap at 99·58 mph, despite a well-oiled rear tyre. But for that handicap, on which he had worked manfully throughout practice, a 100 mph lap was clearly within his and the Honda's capabilities, at a time when no three-fifty had got round at the magic ton, something then achieved only by 500 cc Gileras and MV fours and a brace of Norton big singles.

McIntyre's trouble stemmed from the factory's switch from wet-sump to dry-sump lubrication: under sustained full throttle, such as only he meted out, the oil (which circulated every 30 seconds and so had insufficient time to cool) exceeded 100 degrees C, frothed badly and blew out of the four-pint tank, plastering the left-hand side of the back wheel. From a push start, Mac's opening lap sliced an enormous 48·4 seconds off Carlo Ubbiali's 250 cc lap record and put the Scot nearly half a minute ahead of Gary Hocking, lying second on an MV twin. Mac's second lap (his first flier) actually lopped 5·4 seconds off the Junior (350 cc) record which John Surtees had set the previous year on an MV four.

Alas, the oily tyre increasingly cramped McIntyre's left-hand cornering style and, halfway round the final lap, the tank ran dry and the engine seized at the Quarry Bends. With nobody remotely threatening his lead, Mac handed the race to Hailwood, ahead of Phillis and Redman.

Among the technical changes that contributed to Honda's vastly improved competitiveness was the adoption of barrel-type throttle slides and underslung float bowls in the carburettors, along with generator-powered, energy-transfer ignition using a pair of double-ended, high-tension coils. No longer did the four fail to sustain top revs, although with a useful range of only 10,000 to 14,000 rpm, it was hardly top of the tractability stakes.

Removal of the oil container from the bottom of the crankcase enabled the engine to be lowered. At the same time, the opportunity was taken to unite the fairing sides with a smooth underbelly. Engine power for the twin and four had crept up to 21 and 42 bhp respectively (it crept still higher as the months rolled by). Slim, well faired and reasonably light (231 lb for the four), the Hondas were in a class of their own. By the end of the season, Tom Phillis (125 cc) and

Above: *handicapped by too much oil on the rear tyre and not enough in the engine, Bob McIntyre rounds Whitegates on his 99·58 mph record lap in the 1961 Lightweight 250 cc TT. Before the engine seized on the final lap, he was far ahead of both the opposition and his own Honda team-mates, who filled the first five places*

Desmodromics, Honda assured us, had been tried but abandoned because they proved less reliable and gave no more power, which was 38 bhp at 13,500 rpm for their two-fifty by TT time. As the season wore on, power was pushed up to 20 bhp for the twin and 40 for the four, and the frame's single spine was replaced by a duplex structure with the top and down tubes crossed over behind the steering head (featherbed Norton fashion) and the engine still an integral part of the frame, to which it was attached at four points – one by the exhaust cambox, three behind the gearbox.

On the riding side, the team was strengthened by the inclusion of Rhodesian Jim Redman, who was eventually to contribute six of Honda's world championships and six of their TT victories. The Italian lightweights still trounced them in the grands prix, however, and when the Japanese engineers went home at the season's end, it was not to lick their wounds but to sort out the engines' tantrums and find race-winning performance.

Massacre

Although nobody suspected it, that 1960–61 winter was the calm before a storm of unprecented fury. It broke over the Isle of Man the following June, when Honda simply massacred the opposition, their riders monopolising the first five places in the two Lightweight races. Mike Hailwood won

To keep overall width to a minimum, the exhaust pipes of the 1964–65 Honda 50 cc twin were swept round to the opposite sides of the nine-speed engine

Mike Hailwood (250 cc) had put a stop to Carlo Ubbiali's succession of lightweight titles for MV.

1962

For 1962, Honda spread their attack both up and down the capacity scale, building a five-speed, double-knocker single for the newly-introduced 50 cc class and boring the four to 47 mm (285 cc) to challenge MV supremacy in the 350 cc class.

Virtually a 40 × 39 mm, shrunken half of the 125 cc twin (which had switched from bevels to a train of spur gears for the camshaft drive), the tiddler arrived in Europe with 9–10 bhp at 14,000 rpm, a top speed of 85–90 mph and a thirst of 50–60 mpg. Weight was a mere 132 lb and tyre size a skinny 2·00 × 18 in. In spite of Taveri's forceful riding, however, it lacked the legs of Enrst Degner's Suzuki two-stroke single, both in the TT and, eventually, in the world championship.

Incredibly, Honda twins again filled the first five places in the Lightweight 125 cc TT. Making full use of one or two bhp more than he had in 1961, Luigi Taveri carved 28·6 seconds off his own lap record during his winning ride, and went on to clinch the world championship.

In raising the power of the two-fifty to 46 bhp, however, Honda met elusive misfiring that tarnished their reliability, so that they filled "only" the first three places in the Lightweight 250 cc TT and failed to match their 1961 speeds. Derek Minter blotted his copybook in the factory's eyes by winning,

ahead of Redman and Phillis, on a spare machine borrowed and entered by Hondis, the British importers, but it was Bob McIntyre who again set the race alight. A scintillating opening lap at 99·06 mph put him handsomely in the lead, a stupendous 34·6 seconds ahead of his team-mate Redman and 44 seconds up on Minter. It was a one-man race and nobody in his senses would have bet against the first 250 cc ton lap. But Mac had covered only 12 miles of the second lap when the exhaust howl became a stutter as half the ignition went dead.

Less happy still was Honda's showing in the Junior race, where both 285 cc machines packed up. But the factory debugged them quickly enough for Redman to match the MVs of Hailwood and Hocking in the 350 cc title chase. And when the engine was stretched to 49 × 45 mm (339 cc) for the Ulster GP, Redman clinched the championship, to add to the 250 cc title that was already his.

1963

So enormous and so surprising had Honda's impact been, both on the world championships and on the TT races which they rated so highly, that they seemed to have discovered a short cut to invincibility. But their meteoric rise had spurred rather than demoralised their rivals and 1963 brought ominous signs of the impending two-stroke threat.

Only in the 350 cc class was that threat absent. There, with Geoff Duke's resurrected Gileras showing their age, the only rider who could mount anything remotely resembling a serious challenge to Honda was Mike Hailwood on the MV four. Their pride bruised by the loss of the world title the

The opposition's view of Honda's first MV-eater – the 339 cc (49 × 45 mm) version raced by Jim Redman giving 52 bhp in 1963. Note the snug fit of the fairing round the engine, also the profiled fuel tank

previous season, MV concocted a gigantic twin-leading-shoe front brake for Mike's Junior TT machine, hoping he could offset his deficiency in speed and acceleration by later braking. Mike, however, wore out the brake in a forlorn bid to keep up with the Honda. With 52 bhp on tap, Redman shrugged off MV's desperate gamble, not only in the Junior TT but also by hanging on to his world 350 cc title, proving once more that an overpowered two-fifty (which his Honda virtually was) is more than a match for an underpowered five-hundred, such as the MV and Gilera fours.

Redman retained his 250 cc title, too, but it was a close-run thing. By bringing his wonderful Moto Morini single home first at Montjuich Park, Hockenheim and Monza, Tarquinio Provini kept the championship wide open until the final race, in Japan. Mike

In 1964, Honda got back on top of the 125 cc class by changing from a twin to a four. Here Jim Redman, the eventual winner, slipstreams Phil Read (on an air-cooled Yamaha twin) in the Dutch GP

Hailwood demonstrated the potential of MZ's water-cooled twin by winning at Sachsenring. And, on a sister-model, Alan Shepherd matched the winner's speed at both Hockenheim and Monza after early pit stops had spoiled his chances of winning. More significant, as it turned out, Fumio Ito won the Belgian GP on his air-cooled Yamaha twin (virtually an oriental MZ) and chased Redman home in the TT and the Dutch and Japanese GPs. In the TT, indeed, the burly Japanese led Redman for the first two laps, only to throw away his chance of glory by dallying over his pit stop.

Throughout the season, there were rumours of a water-cooled Suzuki square four with enough power to blow all other two-fifties off the tarmac. As it transpired, that model was the least of anyone's worries (except Suzuki's!), but Honda were not to know that. They could hardly discount the threat, for the square four's engine was thought to be a double-up of the 125 cc twin which, even in air-cooled guise, had heaped humiliation on their own double-knocker twins all season.

Those little Suzukis filled the first three places in the TT, led by the brilliant New Zealander Hugh Anderson, who went on to

relieve Luigi Taveri of the world crown. Anderson scooped the 50 cc championship too, from which Honda had already pulled out and scurried back to the drawing board. But in the tiddler TT, Anderson was led home by Suzuki's Mitsuo Itoh (the first Japanese TT winner) who gave Honda something to think about by adding nearly 4 mph to the race speed for a power increase of only 1 bhp.

1964-65

Honda were on the run and, recognising the two-stroke's growing superiority in bmep, started to cut cylinder size (hence stroke length) to gain power from higher peak revs. They re-entered the 50 cc ring with an incredibly slender, nine-speed twin weighing only 4 lb more than the single, pushing out 15 bhp at 19,000 rpm and easily topping 100 mph. With a bore and stroke of 33 × 29.2 mm, valve diameters of only 12 and 13 mm (exhaust and inlet respectively), 10 mm central plugs and high-compression pistons with squish segments front and rear, the engine looked like a tiny version of the four with the right-hand cylinders cut off. Even the crankshaft resembled the left half of a four-cylinder one, with the crankpins spaced at 180 degrees for better primary balance and lower pumping losses at the expense of uneven firing intervals.

The widest part of the machine was the handlebar, for which the FIM minimum

With four cylinders instead of two, Luigi Taveri wins the Lightweight 125 cc TT for Honda in 1964 on his way to regaining his world title from Hugh Anderson (Suzuki)

was 18 in, but even there the grips were mounted 2 or 3 in inboard to bring the rider's arms farther in. Also contributing to the narrowness was a cross-over layout for the exhaust pipes. Tyre sizes were 2.00 and 2.25 × 18 in and thin aluminium discs were clipped to the spokes to smooth out the eddies behind the tyres. Equally surprising, the

front brake was of pushbike type, with a caliper gripping the wheel rim to form, in effect, an 18 in disc brake.

When the diminutive Irishman Ralph Bryans chased Hugh Anderson home in the 1964 TT, Suzuki started to fret. But during the few meetings it took Honda to debug their little screamer Anderson piled up valuable points and, by the time he notched up his fourth successive win (in Finland), Suzuki's worries were over: his 50 cc title was safe for another year. By the season's end, however, Bryans had turned the tables

and scored four consecutive wins himself. This made him a clear favourite for the 1965 title, which he duly won despite Suzuki's switch to two cylinders and water cooling.

In the 125 cc class, Honda's response to the drubbing Suzuki had given them in 1963 was to pension off their ageing twin and replace it with an eight-speed, 35 × 32 mm four, giving 25 bhp at 16,000 rpm. This immediately displayed an unprecedented blend of speed and wrist-watch regularity, just as Suzuki inadvertently sacrificed reliability while squeezing a few more knots out of their air-cooled twin. Taveri made the most of the situation: in nine rides, he scored five wins (including the TT) and four second places, to grab his title back from Anderson. But that gave Honda only a temporary reprieve from the two-stroke threat.

For 1965, while Honda's effort suffered from their preoccupation with Formula 1 car racing, and Taveri was plagued by chronic misfiring for half the season, both Suzuki and Yamaha adapted their twins to water cooling. The consequent improvement in stamina and performance enabled Yamaha (through Phil Read) to turn the tables on Taveri in the TT, and Anderson to do the same most emphatically in the world championship. Before the season was out, though, there were signs that Honda were buying time by extending their successful 50 cc technology into the 125 cc class for a comeback in 1966.

No consolation

The monumental flop of Suzuki's 54 bhp, water-cooled 250 cc square four in 1964 underlined the old truism that races are won on the tarmac, not on the dynamometer. But that was small consolation to Honda: Fumio

Ralph Bryans and his Honda twin at Assen, on the way to the 1965 world 50 cc title. The front-brake shoes work on wheel rim just behind the fork sliders. Aluminium streamline discs were removed from the front wheel because of high winds, although retained at rear

Ito's performance the previous year had revealed the potential of Yamaha's air-cooled twin and when Phil Read took it over he promptly robbed Redman of his title. This he did by toying with Jim, shadowing him wherever he could and using the two-stroke's edge in speed to romp past in the closing stages. Had Yamaha not bartered their 1963 reliability for their 1964 power increase, Read might have won the TT too, instead of breaking down on that exacting course after making the fastest lap.

Again Honda were quick to react: by the time of the penultimate grand prix, the Italian in September, their five-year-old four had been superseded by a 39 × 34·5 mm six no wider across the fairing than even the singles in the class. With eight speeds and 54 bhp at 15–16,000 rpm, it seemed a good answer to the Yamaha twin. But, on its Monza debut, a misfire blunted its speed and poor handling curbed Redman's zeal, so that he could finish no higher than third while Read clinched the world title. Two months later in Japan, the teething troubles seemingly solved, Redman and the six were uncatchable and prospects for 1965 looked rosy.

Unfortunately for Honda, it did not turn out that way: Redman struck a thoroughly bad patch, eventually coming to the start grid only six times to Read's 12, and the factory's Formula 1 commitments led to half-hearted machine preparation; for example, Jim's gearbox packed up while he was leading the French GP at Rouen. Continuing his 1964 cat-and-mouse tactics,

Jim Redman gives Honda's 250 cc six its race baptism in the 1964 Italian GP at Monza. A misfire and poor handling prevented his finishing higher than third

Read demoralised the Honda camp with four straight wins. There were occasional glimpses of hope – in the Isle of Man, where the Yamaha again lacked winning stamina and broke its crankshaft while Read was leading; at Spa Francorchamps, where Redman gained more from the six's speed than he lost from its camel-like cornering; and at Sachsenring, where Read was supposedly nursing his engine for the following week's Czech GP at Brno. But the hopes were forlorn and Read had no difficulty in notching the three more wins he needed for maximum points.

It was only after Read had thus consolidated Yamaha's grip on the 250 cc title that Honda saw the way ahead, when Mike Hailwood rode the six for the first time in the Japanese GP at Suzuka. His pithy criticism of the handling made the Japanese headlines but he won the race almost contemptuously. With Mike on their payroll for 1966, thought Honda, they could capitalise not only on his youth and dash but also on his long experience of taming even bigger "camels".

Redman's experiences in the 350 cc class, meanwhile, were much happier. With the cylinder dimensions flattened a shade to 50 × 44·5 mm for a full 349 cc, he brought his title tally to three on the trot in 1964 with a virtual walkover, winning every grand prix in the series. Although Giacomo Agostini's exuberance on the MV 12-valve three the following year often camouflaged a slight power deficiency, the wily Redman made good use of his extra speed to hang on to his championship.

1966

"Coming events cast their shadows before" and part of the 1966 pattern was discernible at the Japanese GP the previous October. Not surprisingly, in view of the success of the 50 cc twin, the five-cylinder one-two-five, ridden by Bryans and Taveri, had the legs of everything in its class at Suzuka. Only a trivial fault kept Taveri from winning and, in 1966, he again snatched the championship back from Anderson, so winning his third 125 cc title in five years. With the same cylinder dimensions as the tiny twin (33 × 29·2 mm), the five spun out 30 bhp at 18–19,000 rpm and comfortably topped 125 mph. It had dry-sump lubrication and needed a pair of oil coolers. The middle exhaust pipe, incidentally, swept behind the two on the left, back and up over the clutch, then across the frame to terminate under the rider's right thigh.

Significantly, though, it was no longer Anderson's Suzuki twin that yapped at the Honda's heels but Yamaha's 14,000 rpm twin, with forced water cooling and auxiliary oiling of the engine bearings. When all three works Hondas were slowed by faulty carburation in the TT, it was Bill Ivy who won on a Yamaha twin, followed by his team mate, Phil Read (who had won on a similar model the previous year). Ivy emphasised the challenge by finishing the season with four wins to Taveri's five.

The full signicance of this development, however, was that Yamaha had already doubled-up that engine into a 250 cc vee-four, which made its track debut towards the end of 1965. Although its speed was wasted at its Monza baptism, when plug fouling put Read a lap adrift, and at Suzuka, where he threw it away, the one-two-five's performance clearly showed what we could ultimately expect from the two-fifty.

In the 50 cc class, Bryans and Taveri sustained Honda's slight edge on Suzuki throughout 1966 and, right up to the Japanese GP, it seemed probable that Taveri would relieve his team mate of the individual title. But Honda boycotted the event because it was moved from the Suzuka circuit (their test track) and Suzuki's new signing, Hans-George Anscheidt (from Kreidler) was able to snatch the championship, although Honda kept the manufacturers' title.

Hailwood's mastery of the 250 cc six finally put it where it belonged – at the top of the 1966 championship heap, its first unhappy year now forgotten. There was no shortage of opposition, however, for Read, who started the season on the air-cooled twin but soon switched to the vee-four, fought to the very last. Hailwood nevertheless gave him a dose of the medicine Read had handed to Redman during the previous two years, although Mike's trump card was not so much all-out speed as a combination of dependability, handling and engine braking.

To meet the challenge of Agostini and his 12-valve MV in the 350 cc class, Honda put Redman's four on one side and gave Mike a bored and stroked version of his two-fifty (41 × 37·5 mm = 297 cc). Despite giving away 53 cc, it was unbeatable: in rattling up the six wins that gave him maximum points, Mike well-nigh demoralised Ago, who had to rely for his three victories on Hailwood's bike packing up on the Sachsenring and the Isle of Man, and on Mike not starting at Monza, since the issue was already settled by then.

Honda's chief bait in attracting Hailwood from the MV camp had been the promise of a really up-to-date five-hundred, so racegoers found it incredible that Honda virtually made a gift of the individual 500 cc championship to Agostini with an appalling demonstration of how to lose friends and infuriate people. It is true that Ago proved himself not only the most formidable rider Italy ever produced but also a worthy world champion by any standard. True, too, that MV soon got the hang of the four-valve set-

For 1966, Honda extended their successful 50 cc technology into the 125 cc class and produced this five-cylinder engine. With 30 bhp at 18–19,000 rpm, it gave a top speed of 125 mph. Note the route of the middle exhaust pipe, which sweeps over the clutch and across to finish under the rider's right thigh

up, then got wise enough to abandon their big four and scale-up the 12-valve three-fifty – first to 420 cc, then to full size. But Honda's questionable strategy and half-hearted servicing were equally responsible for the destiny of the individual title.

Sentiment, not sense

At the time, Hailwood and the big Honda, difficult though it was to handle, were more than a match for any other man/machine combination in the world, as emphasised by his Senior TT win, nearly three minutes ahead of Ago, with a lap record of 107·07 mph. But sentiment rather than sense persuaded Honda to let the loyal Redman rather than the incomparable Hailwood spearhead their 500 cc attack, and they squandered Mike's energies in totting up ten 250 cc wins when only the first seven were necessary to snatch that championship from Phil Read.

With wiser team strategy (or hindsight!) Hailwood rather than Redman could have claimed the individual points for the big Honda's initial win at Hockenheim, and for its subsequent victory at Assen, where Ago finished a mere 2·2 seconds behind Jim. For Redman's points were useless once he broke his arm at Francorchamps eight days later. Anyway, Ago was too good for him once the MV engine was full size. Even so, Mike still had the individual title within his grasp

when the crankshaft came apart at Monza, a failure for which, in prouder times, the mechanic responsible might have been expected to commit *hara-kiri*.

Throughout 1966, Honda's superiority on the tracks was such that they won close on 70 per cent of the classic races they contested, with five different makes sharing the remainder. But the net result of their shortcomings in organisation and servicing was that their riders won only three of the five individual solo titles, instead of making a clean sweep, which the factory achieved in the manufacturers' championships.

Technically, the five-hundred was in the old Honda tradition: a 16-valve four (57 × 48 mm for 489 cc) with the cylinders abreast. Dull, maybe, but a long stride ahead of MV's old, eight-valve four and a better bet, given good enough handling, than the Italian 12-valve three, for Honda could always put four cylinders into the width that MV needed for a three and so gain a power advantage. Some of us had hoped for something really exotic – a vee-eight or vee-twelve – but it was not necessary. The four's 85 bhp at 12,000 rpm was more than enough and the maximum the factory squeezed out of the engine (93 bhp at 12,300 rpm) was of academic rather than practical interest.

1967

Blissfully unaware that the management would opt out of classic racing altogether at the end of 1967, the race shop switched that year's 50 and 125 cc efforts from the track back to the drawing board, to cope with the threats from Suzuki and Yamaha respectively. Word leaked out of a three-cylinder

fifty with even more power and dizzier revs than the 18 bhp at 19–20,000 rpm that the twin was eventually giving. There was no hint of the shape of Honda's answer to Yamaha's 125 cc vee-four but most likely it would have been a smaller version of the straight six.

As it was, Anscheidt and Suzuki took the 50 cc titles, Ivy and Yamaha the 125 cc. Only in the 250 and 350 cc classes did Honda and Hailwood maintain their authority, for Honda were robbed of a third manufacturers' award, in the 500 cc class, where Agostini's grip on the individual crown proved too strong to break.

In all three classes, the state of the art in 1967 was crystallised in a magnificent TT week, when Hailwood scored his second treble, winning the Lightweight 250 cc and Junior races so emphatically that the opposition might have been asleep, but winning the Senior only after a tremendous battle with Agostini and a heroic struggle with a loose twistgrip.

From a technical viewpoint, those races were enormously instructive, demonstrating the folly of going for engine power at the expense of handling, and emphasising the supremacy of the TT course in driving that lesson home to those designers and development engineers wise enough to heed it. Honda confirmed that Mike had 60 bhp at the business end of the twistgrip in the two-fifty, 65 in the two-nine-seven and 85 in the five-hundred. His lap records were a carefree 104·5 and 107·73 mph in the 250 and 350 cc races (the latter from a standing start) and an extremely hairy flier of 108·77 mph in the Senior. The diminishing returns on power were obvious: Mike's Junior

Power – too little and too much. In 1967 Mike Hailwood lapped the TT course at 104·5 mph on a 250 cc Honda six with 60 bhp, 107·73 mph (from a standing start) on a 297 cc six with 65 bhp, and at 108·77 mph on a 500 cc four with 85 bhp. On his two-fifty (left) he prayed for more power. The two-nine-seven (below) gave him a carefree ride. But the five-hundred (right) was a nightmare because of hairy handling

bonus of 5 bhp pushed his lap speed up by 3·23 mph, whereas the extra 20 bhp of the Senior bike was worth a paltry 1·04 mph. Indeed, it might have been worth nothing at all if Mike had really pushed his Junior bike on a flying lap, but there was no need since his opening lap put him a monumental 48·6 seconds ahead of the redoubtable Ago and Mike won, easing up, by more than three minutes.

Embarrassing power

Mike confirmed my reasoning afterwards. "On the two-fifty," he said, "I was praying for more power everywhere. On the two-nine-seven I did so occasionally, though not very often. But the five-hundred's power was a sheer embarrassment. About 70 bhp would be ideal for the course."

Nowadays, the optimum would be higher because tyres have grippier tread compounds and larger contact areas, the road surface is less bumpy, suspension is more sensitive and steering perhaps steadier. But the underlying fact remains that sheer power is not the prime requirement in a racing solo, especially at the top end of the capacity scale.

By the end of the season, however, Yamaha were pushing Honda in the 250 cc class as well as the 125. The vee-four two-stroke had never been short of speed. Now it had acquired dependability (it survived the 226 miles of the TT in full vigour for Phil Read to finish second to Hailwood) and the engineers were beginning to get to grips with its handling.

The 350 and 500 cc classes (including the sidecars) were still four-stroke strongholds, but it seemed that 1968 might finally resolve the two-stroke/four-stroke issue in the smaller classes. Alas, any such showdown was pre-empted by Honda's withdrawal and the four-stroke camp practically went into mourning.

One of the most colourful technical periods in classic racing had ended and Honda had proved the benefits of sticking to first principles: shorter and shorter strokes to raise peak revs without pushing mean piston speed much above 4,000 ft/min; deep breathing and mechanical safety through paired valves; efficient burning through central plugs and squish segments; minimum friction through ball and roller bearings; light weight for acceleration, braking, climb and handling; small frontal area and low drag for speed.

To match them for power at comparable revs (some 11,000–12,000 rpm for 125 cc cylinders), a four-stroke would have to produce a bmep of 280 psi, whereas Honda had previously topped out at about 200 and even lower-revving Formula 1 car-racing four-strokes had never bettered 220.

Honda's strategy was nothing if not logical. First they settled on the largest class (500 cc), where the premium on sheer engine power is lowest; then they set about exploiting even farther the basic principles that had served them so well in their heyday. Accepting, as they had to, the two-stroke's increased superiority in bmep (in effect, bhp/litre/1,000 rpm) they sought to narrow the power gap by lifting peak revs to astronomical heights (for cylinders of 125 cc).

By choosing a stroke of only 36 mm, they kept mean piston speed down to 4,250 ft/min at an unprecedented 18,000 rpm. To maintain valve control and breathing at that speed, they put eight tiny valves in each cylinder – in two rows of four, which meant forsaking round cylinder bores for an elongated shape and fitting twin-choke carburettors. And to speed up burning in such

Backs to the wall

When Honda eventually sought to regain their former eminence by re-entering the grand-prix fray late in 1979, the situation was much more daunting. In the intervening 12 years the two-stroke had not only swamped the remaining four-stroke strongholds; it had also progressed so far in specific power (bhp/litre) that it was widely doubted in engineering circles whether any four-stroke with poppet valves could hope to match it on that basis. In engineering parlance, the top two-stroke engines were then producing a brake mean effective pressure (the average useful pressure on the piston crowns throughout a complete engine cycle) of 140 to 150 psi and there was still no sign of an end to their advance.

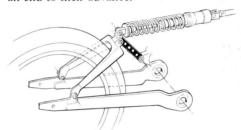

Left and below: *with the rear fork pivoted on the sprocket axis to eliminate chain snatch, Honda were unable to use a triangulated structure, which would have fouled the ignition boxes and oil catch tank. Hence the pivoted U-link connected to the suspension strut by a tie rod*

With the radiator cowlings removed, Mick Grant gives the NR500 Honda a pre-race tryout at Donington. Steering inertia seems high, with fork springs and brake calipers in front of the fork legs which are themselves ahead of the wheel spindle

wide combustion chambers they put two plugs in each.

As to the bike as a whole, they decided to minimise its power requirement by making it light (242 lb), small (only 16 in wheels and a slim V-four cylinder arrangement) and "slippery" (through a relatively smooth aluminium monocoque frame) – in essence, the old Moto Guzzi formula resurrected.

Front and side views of the Honda NR500 water-cooled V-four engine. Cylinder angle is 100 degrees. Each cylinder has a stroke of 36 mm, eight valves, two plugs, a twin-choke carburettor and transistorised ignition. Useful power range is from 11,500 to 18,500 rpm

It was a gamble. In the first place, the percentage power deficit to be offset was considerably greater than in Moto Guzzi's day. Moreover, phenomenal tyre developments meant that the whole contest between the bludgeon of power-at-any-price and the scalpel of light-low-and-slippery was now fought out twice as far up the bhp scale.

At this exalted power level, the exploitation of ultra-high revs is subject to the law of diminishing returns – as mounting friction losses overtake hardwon power gains; smaller ports lose efficiency because of the increasing ratio of skin friction to cross-sectional area; and extended valve timings restrict the compression ratio through the need for increased valve/piston clearance at tdc overlap.

Not surprisingly, Honda's debut with the NR500 (in the British GP at Silverstone and the French GP at Le Mans) was much less promising than their original debut 20 years

earlier. Not only were the engines temperamental starters and pathetically short of power (being outsped by many three-fifties) but handling was below par too.

Besides the fundamental problem of all ultra-light machines – a low ratio of sprung to unsprung weight, so that the "tail tends to wag the dog" – they seemed to suffer from a relative lack of torsional stiffness in the rear fork and excessive steering inertia resulting from the concentration of the mass of the fork legs, spring units and brake calipers too far from the steering axis. Unnecessary steering inertia makes the response more sluggish and less precise.

At the time of going to press, it remained to be seen whether Honda would achieve their aim (and so establish a new standard in four-stroke technology) or be forced to accept the two-stroke's invincibility under the existing FIM formula.

BMW make a comeback

In common with other prewar and wartime designs that owed either their performance or their potential to supercharging (eg, the Gilera four in the first case and the AJS Porcupine in the second), the BMW flat twin had its guns well and truly spiked by the FIM's postwar ban on supercharging. A further handicap for German race engineers was the FIM's refusal to readmit their country to classic racing until 1951. What with the technical problem of converting their engine to atmospheric induction and the track problem of finding a worthy successor to the ageing Georg Meier, it was no wonder that late-starters BMW failed to figure in the early postwar headlines.

Notwithstanding brave and skilful performances by German 500 cc champion Walter Zeller in the mid-1950s, they never did regain their prewar stature in solo racing. Instead, under the technical guidance of the tall, lean and aristocratic Dipl Ing Alex von Falkenhausen, they established the longest and most emphatic monopoly in world championship history by dominating the sidecar class for 20 years, despite producing the Rennsport machine in only small quantities and over no more than two or three years (although spares were made for considerably longer).

The Mustang, their first racing machine under the new rules, looked for all the world like the prewar blown job shorn of its compressor and fitted with a pair of carburettors. It had the old, plunger-type rear springing and a telescopic front fork, and its 43 bhp at 8,000 rpm, while not to be laughed at, was hardly enough to earn it international renown.

It took no more than a year or two for BMW to abandon this anachronism and field a model that was entirely up-to-date. It had pivoted forks at both ends and a main frame comprising an oval-section top tube and duplex loops. For the first time, the drive shaft was enclosed in the right-hand fork arm. The front brake went to twin leading shoes, the wheel rims to light alloy. The double-knocker engine originally had square cylinder dimensions (68 × 68 mm) and an included valve angle of 60 degrees, but the bore and stroke were soon changed to 66 × 72 mm and the valve stems spaced at 82 degrees. Surprisingly, the bike weighed no more than 275 lb, so its 50 bhp at 8,500 rpm put it pretty well in contention for performance.

Right from the start, various types of fuel injection were tried in the quest for power on the works machines, although carburettors were standardised on the slightly detuned catalogue Rennsport model, first marketed in 1953. With the long-stroke cylinder dimensions, this had the compression ratio lowered to 8:1, producing 45 bhp at 8,000 rpm.

The BMW's potential was shown when Zeller, on his very first visit to the Isle of Man, lay ninth in the 1953 Senior TT before stepping off in the second lap. His engine on that occasion was fitted with the second stage of the fuel injection – an axial squirt into each air trumpet. Although injection gave more power, carburettors were eventually preferred for twisty circuits on account of their more responsive acceleration.

When Zeller returned to the Island for his second TT three years later, his engine not only had carburettors but also the latest, oversquare cylinder dimensions of 70 × 64 mm (by then the long-stroke Rennsport was no longer in production). His fourth place at 94·69 mph was all the more remarkable

On Walter Zeller's immaculate fourth-place BMW, the author finds the steering uncannily true during an evening test on Senior TT day, 1956. Fifth gear could not be pulled properly as a result of overgearing following the last-minute removal of the dustbin fairing

because he was able to use only the lower four of his five gears, the bike being geared for a dustbin fairing, which he dispensed with at the last minute, too late to lower the overall gearing to suit.

On race-day evening I kept a rendezvous with Zeller, von Falkenhausen and the BMW mechanics high on the Snaefell Road and I was as keen to find out the truth about BMW handling as I was to sample the engine performance. Despite its seven arduous laps, the bike was as clean as it was on the start grid and no adjustments had been needed. On a pair of soft plugs, I rode back and forth up to 7,000 rpm to get the hang of the bike. I need hardly have bothered: the steering was rock-steady, the firing clean from 4,000 rpm upward, the acceleration tremendous yet ultra-smooth and the braking immensely powerful. The fact that both front shoeplates were anchored directly to the fork arms (no pivoted linkage) meant that hard braking tended to extend the fork and stiffen the springing. But that was a deliberate arrangement, to prevent the sudden dipping of the nose (under weight transfer) that could initiate gyroscopic precession in the longitudinal crankshaft and cause yawing.

With the hard plugs in, I revelled in the full 9,000 rpm and soon confirmed the over-gearing. While the bike repeatedly rocketed up to 130 mph in fourth, it would not pull top. With the dustbin fairing fitted, that gear had been good for a further 10 mph.

Analysing the handling

I tried to provoke the alleged torque effects on handling but failed. A brutal standing start merely caused a wheelie, after which harsh upward changes lifted the bike's nose as it gave the forward lurch characteristic of a heavy flywheel, with only the slightest steering twitch. Harsh downward changes just gave powerful engine braking. High-speed steering was uncannily true and stability was 100 per cent on full bank; Zeller, indeed, had worn flats on both cam covers. Significantly, though, the hydraulic steering damper gave rise to a mild, low-speed roll (reminiscent of overtightened head bearings) whenever I pulled in to compare notes, suggesting a stiff setting.

The only way I could get Zeller's bike to rock sideways was to slip into neutral (or declutch) and blip the throttle. You can produce this effect on any BMW at a standstill and I did so on the move, but only with the drive disengaged. This confirmed the theory that, so long as the drive is fully engaged, the only significant torque reaction is that trying to loop the machine backward around the rear wheel. In neutral, however, blipping the throttle tends to rotate the crankcase in the opposite direction to the crankshaft, while snapping the twistgrip back reverses the effect, so causing a lateral rock. But this technique is artificial;

in practice, the only time the crankshaft is speeded up or slowed down with the drive disengaged is momentarily, while changing gear on the clutch.

This was brought home to me forcibly two years later, when testing Dickie Dale's Rennsport BMW, which had much softer steering damping than Zeller's. So long as I declutched, upward changes provoked a pronounced steering flutter. But as soon as I took Dickie's advice to ignore the clutch and thumb the ignition cut-out instead, the flutter disappeared. It is always nice to get such practical confirmation of an engineering theory.

Von Falkenhausen told me that Zeller's engine gave 58 bhp at 9,000 rpm on carburettors and an extra 3 bhp when injected (for ultra-fast circuits such as Monza and Francorchamps). A year earlier, he had laid bare a 1954 works engine for analysis by Alan Baker (my predecessor as technical editor of *Motor Cycle*). That was a long-stroke unit and since the only major modification afterwards was the change to 70 × 64 mm, the engine was representative of BMW racing practice throughout their postwar heyday.

Injection pros and cons

In the first fuel injection experiment, said Falkenhausen, fuel was squirted at an angle through the wall of the inlet tract, between the flat (guillotine) throttle slide and the valve. Next came the squirt into the trumpet, as used by Zeller on his TT debut. Finally, a high-pressure system was devised, in which fuel was pumped directly into each cylinder head at 570 psi, through a nozzle opposite the sparking plug. Inlet tract dimensions were 32 mm diameter at the head face, 8 in from trumpet mouth to guillotine and $4\frac{1}{2}$ in from there to the valve. To allow ample time for mixing, the fuel was injected well before the end of the inlet phase, though timing was not critical to within 10 degrees.

The absence of obstruction in the inlet ports on full throttle and the more thorough atomisation of the fuel not only boosted power by 3 bhp but cut specific fuel consumption by 15 per cent too. On full load, the engine used only 0·44 lb/bhp/hr, a remarkably low figure. But carburettors, with the customary cylindrical slides cut away on the leading edge, gave finer mixture

control at intermediate throttle openings and this accounted for their use on give-and-take circuits. (For all that, when Helmut Fath won the sidecar championship on an injected BMW in 1960, one of the most striking features of his engine was its tractability.)

Supported in three main bearings (a self-aligning roller and two balls), the sturdy crankshaft assembly comprised hollow mainshafts integral with their crank cheeks, hollow crankpins and an elliptical centre web, all pressed together and secured with expander plugs. To keep the crankshaft short and minimise cylinder offset, the big-end eyes of the thin flat connecting rods were recessed into counterbores in the middle web. And to keep engine width in check, the rods were 10 per cent shorter than the customary "double-stroke-length". The one-piece crankcase was a magnesium-alloy casting and reduction gears in the front compartment drove the first camshaft bevel gear, the magneto (on top of the case), the timed breather and the injector pump on the front cover. A double delivery pump took oil from the five-pint sump and fed it to the cam gear (through jets) and to the main

The BMW flat-twin engine with which Willi Noll won the 1954 world sidecar championship. Points of interest include: close-coupled overhead camshafts and straight rockers; ultra-slim connecting rods; self-aligning rear crankshaft bearing; four rings per piston; injector pump on front cover, with nozzles opposite sparking plugs and flat throttle slides; flywheel clutch

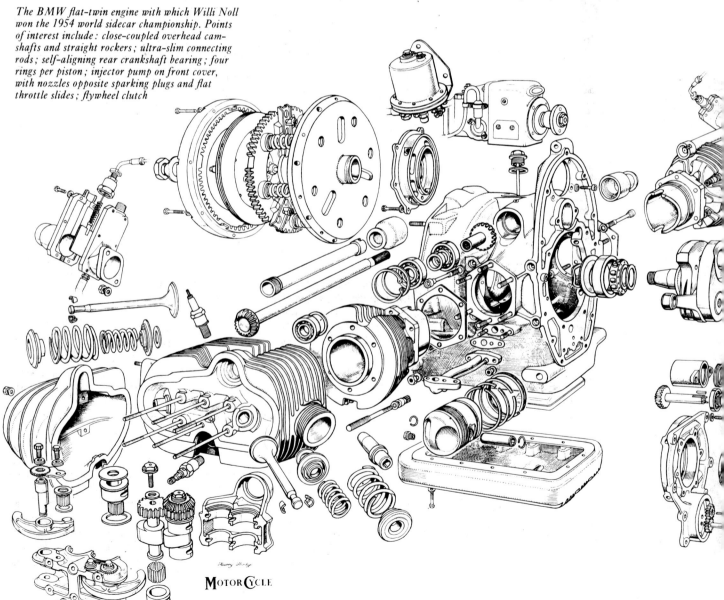

bearings, from which the big ends were supplied centrifugally. Return was by gravity.

Diecast in light alloy, the cylinders had either shrunk-in liners or hard-chrome bores. Four rings per piston (three compression, one scraper) seemed a throwback to supercharging practice, where an extra ring was necessary to help get heat away from the crown. Squish areas boosted compression to 10·2:1, valve sizes were 40mm inlet, 36mm exhaust, and the inlet downdraught was 15 degrees. Strangely, valve timing was symmetrical. Thus the 120 degrees of overlap was equally spaced around top dead centre and, since each valve had an opening duration of 320 degrees, exhaust opening and inlet closing were both 80 degrees from bottom dead centre.

The unusual idea of using valve rockers with twin overhead camshafts seemed to make nonsense of the chief reason for double knockers – to beat valve float by reducing reciprocating weight. But the arrangement of the two camshafts, close-coupled by a pair of small pinions, reduced engine width by making the valve gear "shallower" than it would have been with no rockers and the

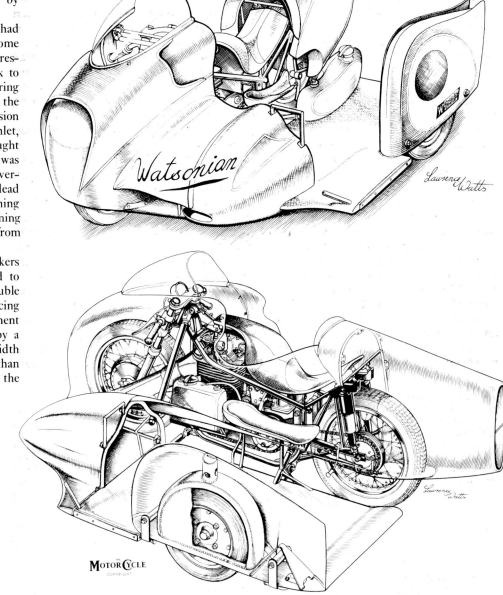

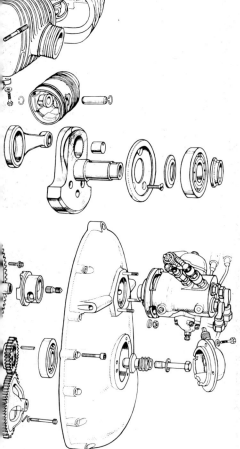

Early developments in streamlined "prayer mats". Top: Eric Oliver's 1953 Norton-Watsonian kneeler outfit, with special chassis, extensive aluminium fairing and the fuel tank alongside the rear wheel. Above: Oliver's 1954 Mark II streamliner, with 10in diameter sidecar wheel surrounded by a fuel-containing mudguard. An electric pump supplied fuel to the carburettor of the standard Manx Norton engine

usual train of five gears connecting the camshafts. BMW also claimed that less power was lost through friction between the coupling gears. Anyway, 9,500 rpm could be used without valve float and, should development have eventually overtaken that limit, Falkenhausen had desmodromics in mind.

Flywheel diameter was about 9in and the single-plate dry clutch was ventilated through air ducts in the housing. Unlike the roadster engines, there was no primary reduction from clutch to gearbox input

shaft, so that the racing engine ran in the opposite direction to the roadster's. Naturally, the gears were all-indirect and top-gear reduction was 1·3:1.

Two decades of sidecar monopoly

Any disappointment BMW felt at their failure to offer a serious challenge to the big Italian fours was swamped by delight over their shattering impact on the sidecar scene. By the time they quit the solo classics in 1958, their crews had already rattled up their first five consecutive world championships (including four TT victories on the trot) and that was just the start: once Eric Oliver and Norton had shot their final bolt in the 1953 championship and 1954 TT, the list of sidecar crews who achieved glory through BMW power reads like a catalogue of all-time sidecar greats, starting with Noll/Cron and finishing with Enders/Engelhardt. With 19 individual champion-

Italian idol Giacomo Agostini drifts his 350 cc MV Agusta four in his home grand prix

The BMW crew who put an end to the Norton reign in the world sidecar championship – Willi Noll and passenger Cron drift their way to victory in the 1954 German GP at Solitude

ships, 19 manufacturers' titles and 19 TTs to the credit of that incomparable power unit, it is simpler to pick out the rare exceptions to its success in a span of two decades.

In the grands prix, Albino Milani won for Gilera at Monza in 1956 and 1957, while Florian Camathias used an ex-works Gilera engine to win the Spanish round in 1964. Between these Italian successes, Chris Vincent drove his BSA twin to an un-

As evening shadows lengthen on Snaefell, Alan Baker (then technical editor of Motor Cycle) *shows great courage in making his debut on a racing platform, while the author is disconcerted by the right-hand sidecar. The outfit is Fritz Hillebrand's 1956 TT-winning works BMW*

expected and unusually slow win in the three-lap 1962 TT – by courtesy of Camathias, who crashed his BMW while leading on lap 2, and world champion Max Deubel, who seized his while leading on the final lap. BMW's championship defeats were much more significant: Helmut Fath, who had won the title for BMW in 1960, took it again on his home-built Urs four in 1968; Horst Owesle drove that same outfit to its second championship three years later. Finally, of course, Rolf Steinhausen heralded the two-stroke avalanche with his Konig success in 1975.

The technical background to BMW's phenomenal run of success was not only sound design and superb engineering (as shown by the immaculate finishing condition

of their outfits), but also the engine's uncanny suitability to sidecar racing, a blessing never envisaged when Max Friz laid out their first transverse flat twin in 1923. Whereas the engine's inherently low centre of gravity could not be fully exploited in a racing solo without sacrificing cornering clearance, its width was no disadvantage in a sidecar outfit, where there was practically no limit to how low it could be slung. In those days, when tyres were less than half today's width, harder in compound and patterned (not slick), the ultra-low centre of gravity facilitated drifting in both directions. The engine's smooth running and high torque were a boon, while its cylinders and heads were marvellously placed for cooling. Finally, for such arduous duty, shaft drive was ideal.

Like the Norton/Watsonians that preceded them, the earliest BMW outfits were virtually Rennsport solos with sidecar platforms bolted on – Steib at first, then BMW. It was on two such outfits – the Schneider/Straus BMW/Steib that won the 1955 TT and the winning Hillebrand/Grunwald all-BMW outfit of the following year – that I filled an obvious gap in my experience of "testing the winners" for *Motor Cycle*.

Reverse technique

Unfortunately, I was not able to judge the outfits as satisfactorily as I would have liked. In the first place, the disconcerting arrangement of a right-side chair and "wrong-way-

Max Deubel's BMW sidecar outfit was just about the lowest of the non-kneelers. Here, despite Emil Hörner's acrobatics, he lifts the sidecar wheel as he rockets out of the Governor's Bridge dip to win the 1965 TT

round" pedals cramped my enthusiasm. Then I lacked the comforting assistance of the regular passengers (who could blame them?). My colleague Kevin Gover (who volunteered in 1955) had played ballast to Eric Oliver once or twice but was as confused as I was by the need to reverse his instinctive technique. And Alan Baker ("persuaded" in 1956!) was entirely new to a racing platform. This combined lack of appropriate experience immediately brought to light the sensitivity of a racing outfit. What with Gover clambering around to try out all the handholds as we first belted up the relatively straight Mountain Mile, and Baker over-enthusiastically "throwing his weight about" on quite mild bends, my first impression of both outfits was one of frightening instability. Once we had established a modicum of co-operation, however, the impression was dispelled and we began to appreciate the controllability of both outfits, although not really enough to notice the benefits of Hillebrand's smaller (16 in) wheels and lower frame, except that wheel-spin coming out of right-handers was more pronounced on Schneider's higher outfit.

Other differences included Schneider's front-wheel cowl and Hillebrand's dustbin

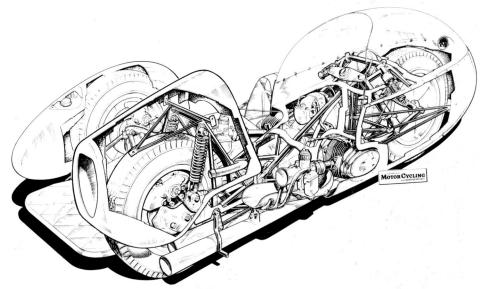

An ultra-low and beautifully streamlined BMW kneeler built by Fritz Scheidegger in 1962. The front fork is pivoted, all three wheels are disc braked, and each carburettor has float chambers both sides to stabilise fuel feed in corners. . Scheidegger was world champion in 1965 and 1966. He won the TT in 1966 after finishing second in 1961, 1963 and 1965

fairing; and Hillebrand's five speeds and 9,000 rpm limit compared with Schneider's four speeds and 8,500 rpm. Both bikes were geared for the 10¾-mile Clypse circuit (lower gearing than for the Mountain course) and we reached 105 mph (8,600 rpm in top) in

1955 and 110 mph in both fourth (9,000 rpm) and top in 1956. In the races, these speeds were exceeded by 10 mph or more on the drop from Hall Corner to White Bridge. In the circumstances, my chief inpressions were of the outfits' straight-line performances, both when piling on speed and when killing it. So vivid was the acceleration that the steering correction necessary to resist the pull to the right was quite conscious. Yet, however hard I braked, there was no trace of directional bias: all three brakes (hydraulic drums) were connected to the pedal and beautifully proportioned.

Opposite, top: *In the final version of the MV Agusta, the four-cylinder engine doubles as the bottom frame member*

Opposite, bottom: *Riding the all-conquering 350 cc Honda four, Jim Redman rounds the Governor's Bridge hairpin in winning the 1965 Junior TT*

Above: *World champions Klaus Enders and Rolf Engelhardt snapped on their BMW outfit in the 1973 Belgian GP at Francorchamps*

Birth of the kneeler

In the mid-1950s, bolted construction soon gave way to integral chassis; as they got lower and wheels got smaller, the BMW element in most outfits was confined to the engine, drive-line and front and rear forks. Not until five years after Eric Oliver had shown the way did kneelers (with side petrol tanks) start to catch on as a means of reducing frontal area and lowering the centre of gravity still · farther. Even then, Max Deubel, who set a record with four consecutive titles from 1961 to 1964, persisted with a conventional sitting position and the tank above the engine.

During that period, Deubel enjoyed full works support (the factory withdrew at the end of 1964) and it was to offset the extra power of the works engines (Florian Camathias had one, too) over his production Rennsport that the great Fritz Scheidegger built his first kneeler in 1960.

His 1964 version measured only 26 in to the top of the steering column and a contributory factor was the use of 10 in Mini cast-magnesium car wheels at the front and side. The standard · shaft-drive unit, however, dictated the use of a 16 in wire wheel at the rear and a maximum tyre width of 3·5 in.

Although Scheidegger beat Deubel for the championship in 1965 and 1966, this limit on rear-tyre width was contrary to the trend towards wider treads for greater traction. An expensive solution was found by Klaus Enders (champion in 1967, 1969, 1970, 1972, 1973 and 1974). In 1972, his ultra-low kneeler had as wide a rear tyre as any at the time ($6\frac{1}{2}$ in) – on a beautifully home-made cast-magnesium wheel.

As the Rennsport engines became ever more ancient and the supply of spares dwindled, so the cost of staying competitive rose and the small number of ex-works engines became priceless. In this climate, success depended largely on engaging the best BMW tuner and building the most up-to-date chassis. Engine power probably never exceeded 65 bhp and the last BMW to win the world title (Enders' kneeler in 1974) was prepared by Dieter Busch. Contributing to its ultra-low height was a very short steering column, with a U-link pivoted front fork, a pivoted rear fork with right-side suspension strut, a welded sheet-metal chassis and small-diameter cast wheels containing four hydraulic, twin-leading-shoe brakes (two at the front), although the use of disc brakes had been spreading for several years by then.

But Helmut Fath had already shown that 10 per cent more power for the same height could be decisive; and now König outboard engines (disc-valve, flat-four two-strokes) were making four-strokes of any sort look underpowered. Unfortunately, they needed a separate gearbox and clutch, with chain

Worthy new sidecar champions. Putting an end to Max Deubel's four-year reign, the lanky Fritz Scheidegger and passenger John Robinson won their first title in 1965. Here they drift their BMW kneeler to victory at Assen

primary drive as well as secondary, and it was chiefly transmission failures, notably on Rolf Steinhausen's and Jeff Gawley's outfits, that delayed the two-stroke takeover. Once four-cylinder Yamaha engines became available with integral transmission, that problem was solved and BMW's long monopoly was at an end. But it will be a long time, if ever, before their record is equalled.

Fath gets independent

Unsuspected by BMW, their spares shortage in the early 1960s was to give rise to one of the most glorious achievements in the history of sidecar racing. Had he been able to get the BMW transmission parts he wanted, Helmut Fath might never have had the incentive to build his unconventional Urs double-knocker four – the only four-stroke outfit to interrupt the long list of BMW world champions. (The name was the first three letters of his native Ursenbach.)

By winning the 1960 world title as a privateer, Fath proved not just his driving talent but his prowess as a BMW tuner. And, during the long convalescence following his

Nürburgring crash in 1961, he dreamed of making his comeback on the fastest BMW outfit ever. Alas, the water-cooled flat-four he planned required a plentiful supply of transmission parts; Fath found that spares were allocated strictly on an exchange basis, and he had but one outfit. With phenomenal courage he accepted – and mastered – the challenge of regaining his world title with an outfit of his own design and construction. His efforts were crowned in 1968 and he was all set to retain his championship in 1969 when a late-season prang in a Finnish non-title event put him out of the running and let Klaus Enders back in.

Fath's self-imposed task was much more difficult than his original plan to build a superfast BMW would have been. That would have involved making an ultra-reliable outfit faster. As it was, he had first to create a fundamentally faster outfit; then, faced with the inevitable teething troubles, he had to invest it with reliability. More power, Fath decided, meant more cylinders, but his experience of silk-smooth flat twins left him dissatisfied with the comparative roughness of the conventional straight-four layout. True, the two-up, two-down piston arrangement cancelled out the primary inertia forces, but the secondaries worked in unison to produce a vertical vibration equal in size to the primary from one cylinder and at twice engine speed.

Fath's bold solution was to space the four

Conventional: at the dead-centre positions (diagram a), the upward primary forces exerted by the top pistons cancel the downward primaries from the bottom pistons. However, the secondaries from all four pistons act upward in unison (they are about a quarter the size of the primaries). At midstroke (diagram b) there are no primaries but all four secondaries act downward. Overall result is a secondary vibration at twice engine speed and equal in size to the primary from one piston.
Fath Urs: in diagram (c) the dead-centre and midstroke positions coincide. Hence the primary forces from the top and bottom pistons cancel out while their upward secondaries are opposed by the downward secondaries from the midstroke pistons. There is, however, a slight rocking couple.

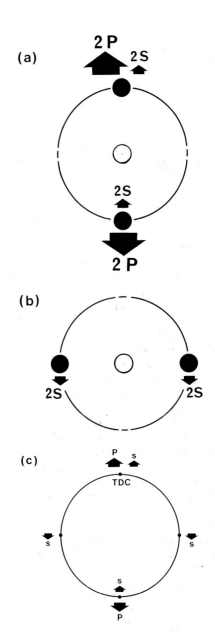

crankpins at 90 degrees, like the points of a compass. As my diagram shows, that arrangement neutralises the secondary inertia forces as well as the primaries, for the price of a small rocking couple (taken care of by four rubber engine mountings). Moreover, the fact that the two midstroke pistons are travelling at maximum speed while the others have stopped to change direction, further contributes to smooth running by providing a "flywheel" effect.

Unfortunately, the 90-degree crank spacing introduced a problem of its own, not because of the uneven firing intervals (90, 180, 270 and 180 degrees) but because, at the peak revs of 14,000 rpm, the smallest of those intervals left less than a thousandth of a second for the battery to re-energise the ignition coil, and that was too short. Even with fully transistorised ignition, the sparks in the extreme right cylinder, which fired 90 degrees after the extreme left, showed signs of weakness from as low as 8,000 rpm. The final solution was to use a separate coil for each cylinder and to make a special contact breaker with four sets of points, spaced at 45, 90, 135 and 90 degrees. Since each cylinder had two 10 mm plugs, the coils were double-ended, to furnish pairs of simultaneous sparks.

There was further unorthodoxy in the crankshaft, which was made in two halves, to reduce torsional and bending stresses and so permit smaller journal and crankpin diameters. The halves were unconnected, save that pinions in the middle of each drove opposite ends of the half-speed countershaft. Each crankpin had its own pair of flywheel discs (eccentric for balance purposes) and each crankshaft half was supported in three roller bearings: the outer crowded and lipped, the others caged and the middle one hard against the outside of the driving pinion.

The slim connecting rods were in titanium, with deep webs round the caged-needle big ends. Each full-skirt piston had only two rings (compression and scraper) and a high dome giving a compression ratio of 9·3 : 1. The pistons worked in separate, light-alloy cylinders with hard-chromed bores. Cylinder dimensions were 60 × 44 mm and, since the single 34 mm inlet and 30 mm exhaust valves (splayed at 67 degrees to one another) left no room for a central plug, the two plugs were set vertically, 35 mm apart. Bench tests proved that the shorter flame travel cut the required ignition advance from 18 to 7 mm. The down-draught angle was 30 degrees and the fuel (supplied by a Bosch pump from a 1·5-litre Borgward engine) was at first injected through nozzles in the port roofs.

Later on, the cylinder head incorporated auxiliary inlet ports, which were parallel to the cylinder axes so that they converged with the main ports at 60 degrees. This arrangement necessitated switching the nozzles to the floor of the original ports, since there was no longer room at the top. Fath would have preferred direct injection into the heads but, with dual ignition, there was no room for the nozzles. The idea behind converging ports is to improve cylinder filling by using the full periphery of the inlet valve (instead of just the upper half) and to get better atomisation and turbulence. Unfortunately, Fath did not realise the scheme's full potential. Since only the original ports were injected (the others just carrying air) the fuel droplets were neither broken down so finely nor distributed so homogeneously as they might otherwise have been. Consequently there was no gain in peak power, although acceleration was improved from 11,000 rpm upward.

The doctor prescribes

A considerable achievement was banishing valve float beyond 15,000 rpm, despite the use of single valves and relatively heavy cam followers (steel rollers supported on needle bearings in sliding blocks). Credit for this went to Dr Peter Kuhn (formerly a lecturer at Heidelberg University). By using thick wire (4·25 mm) and only four coils, he pushed the natural frequency of the springs too high for surge to set in. Then he plotted the cam contour to suit the spring frequency. Naturally, the short length of wire in the springs meant high torsional stresses, so a special wire was imported from Sweden and processed by Fath. Incidentally, the springs were so successful that Fath supplied them to most of his BMW rivals, including 1974 world champion Klaus Enders!

Supported in two ball bearings, the half-speed countershaft drove all the ancillaries as well as the six-speed transmission: the oil pump and contact breaker from the extremities, the camshafts from a sprocket

Opposite, top: *On his way to the 1969 world 125 cc championship – Dave Simmonds at Brno on his Kawasaki side-by-side, disc-valve twin*

Opposite, bottom: *On the first non-disc-valve Yamaha to win a world title – Rod Gould at Assen in 1970*

Above: *With third place in the wet British GP at Silverstone, George O'Dell and passenger Cliff Holland clinch the 1977 world sidecar championship*

in the middle, the injector pump through a train of pinions on the right and the clutch through a pair of reduction gears, also on the right. The first clutch was a six-spring Norton, followed by a diaphragm-spring Borg and Beck. The gearbox was a Schafleitner cluster in a Norton shell.

The camshafts, too, were in right and left halves, clamped to opposite sides of the central sprockets, and each half was supported in two, crowded-needle bearings. Oil from the long, finned magnesium sump was pumped to eight jets directed at the cam/follower contacts, into the outer ends of the crankshaft (for the big ends) and through a crankcase gallery serving the main bearings. Return was by gravity.

Right from its debut at Hockenheim in 1966, the Urs had its rivals beaten for power and speed, but there were snags to be eradicated besides the ignition problem mentioned earlier: overheating (hence the enormous duct in the fairing nose), failure of the long-waisted studs uniting the camshaft halves and, especially on the bumpy TT course, overrevving due to a combination of wheel patter and light flywheels. This not only wore out the rear tyre rapidly but raised its temperature as high as 130 degrees C. The ultimate solution (when Horst Owesle was campaigning the outfit) was to increase tread width from 5 in to 8 in.

In the absence of authenticated bhp figures, there was much wild speculation as to the Urs engine's power. Fath was disdainful: he agreed that the 76 bhp shown on his brake was optimistic but, he said, so was the 68 bhp for a top BMW engine. What the tests did show was a 10 per cent surplus for the Urs and its track performances substantiated that. Indeed, for Owesle's 1971 championship, bench power was boosted to 86 bhp by changing to four Keihin carburettors, higher-lift cams and dry-sump oiling. It is debatable whether Owesle's track talent would have taken him to the top without such a healthy power advantage.

In classic racing, really great rider/tuners have never been plentiful. Certainly none has surpassed Fath for all-round talent and persistence.

Four cylinders and eight inlet ports – Helmut Fath's Urs engine in its 1968 guise, with fuel injection (into lower ports) and wet-sump oiling. Later on, power was boosted by conversion to Keihin carburettors, higher-lift cams and dry-sump oiling

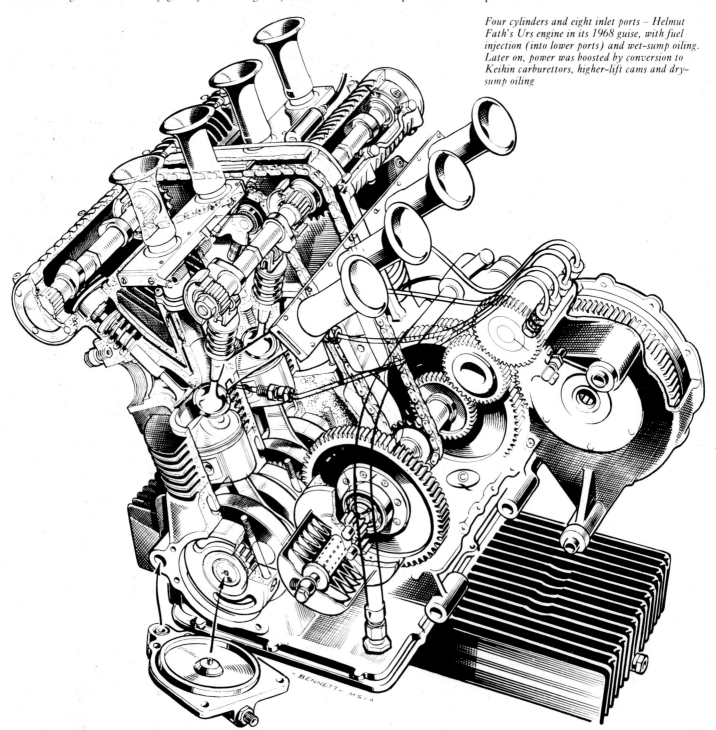

TWO-STROKES SUPREME

IN retrospect, the postwar ban on super-charging had a much greater effect on two-stroke design than merely robbing the top-dog DKWs of the cornerstone of their prewar power superiority. It also greatly curtailed engine designers' scope for variety and novelty. In the 1930s, fresh and exciting layouts almost fell over one another as they tumbled off the DKW drawing boards. Yet, in a period three times as long since the war, and with more than a dozen two-stroke manufacturers applying their brains to racing design and development, only two basic engine types have emerged – those with piston-controlled induction and those with disc valves.

True, there is plenty of variety in cylinder arrangement – single cylinders come prone as well as upright; twins have their pots either in tandem or abreast; and fours may be in square formation, all-abreast or in horizontally opposed pairs. But all of them fit into one or other of those two induction categories.

This is not to ignore the prodigious amount of thought, calculation and experiment that have been applied to the problems, first in Europe, then in Japan. It simply illustrates the fact that, without super-charging, two-stroke designers are at the mercy of natural inlet and exhaust resonances in their quest for power. Harnessing these pressure fluctuations is the only way to improve cylinder scavenging and filling at ever-higher rpm.

Both before and after the war, most racing two-stroke development has been concentrated on countering the disadvantages of symmetrical port timing, which is itself an inevitable consequence of the engine's mechanical simplicity. This unwanted symmetry has two fundamental drawbacks – it curtails the length of the inlet phase (if port closure is not to be so late that some of the gas is blown back out of the crankcase by the descending piston); and it allows some of the charge in the cylinder to escape through the exhaust port immediately the transfer ports have closed.

Up to 1939 (Chapter 3) the brevity of the inlet phase was offset by the high pressure at which the charge was pumped in and the comparatively low revs at which the engine ran, while the loss to the exhaust was kept in check by the split-cylinder arrangement which – besides separating the ports physically – closed the exhaust *before* the transfers, not after.

1967 125 cc champion Bill Ivy and Yamaha team mate Phil Read in the Spanish GP

No option

Today – with engine speeds doubled (hence inlet duration halved) and induction pressure available only from natural resonances – there is no option but to lengthen the inlet phase as much as possible. To this end, a disc valve is a blessing. By uncovering the port as early as, say, 40 degrees after bottom dead centre, it permits a duration of well over 200 degrees without the ultra-late closure that would otherwise result in significant blowback through the carburettor.

This arrangement was pioneered for grand prix racing by MZ's Walter Kaaden and copied by every other constructor, including Yamaha on their world-beating 125 and 250 cc twins and vee-fours. The alternative is to retain piston control of the port, lengthen the duration as much as possible and resist blowback by so tailoring the inlet tract that a powerful pressure pulse is reflected back from the carburettor mouth to the port just as the descending piston is trying to reverse the gas flow. (Another way of preventing blowback is to put an automatic reed valve in the inlet tract. But the sacrifice in peak power, through cluttering up the tract, is unacceptable in classic racing with its 500 cc limit, although of little consequence in 750 cc racing where the premium on sheer bhp is not so high.)

Yamaha switched from discs to piston-controlled induction for commercial, not technical, reasons once they knew the FIM

intended to outlaw their vee-fours at the end of 1969 by restricting 125 and 250 cc engines to two cylinders. With Honda and Suzuki no longer running works teams, Yamaha reasoned that they could hold their own with machines looking like souped-up versions of their roadster twins, despite their lower peak power, narrower torque range and heavier fuel consumption compared with disc-valvers.

They were right. After Dave Simmonds (on a 125 cc Kawasaki disc-valve twin) and Kel Carruthers (on a 250 cc double-knocker Benelli four) had taken advantage of the 1969 lull while Yamaha were changing course, Yamaha's slim piston-valvers enjoyed a good championship run in the 250 cc class. Later they took over from MV in the 350 cc class (with a bored-out version of the twin, although four cylinders are allowed there), and later still they reached the top of the 500 cc and sidecar classes, with a straight four that was virtually a pair of 250 cc twins side by side.

Eventually, however, the disc-valver's technical superiority asserted itself. Its only technical drawback had been excessive width across the carburettors so long as the two cylinders were placed abreast – and that problem only arose from 250 cc upward. This width necessitated substantial bulges or blisters on the fairing sides, which increased frontal area and could even restrict cornering clearance.

The solution, again pioneered by Kaaden (in 1969), was to arrange the cylinders in tandem and couple their crankshafts by a pair of gears, on the grounds that the tiny friction loss in the gears was a small price to pay for combining an ultra-slim profile with the disc-valver's superior engine performance. Unhappily, MZ never reaped the reward of this layout – Kaaden had always had to work within a derisory budget and MZ quit racing soon afterwards. But the idea was not lost on Kawasaki, whose tandem twins easily won both 250 and 350 cc championships in 1978 and 1979.

The other problem arising from symmetrical port timing – loss of fresh gas to the exhaust immediately after the transfer phase – is the same for both types of engine. This escape is resisted by reflecting a powerful pressure pulse back to the exhaust port towards the end of the concurrent transfer and exhaust phases. The reflection comes from the reverse-cone portion of the exhaust box, and is only one of several functions of

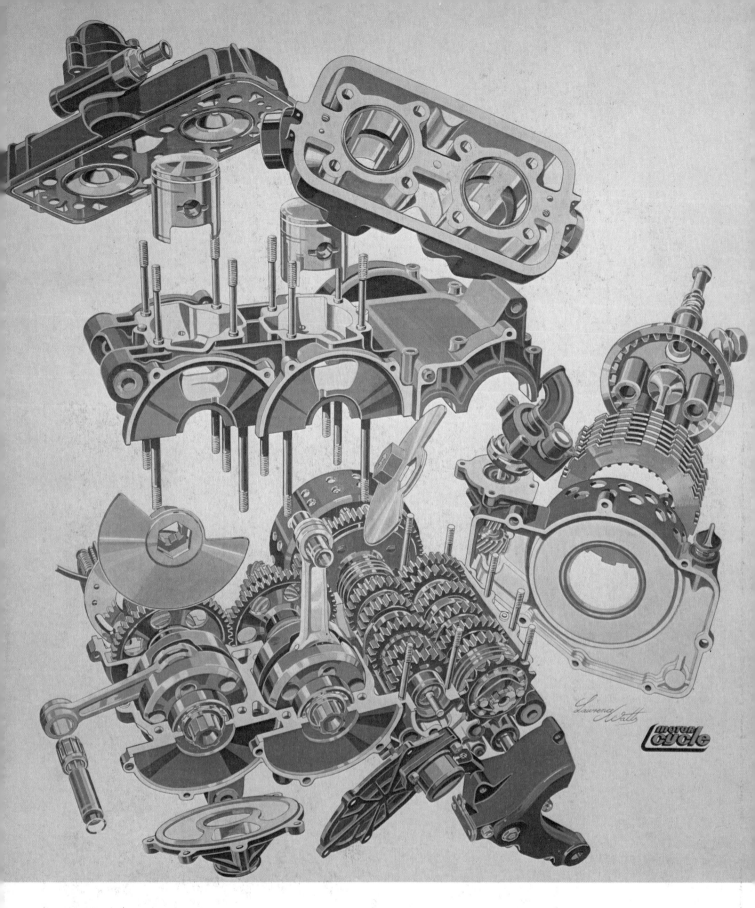

Above: *Exploded view of Kawasaki's world-beating 250cc tandem twin. Direct coupling of the two crankshafts involves overlapping of the fibre inlet discs; both pistons move in step to eliminate horizontal vibration. Exhaust ports are at front and rear of the cylinder block. The pistons have single rings and the combustion chambers have wide annular squish bands. Front crankshaft has the ignition unit on the right; rear crankshaft drives clutch, water impeller and tachometer*

Opposite, top: *Ghosted view of the Kawasaki tandem twin that Kork Ballington rode to the 250 and 350cc world championships in 1978 and 1979*

Opposite, bottom: *Follow my leader. Tom Herron leads Akihiko Kiyohara, Takazumi Katayama and Mick Grant through an S-bend in the 1977 French GP*

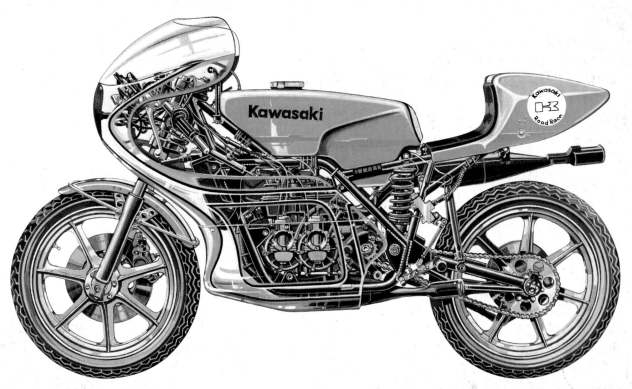

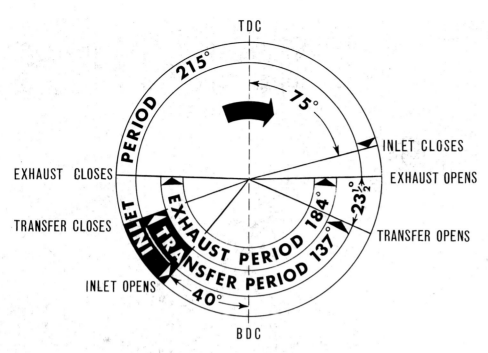

TDC

PERIOD 215°

75°

INLET CLOSES

EXHAUST CLOSES

EXHAUST OPENS

INLET PERIOD

TRANSFER CLOSES

EXHAUST PERIOD 184

23½°

TRANSFER PERIOD 137

TRANSFER OPENS

INLET OPENS

40°

BDC

Port-timing diagram for the 1965 MZ 250 cc disc-valve twin, peaking at about 11,000 rpm. All phases are time-based, hence higher peak revs tend to require longer angular timings

In the sunshine at Clermont Ferrand early in 1964, MZ's ace development engineer Walter Kaaden (left) chats with the author. At Sachsenring that year Mike Hailwood showed the 250 cc MZ's potential by breezing past a Read/Redman championship tussle as if they had the brakes on

today's complex exhaust systems.

There are two dramatic proofs of the racing two-stroke's total dependence on natural resonances. First, when an exhaust box splits (usually through high-frequency vibration) all useful power immediately evaporates. Second, should a disc valve jam wide open during a full-power bench test the engine continues to run unimpaired, so precisely is the disc timing phased with the

inlet-tract resonances. As soon as the throttle is closed, of course, and the revs drop below the resonant speed, the engine dies.

Naturally, as peak revs have been pushed higher and higher over the years all port heights have had to be increased, for duration is a function of time not crank angle. As a result, exhaust-port height is now approximately half the stroke length, so that pressure is applied to the piston crown for only half its downward travel on the firing stroke.

Stamina

Harnessing the resonances is not the only headache for the two-stroke engineer. There are the intractable problems of breeding stamina into the engine and ridding it of the nasty habit of locking the rear wheel too suddenly for the rider to grab the clutch. These problems stem from distortion of the cylinder, which has to handle hot exhaust gas on one side, cool transfer charge on the other, and borderline lubrication, which is dictated by the linking of crankcase and cylinder via the transfer ports.

With air cooling, the inevitable cylinder

This head-on view of MZ's water-cooled 250 cc side-by-side twin shows the embarrassing width across the two side-facing carburettors. Front fork is Norton

The year after Yamaha withdrew their vee-fours (1969), Kel Carruthers robbed Phil Read of his world 250 cc championship on a double-knocker Benelli four. Here Carruthers leads Read's Yamaha twin in the Italian GP at Imola

distortion first precludes the use of piston clearances small enough for the crispest pumping and best possible seal between exhaust port and crankcase (both necessary for optimum torque). Then, at best, it blunts the engine's initial power once it reaches its highest running temperature. At worst, it causes piston seizure – the more abruptly because of the scarcity of oil.

The twofold cure (or palliative) is water cooling – preferably with an impeller, not thermosiphon – and smaller cylinders, hence more of them for a given cylinder capacity. By equalising cylinder temperature all the way round, water cooling eliminates distortion so preventing power from falling

off with rising temperature and permitting piston clearances to be halved, to the benefit of torque.

Smaller cylinders mean cooler pistons, since the crown area absorbing heat is reduced as the square of the ring length through which much of it is dissipated. Also, piston seizure is less dramatic the more cylinders there are. Two, three or four pistons are unlikely to seize at the same instant – some try to soldier on and so the rider gets a mite more warning. From this standpoint, the FIM's 1969 limit on cylinder numbers actually made two-stroke racing potentially more dangerous, especially in the 50 cc class where only one cylinder is allowed.

The more serious mechanical failures, however, are those caused by under-lubrication of the connecting-rod bearings, albeit of the hardy needle-roller type nowadays. Use enough lubricant to keep the

big-end and small-end bearings happily oiled and cooled and you will hopelessly contaminate the charge and foul the sparking plug. Cut the oil enough to banish all risk of plug fouling and a bearing may well disintegrate.

A wise move here is to transfer the close lateral clearances necessary for connecting rod location from the big end to the small end, as in the Suzuki RG500. With such close clearances, angular rubbing builds up heat – and there is a great deal less angular rubbing at the small end than at the big end.

Either way, though, the plug presents a problem. It not only has to resist fouling (even with as little as three per cent oil in the fuel), it also has precious little time to cool between firing strokes. A grade that runs hot enough to burn off any oil may well burn a hole in the adjacent part of the piston crown; a colder-running grade, while safer for the piston, may not be immune to fouling.

Most grand-prix engines now rely solely on automatic petroil lubrication, with anything from two to six per cent of oil mixed with the fuel. The pump systems common on roadsters (in which pump stroke varies with throttle opening) are designed to cut down the oil supply at small throttle openings. Since a grand prix engine normally operates on full throttle, such a refinement is unnecessary, although some makers (notably Suzuki and Yamaha) used to supplement the petroil with a meagre pumped supply to the crankshaft bearings.

DKW start afresh

Sheer pride and knowhow made it inevitable that DKW would be the first two-stroke factory to make grand-prix headlines after the war, even though the partition of Germany forced them to quit their Zschopau home in the East and make a fresh start in Ingolstadt in the West – and even though they had never made an unblown racing machine before 1951, when Germany was readmitted to the FIM.

Anticipating the much higher engine

First of the tandem twins – 125 cc MZ with geared cranks, originally tried in 1969. It gave 32 bhp at 13,000 rpm but had too narrow a torque spread

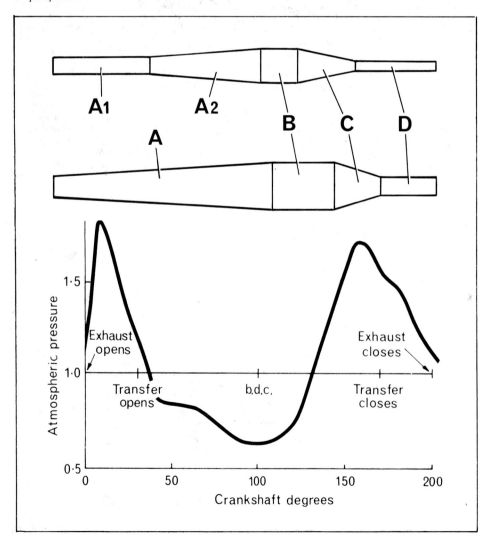

A modern two-stroke exhaust system makes use of two facts:
1 a pressure wave travelling along an open pipe is reflected from the end as its opposite (ie, a positive wave goes back as negative and vice versa).
2 a pressure wave travelling along a closed pipe is reflected from the blank end without change (ie, positive remains positive and negative remains negative).
In these typical exhaust systems, the functions of the various parts are:
A From the end of A1, the exhaust pulse is reflected back as a depression to help scavenge the cylinder and pull in fresh gas from the crankcase around bottom dead centre. The effect is enhanced by the megaphone section, A2. The fully megaphoned alternative (A) usually indicates a higher degree of tune (more peaky power curve). Sometimes the megaphone has a triple taper to harness secondary reflections.
C The reverse cone is virtually a blank end (with an escape hole in the middle). It reflects a positive pulse back to the port to resist the loss of fresh gas at the end of the transfer phase.
B Since the length of A (or A1 plus A2) is precisely calculated, as is the distance of C from the cylinder, the parallel section B simply spaces out the two tapered portions.
D Since section C has also to let the exhaust gases escape to atmosphere, the diameter of tailpipe D is the minimum necessary for this; a larger hole would weaken the ram pulse unnecessarily. Tailpipe length is not critical, provided the negative pulse it reflects back to C does not detract from the ram pulse

Lower illustration is an approximate exhaust-port pressure diagram for an early racing 250 cc twin, with resonant exhaust system, at 11,000 rpm. A depression at bdc (from section A) without a subsequent ram pulse (from section C) would give heavy fuel consumption and low torque. A ram pulse without sufficient prior depression would push burnt gas back into the cylinder, so reducing volumetric efficiency

speeds that would be necessary for competitive power, they ruled out the split-cylinder arrangement both on account of the weight of the articulated connecting rod assembly and the impossibility of filling a divided cylinder in the much shorter time available. To start with, they settled on an inclined 125 cc single. And although that committed them to symmetrical exhaust and transfer timing (unlike their prewar engines), they avoided the restrictions of symmetry on the inlet side by using a gear-driven cylindrical rotary valve across the rear of the crankcase.

Soon this engine was doubled-up into a 250 cc parallel twin, with a long tubular inlet valve feeding the left and right crankcases alternately from a single carburettor at one end. The obvious drawback here was the unequal length of the two inlet tracts, and the equally obvious solution was to swing the rotor through 90 degrees to lie fore and aft between the two crank chambers. The carburettor then fed the rear end of the valve while the magneto was driven by the front end.

Although the ageing Siegfried Wünsche rode one of these machines into third place in the 1953 Lightweight 250 cc TT, it was

Above: *changing from one cylinder to two in 1963, the 125 cc Suzuki gained both speed and stamina. Here Hugh Anderson wins the TT on his way to the world championship*

Below: *to supplement their three-per-cent addition of oil to the fuel, Suzuki introduced this auxiliary big-end lubrication on their twins in 1965. The pump is driven by the gearbox and draws oil from a reservoir in the seat tail*

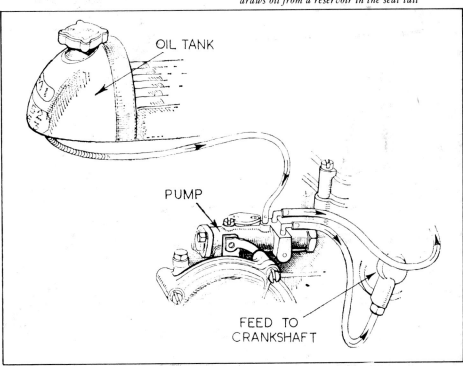

OIL TANK

PUMP

FEED TO CRANKSHAFT

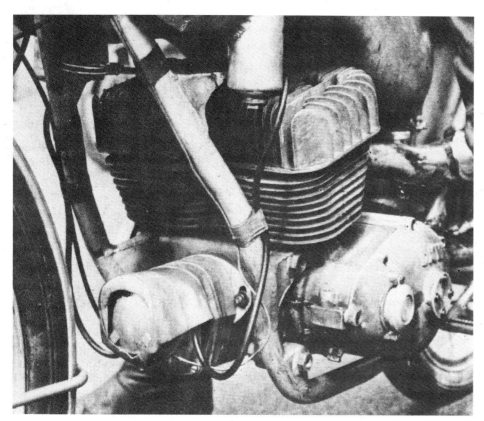

Immediate ancestor of the 350 cc DKW three, this 250 cc parallel twin had a cylindrical rotary inlet valve situated fore-and-aft between the two crank chambers, with the carburettor at the rear and the magneto at the front. The third cylinder eventually took the place of the magneto

mensions from 54×54 mm to $53 \times 52 \cdot 8$ mm. Thus the peculiar cylinder layout, with the end ones inclined forward 15 degrees and the middle one prone, was an accident of development, not the result of a high-falutin' design principle.

Each cylinder had its own Dellorto carburettor and a six-cylinder magneto was driven at half engine speed by a pair of gears at the right-hand end of the crankshaft. To suit the magneto, the three firing strokes had to be evenly spaced (one every 120 degrees). So, with the middle cylinder 75 degrees out of line with the others, only the outer crankpins were spaced at 120 degrees to one another – the middle pin was 45 degrees out of phase with the right-hand one.

With 31 bhp at the rear wheel, the three was initially a bit short of competitive power and none too reliable either. Wünsche rode the prototype in the 1953 Junior TT and retired. The following spring, DKW took the bull by the horns and separated the racing and technical departments. Jacob became team manager while chief technician

Debut of the DKW three in Switzerland. At that time, it had a large bevel-driven magneto, a telescopic front fork, no intake gauzes and no hydraulic control for the brakes

clear to the engineers that its high-speed power potential was limited by the long and tortuous gas path and the relatively slow port opening of the small-diameter tube compared with a large-diameter disc. (One of the factors governing the strength of a pressure pulse is the speed of port opening.)

So, in the winter of 1952–53, the engine was converted (by engineers Woolf and Jacob) into a 350 cc three by abandoning the rotary valve in favour of piston-controlled induction, putting a horizontal cylinder (with longitudinal finning) in place of the magneto and reducing the cylinder di-

These works pictures show how compact was the five-speed power plant of the DKW three. The domed intake gauzes were said to stabilise airflow. On the right-hand side of the crankcase is the contact breaker, on the left the generator for the revmeter. The pedal is the gear change, not kickstarter!

Helmut Görg was given the task of squeezing more power out of the engine and simultaneously improving its reliability.

Görg's admirable thoroughness and energy paid off very quickly. By midsummer 1955, August Hobl had not only sewn up the German 350 cc championship but was also harrying Bill Lomas in the classics with speed and acceleration to spare, finishing second to the Moto Guzzi star in both the Belgian and German GPs. Even that early in the Deek's development, Moto Guzzi team manager Fergus Anderson paid it the compliment of saying that it would have toppled the Italian single from its world perch if only the teams had swopped riders.

By that time Görg had already squeezed no less than 33 per cent more power out of the engine (42 bhp at 9,700 rpm) and Hobl's unfaired bike had streaked past John Surtees' works 350 cc Norton in front of a packed grandstand at the Nürburgring as if John's brakes had jammed on. For 1956, the riders had even more power on tap – 45 bhp at 9,500 rpm – and with it the utmost reliability, an average fuel consumption no worse than 30 mpg and a top speed of 140 mph, thanks to a fairing developed at Munich Technical College that cut air drag by 35 per cent.

It was back in 1955, the day after Hobl

Final version of the 350 cc DKW three with full frontal streamlining and faired seat. Note the long pivoted torque arm for the hydraulic rear brake

had chased Lomas home in the Belgian GP, that I went to Ingolstadt to find out how Görg had managed to improve the three so much and so quickly. We soon discovered that neither of us spoke a word of the other's language – and although a secretary was co-opted as interpreter, on the strength of her wartime fraternisation with an American GI, it transpired they had somehow never got round to discussing two-stroke technology! So Görg and I reverted to sign language and prolific sketches – and quite successfully, too.

In a nutshell, he had gained power chiefly by developing the exhaust boxes, port timing, and piston and head design (a fraction was also saved by scrapping the big magneto in favour of a six-volt battery and three coils). Stamina had been improved by stiffening the crankshaft assembly, enlarging the main bearings, improving lubrication and preventing the ignition timing from

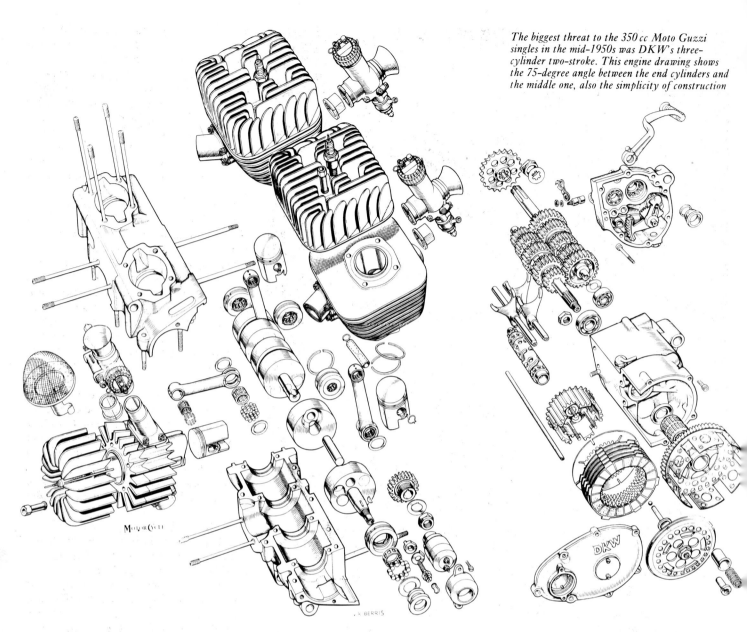

The biggest threat to the 350 cc Moto Guzzi singles in the mid-1950s was DKW's three-cylinder two-stroke. This engine drawing shows the 75-degree angle between the end cylinders and the middle one, also the simplicity of construction

straying at high revs. Görg also scrapped the telescopic front fork for leading links and fitted massive duplex twin-leading-shoe hydraulic brakes to both wheels to compensate for the two-stroke's weak engine braking and the reduced air drag of the dustbin fairing.

In more detail, port grinding was no longer done by hand. Instead, for absolute consistency, an internal jig was used for the cylinder muff and an external jig for the liner. Port layout was basic – large ovals for the inlet and exhaust, two rectangular transfers each side. After grinding, all ports were checked for timing with a protractor. Then, all cylinders were individually power tested on a dummy crankcase and matched before assembly into a complete engine.

The piston skirts were cut away at the sides to shorten the transfer passages in the magnesium-alloy crankcase, and precisely ground at the rear to ensure accurate inlet timing. The carburettor size was increased to 28 mm. Steeply domed gauzes were fitted over the intakes to stabilise airflow and

Helmut Görg (right) and August Höbl astride one of the sleek 125 cc DKW singles

keep out grit, while plastic sleeves insulated the carburettors from cylinder heat in the interest of volumetric efficiency.

By deflecting the inlet gas stream downward more steeply, Görg improved big-end lubrication sufficiently for the petroil ratio to be cut from 16:1 (six per cent) in 1954 to 25:1 (four per cent). Regardless of the ratio, however, the small-end bearings had to be changed from fully-floating bronze bushes to needle rollers to stop rapid wear.

A half-moon squish band in the head was ground to match the shallow dome on the piston crown and provide a compression ratio of 12:1 (geometric) – about 7:1 from exhaust-port closure (Japanese reckoning). As with all racing two-strokes, ignition timing was found to be critical and was adjusted to a hundredth of a millimetre. Initially, however, it tended to advance itself at high revs as centrifugal force flung the cam lobe slightly outward, despite the use of

August Höbl shows the difference in frontal area between the DKW 350 cc three-cylinder (left) and 125 cc single-cylinder. Höbl was third in the world 350 cc championship in 1955 and second in 1956

an outrigger bush for the shaft.

The cure was to scrap the bush, drill the lobe liberally and put a long double-row needle bearing close behind it in place of the original ball bearing. Incidentally, an ignition cut-out was fitted for upward gear changes, chiefly so that the throttle could be left wide open to avoid interrupting engine lubrication.

In the six-piece pressed-up crankshaft, stiffness was enhanced by increasing the mainshaft diameter to 22·5 mm (just over $\frac{7}{8}$ in) and the outside diameter of the four roller bearings to 55 mm. Great importance was attached to crankshaft alignment, which was checked by a dial gauge calibrated to a thousandth part of a millimetre. Görg proudly proved the stiffness of the assembly

to me by checking the alignment of a crankshaft fresh from the German GP – the dial-gauge needle remained virtually steady.

Overall crankshaft length was kept down to 11 in, partly by making the connecting rods so slim that they needed a clearance of only 6 mm (less than $\frac{1}{4}$ in) between the flywheel cheeks. Excessive mainshaft wear by the gas seals was overcome by changing them from rubber to metal rings. Crankshaft location, incidentally, was by a ball bearing in the primary drive cover (outboard of the pinion).

Comparison

In the Isle of Man the following year Görg agreed to my trying the lone DKW three that Cecil Sandford had just ridden into fourth place in the Junior TT. Since I rode it immediately after testing Ken Kavanagh's winning Moto Guzzi (page 57), I got a direct

comparison and soon understood why Fergus Anderson and his team had so much respect for the German two-stroke.

Görg's thoroughness was apparent as soon as we lifted the Deek out of the van at the Mountain Box – he produced an anemometer and checked the wind speed at 15 metres a second, appreciably over 30 mph. I half expected him to take my pulse! Fuel on, ignition on, drop the clutch after a few paces – and the clean song from the exhausts was as eager as it was delightful.

At that state of the art of exhaust-box design, there was not so harsh a transition "from nothing to everything" as there is with today's more highly developed piston-valvers. It was just that engine power was moderate until the resonances began to harmonise at 7,000 rpm. From that speed upward, though, the engine kicked so hard that my thumb was hardly off the button until I was in top (fifth) gear. If there had been any more gears I felt I would have gone into orbit – yet the engine felt turbine smooth at all speeds.

So rapidly and smoothly did the revs build up that it was no surprise to find the electric (no-lag) revmeter fitted with a "dead" hand. This was nudged round by the ordinary needle so that at the end of a race it showed the highest revs reached. Since a magnet was needed to return it to zero, it could embarrass a rev-happy rider but was valuable to Görg in diagnosis. The normally used rev range was 7,500 to 10,500 rpm, with 11,000 as the limit, but Görg told me the engine would spin up to 15,000 without distintegrating.

Possibly the wind had abated slightly or maybe Sandford's bike was heavier than Kavanagh's, but straight-line steering seemed even steadier than on the Moto Guzzi. Both suspensions worked superbly and although Görg had warned me of the power of the four hydraulic brakes, I found them velvet-smooth and progressive.

The pedal effort was proportioned 60 per cent to the rear and 40 per cent to the front, leaving the rest of the front wheel braking to be done through the handlebar lever. The snag with such massive brake equipment was its weight; so for slow, tricky circuits the earlier cable-operated single brakes were fitted and the fairing removed.

The turns I had to make in the narrow road at the Guthrie Memorial were distinctly unfair to any racing engine, particularly a petroil-lubricated two-stroke on hard plugs, so my back-and-forth dashes were punctuated by a couple of stops for clean plugs. It was abundantly clear, though, that the three-cylinder Deek had the potential to win a world championship. What a pity the factory quit racing at the end of the year – just when Görg was considering fuel injection, from which he expected a 15 per cent power boost . . .

Above: *wearing an ankle-length stormcoat against the blustery wet weather, DKW engineer Helmut Görg and a works mechanic give the author a push at the start of one of his trial runs on a deserted stretch of the Mountain road in 1956*

Right: *hydraulic control for the rear drum brake on Cecil Sandford's fourth-place DKW three in the 1956 Junior TT*

Building a formula

Even though DKW made their quickfire 350 cc challenge in the full glare of European publicity, few observers in the mid-1950s believed the unblown two-stroke was a serious long-term threat to the four-stroke multis for classic racing. Most folk retained an image of the two-stroke as fundamentally fickle and thirsty and likely to become more so if tuned highly enough to keep pace with the top four-strokes. DKW's withdrawal seemed like the end of a gallant but doomed technical exercise.

Not so. In relative obscurity behind the Iron Curtain, and simultaneously with Görg's efforts, Walter Kaaden was slowly but surely laying the foundations of a two-stroke formula that was ultimately to leave no doubt in anyone's mind that the four-stroke was an also-ran within the FIM's engine-capacity framework.

Trained as an engineer in Chemnitz (now Karl-Marx-Stadt) before the war, Kaaden had not only grown up at a time when the very air of his native Saxony was redolent of

two-stroke magic and success; he also inherited the intellectual stature of his predecessors at the Zschopau factory. After building and racing his own two-strokes, he joined MZ at the end of 1952.

Right from the start he chose a crankshaft-mounted disc valve for inlet-port control (although his phenomenally successful ISDT cross-country machines had piston-controlled ports). He well recognised that the later opening of a piston-controlled

port gave a stronger induction pulse (by virtue of the increased crankcase depression) – and that the pressure pulse subsequently reflected back from the carburettor mouth to resist blowback would therefore be stronger, too.

But – for filling the crankcase and trapping the charge in a high-revving racing engine – his instinct told him that high "suction" was less important than lengthening the inlet period and phasing the port timing to

Ernst Degner, MZ's world-class star, on the Monza start grid for his Italian debut in the 1957 125 cc GP

match the natural frequency of the induction system (including the crankcase).

Kaaden's first racing MZ was a simple 124 cc (54 × 54 mm) single with two transfer ports, two megaphone exhausts, three speeds and a modest output of 9 bhp at 7,800 rpm. Significantly, though, like the prewar DKWs, it had the exhausts at the rear. The advantage of this was that, since the engine rotated forward – hence the piston was thrust against the rear cylinder wall on the downstroke – the gas seal between the exhaust port and the crankcase was better than it would otherwise have been. As a result, torque was crisper and a good rider could always detect the improvement in acceleration.

The seeming disadvantage of rear-facing exhausts – overheating – was obviated partly by using deep cylinder finning, but mostly by machining the rear fins back to keep the port very short and so minimise heat absorption from the outgoing gases.

Within only a few months, higher compression, larger ports, longer timing and changes in exhaust dimensions had boosted power by 30 per cent. By 1954 the peak was 13 bhp at 8,000 rpm and there were four gears. The following year a single exhaust pipe replaced the previous two and its outlet was baffled to resist the escape of fresh charge. (This was the embryo of the modern exhaust box.) Peak power was 15 bhp at 9,000 rpm and MZ riders were winning international races as well as nationals, although the DKW single still had the edge at world-championship level.

By then the MZ's torque spread had become too narrow for four speeds, while both the small-end bush and the East German IKA magneto were jibbing at the revs. So for 1956 there were six speeds, a caged needle-roller small-end bearing and battery ignition. Power climbed a further 10 per cent to 16·5 bhp at 9,200 rpm.

Unexpected

From then on, painstaking development boosted power by an average of nearly 2 bhp a year – but the best single gain came in 1959, when the adoption of a third transfer port, opposite the exhaust, brought an entirely unexpected bonus of 1½ bhp, lifting the peak to 22 bhp at 10,000–11,000 rpm.

The gain was unexpected because the port was introduced not for power but to improve the lot of the small-end bearing, which got hot and bothered again once peak revs rose beyond 10,000 rpm. Since the extra transfer passage was fed via a window high in the front of the piston skirt, the cool, oily gas had to wash over the bearing on its

MZ's first 250 cc rotary-valve twin, in 1954. At that time, each cylinder had two megaphone exhausts. Note the Earles-type front fork

way up. Besides solving the small-end problem, the auxiliary port improved cylinder filling and sparked off intensive research into relative transfer discharge angles and flow rates.

Almost from the start, incidentally, the engine had been doubled-up into a 250 cc side-by-side twin by the simple expedient of splining both crankshafts into a central transmission gear. The broad strategy was to experiment on the single, then incorporate any benefits in the twin.

From time to time, too, some offbeat lay-outs were tried. First (in 1954) was a 125 cc parallel twin – but, with only 12 bhp at 9,000 rpm, it was no match for the single (then giving 13 bhp at 8,000 rpm). Much more complex was a tall opposed-piston single with a crankcase and disc valve at top as well as bottom, and the two crankshafts coupled (by chain) 15 degrees out of phase to give the exhaust piston (the upper one) a permanent lead over the transfer piston.

This layout foundered on the excessive length of the transfer passages from the top crankcase to the ports at the bottom of the cylinder. Again 12 bhp at 9,000 rpm was the limit and again the idea was scrapped.

Finally (in 1956) – with the dual aim of filling the crankcase from the middle rather

121

CYNAR

Right: *Eddie Crooks at the foot of Bray Hill on a 125 cc MZ in 1960. Note the leading-link front fork and the exhaust deflector stupidly insisted on by the ACU*

Above: *the writing on the wall. At Monza, Ernst Degner (MZ) finishes a mere wheel's breadth behind world champion Carlo Ubbiali (MV Agusta) in the 1959 Italian 250 cc GP after having beaten him by a machine's length in the 125 cc race*

than one side, and directing the cool, oily charge straight at the grateful big end – the cylinder was laid flat and the disc moved to the top face of the crankcase, where it was driven by skew gears.

This engine suffered a multitude of ills. Not only were the skew gears unreliable, but the cylinder head screened the barrel and crankcase so badly that piston seizure was chronic and charge density so low that no more than 14 bhp was ever obtained – $2\frac{1}{2}$ bhp less than the regular engine was giving at the time.

Had Kaaden not been so pathetically starved of resources, one or two of those abortive experiments might have been worth further investigation. As it was, his ordinary

engines were responding so well to steady development that they outstripped the best Italian double-knockers by the late 1950s – and the twin even outstripped its own chassis, especially on bumpy circuits, causing Kaaden to try three types of front fork (Earles, leading-link and telescopic) in a desperate bid to tame the handling.

In 1958, a year before the power boost from the third transfer port, Horst Fügner's twin was so fast that only Tarquinio Provini's dynamic riding on the MV kept the East German from winning the world 250 cc championship. Even so, Fügner split Provini and his team mate Carlo Ubbiali in the final reckoning – and top Western stars started clamouring to race the MZs.

Coming events

When they did, in 1959, the tip of the long shadow of impending two-stroke dominance flitted unmistakably across the classic scene.

After pulverising the lap record twice, Luigi Taveri had the Lightweight 125 cc TT well sewn up until an overtight helmet upset his vision – forcing him to ease the pace, so that his hard plug jibbed at the rich mixture and Provini nipped past on the MV.

In the second half of the season, the up-and-coming Gary Hocking took over one of the twins to score four brilliant wins (including the Swedish and Ulster GPs) and finish second in the title chase to Ubbiali, who had been piling up points on his MV all season. In the 125 cc Ulster, too, Hocking led from Mike Hailwood on a Honda twin until the MZ packed up.

When the Italian GP brought the season to a close, Ernst Degner humiliated MV's world champion Ubbiali by beating him on his home ground (Monza) in the 125 cc race and running him second by no more than a wheel's breadth in the 250 cc race.

Had MZ been able to offer Western currency to riders, instead of East German marks that were practically worthless outside the country's borders, Hocking would surely have won both Lightweight titles in 1960. Anyway, Count Agusta took no chances and quickly stepped in with an offer the Rhodesian could not refuse.

From then on, Kaaden had not only to cope with indifferent East German equipment; he had also to rely chiefly on local riders, with occasional spectacular help from Mike Hailwood and Alan Shepherd. Even so, Ernst Degner (MZ's only home rider of world class) dominated the 125 cc class in 1961 and was deprived of the championship only by a ban the FIM imposed on him for the final round in Argentina as "punishment" for having just defected to the West.

While Suzuki and Yamaha then gratefully started to build for the future on the basis of the MZ formula that Degner had taken to Japan, Hailwood and Shepherd time and again proved the genuine MZs to be a match for the world-champion Hondas. Since the team's excursions outside East Germany were heavily curtailed following Degner's defection, Sachsenring was their happiest hunting ground.

There, in 1962, Mike finished only half a wheel behind Redman's 250 cc Honda four after being bumped on the final bend – and Shepherd had been 15 seconds ahead of the pair of them when his engine cut. The following year, the vast East German crowd were

Right: *here climbing out of Ramsey, lone hand Alan Shepherd rides his water-cooled MZ twin into second place behind Jim Redman's Honda four in the 1964 Lightweight 250 cc TT. In the world championship he finished third to Phil Read (Yamaha) and Redman*

Above: *simplicity itself – the 1964 version of MZ's water-cooled 125 cc disc-valve single. Best power at that time was 29 bhp at 11,600 rpm*

Below: *there was not much room left on the crankcase covers of the 1964 MZ 250 cc twin after the carburettors and gear-driven half-speed magnetos were fitted.*

overjoyed when both Hailwood and Shepherd put it across Redman. In 1964, after tailing one of the needle-sharp Read/Redman world championship tussles for a short while, Mike breezed past with a 102·06 mph lap only 1·58 seconds outside the absolute record on a 500 cc MV four (and that in a lap of more than three minutes). Quickly pulling out a lead of 300 yards, Mike made both the Japanese bikes look a bit old fashioned until he got throttle-happy and spun to ground on a slow corner.

· On MZ's relatively infrequent appearances outside Saxony, Shepherd might well have won at Hockenheim and Monza in 1963 but for brief stops for trivial troubles. The following year he won the American 250 cc GP at Daytona, was second to Redman in the Lightweight 250 cc TT and – with an engine skimmed out to only 251 cc – chased Jim in the Junior (350 cc) TT too, until the ignition failed. What those bald facts conceal is that MZ's total strength in the Isle of Man that year was one machine, one mechanic, Kaaden and Shepherd, who was still recovering from a broken collarbone!

Although Derek Woodman and Gunter Bartusch subsequently put up some stirring performances, lack of top track talent and anything like enough development resources condemned Walter Kaaden and his team to an ever losing battle. Such was the machines' potential, however, that even five years later (in 1969), admittedly after Yamaha had withdrawn their vee-fours, Woodman's grossly undergeared twin was the fastest two-fifty through *Motor Cycle*'s TT speed trap at the Highlander. And, in the 1971 Junior race, Bartusch's 300 cc MZ was virtually as fast through the same trap as Giacomo Agostini's full-size MV three, even though the German was practically a TT newcomer and badly put off by the rain.

In 1971, too, both Peter Williams and Chas Mortimer were greatly impressed by the MZ twin. Taking over the second-string model (57 bhp against Bartusch's 60) at the last minute without any practice, Williams naturally devoted the first lap of the Lightweight 250 cc TT to acclimatisation. Yet he had no difficulty in keeping Phil Read's winning Yamaha in sight and was quite confident of overhauling it until the engine tightened as he rocketed out of Governor's Bridge at the end of the lap.

Mortimer had tried the same MZ in the final practice session. With a vast experience of piston-ported Yamahas, he was able to make a direct comparison. The MZ, he enthused, left no doubt as to its extra power. Not only was it much faster but more tractable, too. And it handled better.

Chief problem

Once Kaaden had finalised the basic formula for a grand-prix two-stroke, his major technical problem was ignition. East German contact breakers just could not stand five-figure revs and he had no option but to gear them down to half engine speed, fit an extra set of points and time each set independently on alternate firing strokes. This arrangement was used both with the IKA magnetos and with the battery ignition tried early on. In 1960, dual ignition was tried, too, but gave no advantage.

From 1964, Lucas electronic ignition was adopted. Unfortunately, this method of spark generation was then in its infancy, with transistors borrowed from other applications rather than specially tailored. Also, since the sparks were triggered from one crankshaft only on the twin, the timing in the opposite cylinder was affected by any backlash in the crankshaft coupling. On bench test there was a five-per-cent power bonus but on the track there was a persistent misfire at top revs, so the suspect IKA magnetos were reinstated.

Mixture control, too, created problems until Mikuni carburettors were fitted (along with Krober electronic ignition) in 1971. Previously, the rider had to be relied on to weaken the mixture for slow corners (to prevent plug fouling and ensure clean acceleration); enrich it to prevent seizure on severe climbs and long straights; and determine in practice the precise position of the air lever that gave maximum power. For the race, the main jet size was then adjusted to give the same mixture strength with the air lever wide open – because full closure of the air lever to compensate for too small a jet cut the power by 10 per cent, while a wide-open air control with too small a jet was a recipe for seizure.

Although water cooling (cylinder barrel first, then barrel and head) brought reliability and consistent speed in 1963 – banishing the previous 10 per cent power drop after three minutes on full bore – MZ had to stick to the thermosiphon principle because they could not afford to change to an impeller, which would have permitted a smaller, lower-slung radiator.

To narrow the twin between the rider's knees, the exhausts were switched to the front in 1961; but the consequent blunting of acceleration only confirmed the sealing theory responsible for the rear exhausts in the first place.

The most serious attempt at narrowing the twin, however, was the tandem cylinder arrangement adopted in 1969. Although it was the two-fifty, rather than the one-two-five, that was in drastic need of slimming, the smaller size was used as a guineapig in the usual way, with the idea of transferring the layout to the two-fifty once any problems had been solved.

Unhappily, though, in spite of an initial power boost of 10 per cent (to 32 bhp at 13,000 rpm), the useful torque spread was cut from nearly 3,000 rpm to just under 1,000 and so the extra power was never reflected in higher lap speeds. By 1971 the project was abandoned.

Simplicity

During the years that MZ graced the classic scene I twice went to Zschopau to discuss Kaaden's work with him – in the winter of 1961–62, just after the 125 cc single had become the first grand-prix engine to reach 200 bhp/litre (25 bhp at 10,800 rpm); then four years later to analyse the 250 cc twin. On both visits I was struck by the utter simplicity of the engine construction, the sheer logic of Kaaden's development work and the appalling poverty of his resources compared with those of his Japanese and West European contemporaries.

It seemed unreal, the first time, that such a historic milestone in specific power could have been established by so basic an engine. There were two plain crankcase halves, with a six-speed gearbox bolted on the back; and a three-piece pressed-up flywheel assembly,

The 1959 version of the MZ 125 cc single, showing: the cutaway inlet disc; bevelled flywheel rims; piston window for the third transfer port; main transfer passages angled away from the exhaust; half-moon squish band in cylinder head

supported in three main bearings, with the primary drive pinion on the left and the cutaway disc on the right. On the disc cover was the 27 or 29 mm carburettor and half-speed magneto.

The carburettor had a slight updraught angle which, together with a pronounced bevel on the flywheel rim, directed the charge straight into the space it had to fill (between the wheels and the piston crown). The connecting rod had needle bearings at both ends while the piston had only one ring, giving a fractional power bonus above 6,000 rpm. Its skirt was cut back at the sides to clear the transfer and inlet tracts and holed at the front for the third transfer port.

Deeply finned, the cylinder had square-cut exhaust and transfer ports, with the exhaust machined right back and fitted with a quick-change pipe adaptor. Equally well finned, the head had a half-moon squish band at the rear that concentrated the combustion space at the front and helped deflect the looping transfer streams away from the gaping exhaust port. (The effectiveness of this and the exhaust box was reflected in the fuel consumption of almost 50 mpg.)

Of course, the "secret" of the engine (not apparent in a casual glance) was the cylinder porting and the dimensions of the resonant exhaust and induction systems – calculated in the first place, then refined by painstaking

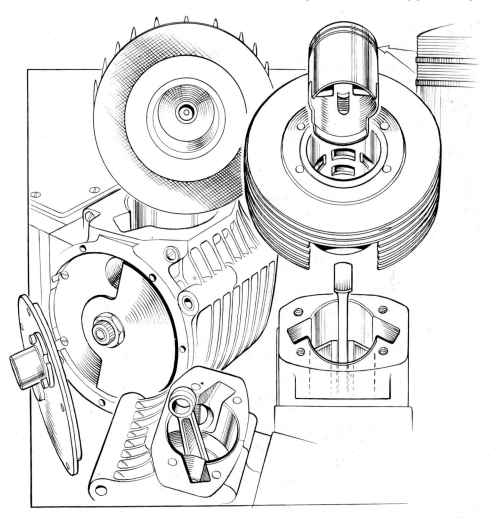

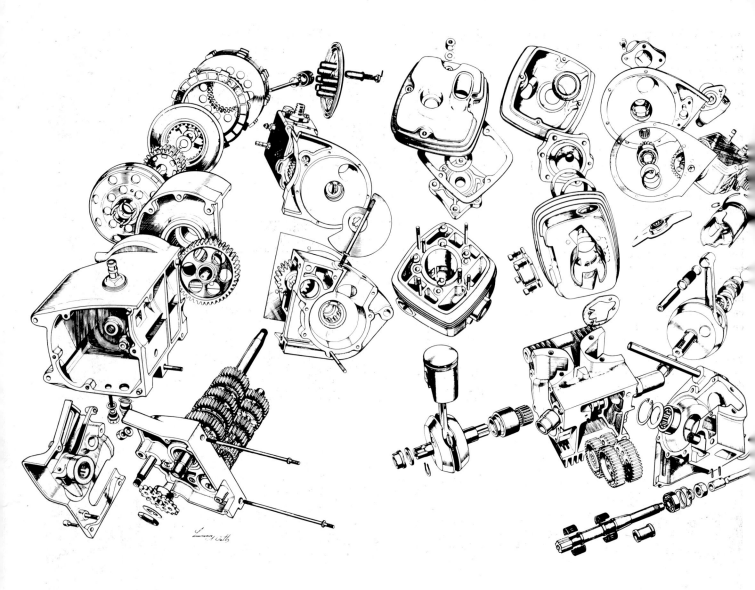

The 1965 version of MZ's 250 cc twin-cylinder engine. Note water passages in barrels and heads; cylinder porting; half-moon squish band; cutaway inlet discs; bevelled flywheels; half-speed, gear-driven magnetos; double power take-off gears and six-speed transmission

experiments. Indeed, it was to speed up otherwise laborious bench tests of dozens of minutely different exhaust boxes that the double-wall pipe adaptor was introduced, with the pipe retained by two springs. This arrangement, now universal, also provides slight flexibility to absorb vibration and so resist cracking.

Green fingers

The engine of the 145-mph twin I examined in early 1966 retained the characteristic simplicity of the earlier single, except that the cylinders and heads were water cooled, the small-end rollers were crowded (not caged) and power was taken off from a common central gear to a jackshaft.

Although specific power had meanwhile climbed by nearly 20 per cent, peak revs were no more than 10 per cent higher –

which clearly indicated better breathing. Indeed, Kaaden had measured a volumetric efficiency of 105 to 110 per cent for the crankcase – and had had to reduce the primary compression ratio from 1·6 to 1·5:1 (ie, increase the crankcase volume by about 40 cc) to accommodate the extra charge without some of it being blown back through the carburettor by the descending piston.

Since port durations are time-based, the increase in peak revs was reflected in a 5–10 per cent extension of the inlet, transfer and exhaust phases. A high price had been paid for the extra power, however, for Kaaden told me the 54-bhp water-cooled twin (by no means the most powerful he made) used twice as much fuel as the 43-bhp air-cooled version on which Gary Hocking did so well.

If Kaaden – with never more than one test bench, and new cylinders supplied (belatedly) in threes – had enjoyed the facilities of his Japanese contemporaries (eight test benches and batches of 50 cylinders), he might have reaped the kudos he deserved. As it was, MZ's failure to win a world championship was a sad victory of politics and economics over technical merit.

I never met a top engineer more modest or

unassuming, more conscientious or dedicated. There was no trace of side in Kaaden's make-up. Above all, he had an instinctive "feel" for two-strokes – the sort of intuition that gardeners call green fingers. Alas, there are no medals for pointing every subsequent successful two-stroke designer in the right direction but his inspiration lives on still in the Japanese and West European elaborations of his basic theme.

Iberian Express

Even outside the Iron Curtain, however, the scope for knowhow and initiative was sometimes drastically curtailed by scarce resources, indifferent materials and lack of funds. An outstanding example of an heroic struggle against such odds was the lone 250 cc (70 × 65 mm) air-cooled Ossa single ridden so spectacularly by Santiago Herrero in the late 1960s.

Despite relative economic backwardness, Spain had long been famous for high-performance piston-valve two-strokes – but the Ossa was a disc-valver. Due to low finance, the Barcelona factory was not able to run a special race shop, let alone a

MZ cylinder liner split vertically through exhaust-port bridge and unrolled. Main transfers are also bridged to prevent ring trapping. Their gas streams converge on front cylinder wall at included angle of 124 degrees and slightly upward. Middle transfer stream is much faster and directed steeply upward

research department – yet designer Dr Eduardo Giro proved that brains are by no means the prerogative of the wealthy factories.

At a time when even water-cooled twins had been outdated by Yamaha's phenomenal vee-fours, Giro had to stick to an air-cooled single for simplicity and cheapness. He knew only too well that his mechanical and heat problems, like his quest for power, would have been greatly simplified if only his brief was for a water-cooled multi. Yet he endowed that primitive Ossa with a phenomenal blend of speed and reliability.

This picture shows Santiago Herrero and the compact layout of the Ossa single without the dolphin fairing. The Ossa weighed 220 lb and its top speed with fairing was about 140 mph

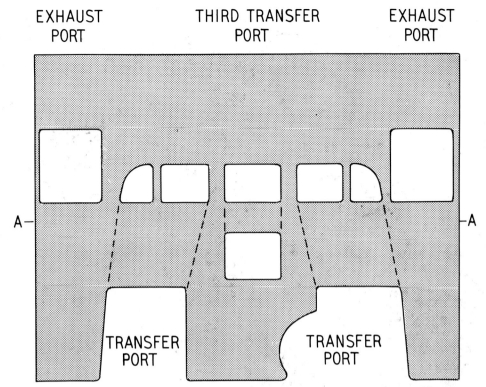

EXHAUST PORT   THIRD TRANSFER PORT   EXHAUST PORT

A—   —A

TRANSFER PORT   TRANSFER PORT

Paddock photograph of the 250 cc Ossa's midriff. The largest carburettor ever on a grand-prix two-stroke (42 mm) was fitted because there was nothing larger! Finning and exhaust dimensions were also unusually large. A welded aluminium monocoque frame holds the fuel and oil. Below the steering head is a diaphragm-type damper

Herrero's third place in the 1969 Lightweight 250 cc TT at 92·82 mph was a stupendous performance, as were his 133·3 mph through *Motor Cycle*'s speed trap at the Highlander and his overall fuel consumption of 30 mpg. That trap speed, indeed, was only narrowly bettered by Derek Woodman's works MZ twin, Rod Gould's works Yamaha twin and Kel Carruthers' works double-knocker Benelli four. In the paddock I spoke to Giro, then 27, about his work. I asked him why he used such a large exhaust port and fitted a 42 mm (more than $1\frac{5}{8}$ in) carburettor.

"I use a 42 mm Dellorto carburettor," he told me, "because I can't get anything bigger! I would prefer 45 mm but nobody makes that size." There were two reasons, he explained, for the enormous diameters of the exhaust and inlet ports. First, larger ports resonate at higher speeds, which he wanted for power. (At that stage he was getting 42 bhp at an incredible 10,000–11,000 rpm.) The second reason was concerned with scale. Doubling a cylinder's linear dimensions (bore and stroke) gives four times the surface area (which governs port size) but eight times the volume to be filled and emptied through those ports. Thus the relative port sizes are halved. It was to minimise this large-cylinder breathing restriction that Giro put the biggest ports he could in his engine.

Another obvious feature of the engine was the great depth of finning, to cool and stiffen the cylinder. Inside, Giro confided, the cylinder head had an unusually large squish area. Between 1 and 5 per cent of oil was mixed with the fuel and supplemented by a small feed to the main and big-end bearings.

With useful power starting at 6,500 rpm, the Ossa put many a more exotic two-fifty to shame for tractability, so that six speeds were ample. The mechanical safety limit was 11,500 rpm; above that, naturally enough for a 250 cc single, everything was liable to disintegrate.

The frame, too, was unusual – a beam structure of pistol-grip shape that doubled as a fuel and oil container. It was rather crudely welded from aluminium-alloy sheeting that helped keep total weight down to 220 lb.

At the time we talked, Giro was clearly delighted that Herrero was leading the world championship, although he eventually finished third. Later in the season, at Assen, there was an experimental water-cooled version of the engine, in which the water

jacket was such a snug fit round the cylinder as to show the shapes of the transfer and exhaust passages. Internally, the engine was unchanged; the purpose of the switch to water cooling was solely to reduce cylinder distortion and so maintain maximum power throughout long races. However, Herrero chose the well-proven air-cooled engine for the race itself. Indeed, when it reappeared in the Isle of Man the following year (1970) the Ossa was still air cooled.

At that time Herrero was lying third in the world championship (behind champion-elect Rod Gould and reigning champion Kel Carruthers, both on Yamaha twins) – and his speed through the Highlander trap had increased to 137·9 mph, little more than 4 mph down on Paul Smart (Yamaha) and Gunter Bartusch (works MZ twin).

Alas, Herrero was caught unawares by molten tar on the fast left-hand bend at the bottom of the downhill 13th Milestone section and died of his injuries. Ossa quit grand-prix racing there and then. As with Dario Ambrosini and Benelli 20 years earlier, Herrero *was* Ossa so far as classic racing was concerned. Without him, Eduardo Giro had no further heart for the valiant technical struggle.

Suzuki take the hint

Nowhere was the MZ lead followed more

Above: *seen at Assen – the 250 cc Ossa engine with water cooling for stamina. The water jacket is an unusually snug fit round the gas passages. The Motoplat ignition generator is on left-hand end of crankshaft*

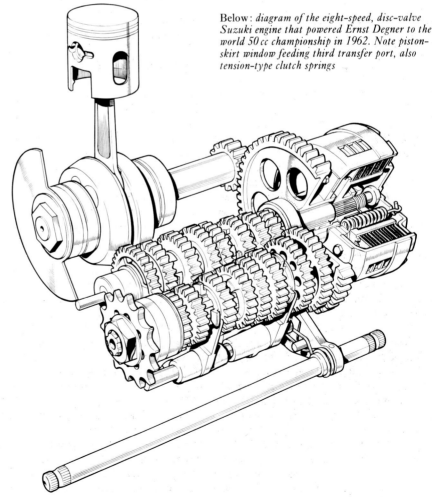

Below: *diagram of the eight-speed, disc-valve Suzuki engine that powered Ernst Degner to the world 50 cc championship in 1962. Note piston-skirt window feeding third transfer port, also tension-type clutch springs*

promptly than at Suzuki, the first Japanese factory to mount a serious challenge to Honda. Before Ernst Degner's arrival, their grand-prix two-strokes were pathetically uncompetitive – high-revving piston-ported machines with a power band almost impossibly narrow. In 1960 they fielded a 125 cc twin (the Colleda). The following year it was partnered by a 250 cc twin that did nothing to dispel the impression that the Hamamatsu engineers were groping in the dark of two-stroke mysteries.

Peaking at 9,500 to 10,000 rpm, the two-fifty was useless below 8,500 rpm, so that the clutch came in for excessive slipping and the six speeds were anything but a luxury. Given the right riding technique, acceleration was startling and top speed 120 mph – but, once the engine was hot, both acceleration and speed were severely blunted by misfiring.

Within a year or two of Degner's arrival, however, Suzuki in particular, and Japanese two-strokes in general, were clearly on the highroad to world domination. Nothing illustrates more plainly the difference between the creative talent of Walter Kaaden (starved of the backing that would have

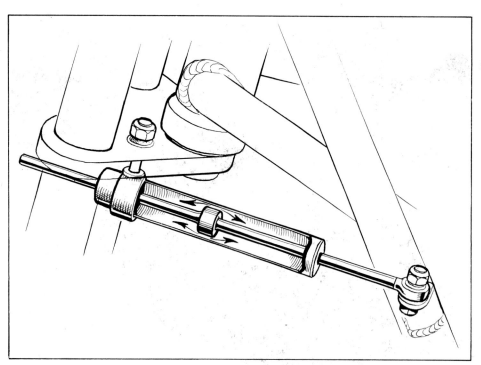

Above: *smallest of the telescopic steering dampers was this one fitted to the 1963 Suzukis. To obviate displacement problems, the piston rod protrudes through both ends of the hydraulic cylinder*

Below: *crankcase of the 1963 50 cc Suzuki single is horizontally split through the three shaft axes. Here Ernst Degner (left) shows the simple construction*

farther up the capacity scale – first with an air-cooled twin, then with a water-cooled square four (both 250 cc) – were notably unsuccessful. It was not until they re-entered grand-prix racing nearly a decade later, with the RG 500 square four, that they shed their lightweight image with a brace of world 500 cc championships by Barry Sheene.

Surprisingly, too, their first MZ copies – a 125 cc single and 250 cc twin – incorporated features Kaaden had already proved undesirable. These were air cooling for the twin and forward-facing exhausts. Whether those mistakes were due to Suzuki's having started their copying before Degner joined them or to the fact that, fine engineer though he was, Degner was not the brain at MZ, is arguable. Either way, Suzuki had to learn at first hand that rear exhausts give crisper torque and that the stagnant pocket of air between the twin's cylinders was a recipe for sudden piston seizure.

There were no such frustrations in the newly instituted 50 cc class. Right from the start, Degner's air-cooled single showed uncanny reliability and he romped to the 1962 world championship via emphatic victories in the TT and three other grands prix. With 10 bhp at 11,000 rpm, he had no difficulty in averaging a higher speed in the TT (75·12 mph) than Cromie McCandless had done on a double-knocker FB Mondial in the first 125 cc event 11 years earlier.

ensured his just reward) and the Japanese genius for developing sound ideas to the utmost through diligent application and incomparably greater resources.

Strangely, during their first spell on the classic scene (up to 1967) Suzuki had to be content with 50 cc and 125 cc successes. Their attempts to extend their influence

Degner's TT win was the first by a two-stroke since 1938. At 40 × 39·5 mm, the cylinder dimensions were virtually square and there were three transfer ports. The updraught carburettor had a 21 mm choke and the magneto was driven from the gearbox. Eight speeds enabled him to keep the revs between 10,000 and 12,000 rpm. Although the frame had full duplex loops, the bike's total weight was a mere 132 lb, including the plastic dolphin fairing, and only one twin-leading-shoe front brake was called for.

That simple air-cooled single stayed on top of the heap for the next two years, thanks largely to the scintillating form of New Zealander Hugh Anderson, world champion in both 1963 and 1964. For 1963 the engine had 1 bhp extra (a total of 11) and one more gear in the transmission (nine in all). The consequent boost to top speed was 6 mph – and it was indicative of the high proportion of race time spent flat-out by the fifties that this increase enabled Mitsuo Itoh (the first Japanese TT winner) to better Degner's 1962 average speed by no less than 3·6 mph.

With 12 bhp on tap in 1964, Anderson added 2 mph to both Itoh's TT race speed and Degner's lap record. Yet neither of the New Zealander's world titles reflected a lack of worthy opposition. True, Honda had thrown in the sponge in 1963, but Hans-

Above: last fling for the single-cylinder version of Suzuki's 50 cc title-holder. At Solitude, Hugh Anderson tucks his elbows between his knees to win the West German GP on the way to his second championship in the class

Below: it was not for want of trying that Hugh Anderson (Suzuki) surrendered his world 50 cc title to Ralph Bryans (Honda) in 1965. Here is a typical picture of the hard-riding New Zealander lapping Gerhard Thurow (Kreidler) in the Dutch GP as runner-up to Bryans

On the way to the first of his three 50cc titles in a row for Suzuki, Hans-Georg Anscheidt screams his 128-lb water-cooled twin to victory in the 1966 West German GP at Hockenheim

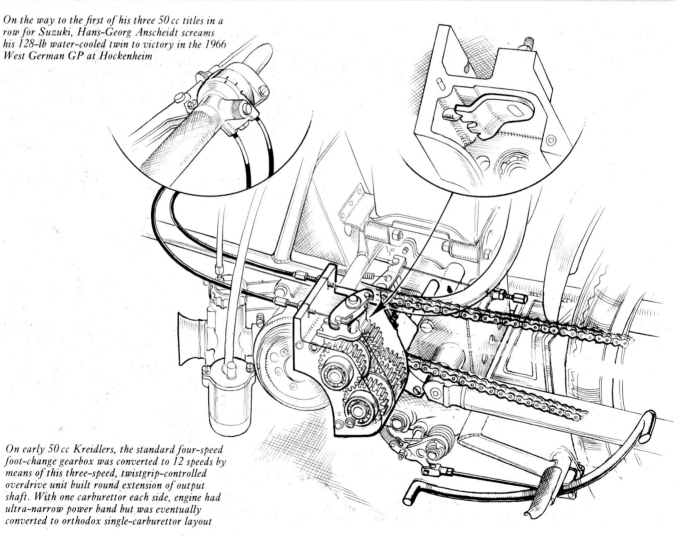

On early 50cc Kreidlers, the standard four-speed foot-change gearbox was converted to 12 speeds by means of this three-speed, twistgrip-controlled overdrive unit built round extension of output shaft. With one carburettor each side, engine had ultra-narrow power band but was eventually converted to orthodox single-carburettor layout

Georg Anscheidt's two-stroke Kreidler might have edged the Suzuki star out of the title but for breaking down in the final round in Japan. In 1964, too, Ralph Bryans' new nine-speed Honda twin (with 15 bhp at 19,000 rpm) finally outpaced Anderson's single and Hugh owed his title that year to the 22 points he had chalked up before the Honda outgrew its teething troubles.

Gears galore

Anscheidt's Kreidler, in contrast to the opposition, was not designed as an out-and-out racer in the first place but was a variant of the Florett four-speed roadster. The engine was unusual in having two disc valves and carburettors, one each side of the crankcase. Most likely this "over-carburetting" was responsible for the embarrassingly narrow power range, a mere 800 rpm in 1963. The engine was a match for any when stoked up to 14,000 rpm but was useless below 13,200!

To provide the large number of gear ratios necessary to make such a tempera-

Seen here at Bedstead corner in the 1964 TT, Hans-Georg Anscheidt's twin-carb 50 cc Kreidler single has 12 gears to enable the rider to keep the revs between 13,200 and 14,000 rpm

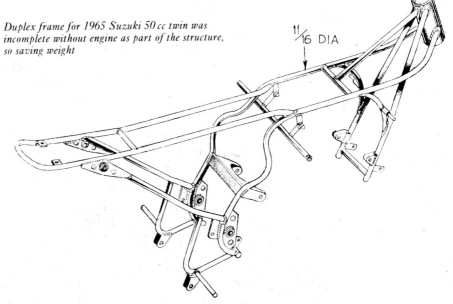

Duplex frame for 1965 Suzuki 50 cc twin was incomplete without engine as part of the structure, so saving weight

mental engine raceworthy, Kreidler hit on the ingenious idea of building a compact three-speed overdrive unit around an extension of the gearbox output shaft. The overdrive was controlled by the left twist-grip, the main box by the usual pedal. Thus there was a choice of 12 close ratios, which could be changed one at a time (hand and foot) or three at a time (foot only) according to circumstances.

Later on, persisting with the twin-carburettor layout, Kreidler obtained more power at the cost of an even narrower rev band and saddled the poor rider with 18 gears – strangely, not by putting six speeds in the main box but by using nine main gears and reducing the overdrive to two.

Scaling down

Suzuki's answer to the Honda twin was to use two cylinders as well and change to

water cooling at the same time. It was two years, however, before they were again dominant enough to win the manufacturers' title as well as the individual (which Anscheidt won for them in 1967 and 1968). Actually, Anscheidt first won the title in 1966 but that was virtually a gift from Honda, who boycotted the Japanese GP at which he clinched it but nevertheless took the manufacturers' championship.

Surprisingly, at 128 lb, the Suzuki twin was even lighter than the original single, and it had duplex front brakes too. Typical of the efforts to save every possible ounce was a new duplex frame, which relied on the engine to complete the structure and in which the main tube diameter was only $\frac{11}{16}$ in.

In its first year (1965) the engine had 12 speeds and gave 14·5 bhp at 16,500 rpm – but not even Anderson's most resolute scratching could prevent Taveri from beating him in the TT or Bryans from snatching his world crown. By the time Anscheidt joined the team, power was up to 16·5 bhp at 17,000 rpm but it was not until the following year (with 17·5 bhp at 17,300 rpm) that Suzuki's tiddlers were really back in business, with a TT win by Stuart Graham as well as Anscheidt's world title.

When switching from Kreidler, the German may have expected some relief from the chore of excessive gear changing.

Above: Stuart Graham pops out of the Governor's Bridge hollow to win the 1967 50 cc TT. His water-cooled disc-valve Suzuki twin had 14 speeds, 17·5 bhp at 17,300 rpm and topped 110 mph. It weighed only 128 lb.

Below: on an air-cooled disc-valve twin, Hugh Anderson spearheads Suzuki's clean sweep of the 1963 Lightweight 125 cc TT. In robbing Luigi Taveri of the world title that year, he forced Honda to abandon their twin for a four

Robbed of his world 125 cc title in 1964 by Luigi Taveri's new Honda four, Hugh Anderson nevertheless trounces the Swiss star in the Ulster GP. Here he flings his air-cooled Suzuki twin into Ireland's corner during his meteoric ride following a first-lap tumble at the hairpin

It is doubtful whether he got it, for the Suzuki twin went from 12 gears to 14 and there was no dual control, only the conventional pedal. So quickly could such a light machine be braked from its top speed of 110 mph for a slow corner that the rider had his work cut out to fan the pedal fast enough.

The engine, which finished up with 18 bhp, had updraught carburettors and a central power take-off to a jackshaft that drove the ventilated clutch on the right and the magneto on the left. Because of the extra width of the gearbox, the final-drive sprocket could not be mounted on the left-hand end of the second shaft, as it otherwise would have been. To bring the chain in close enough to the rear wheel, a short sprocket shaft was mounted behind the gear cluster and driven by a large inboard gear on the second shaft. The oil pump was bevel driven from the first gearbox shaft and the water impeller from the second.

Fascinating though that tiny engine was, Suzuki had a more potent one up their sleeve. Had their battle with Honda con-

tinued beyond the end of 1967, they planned to field a three-cylinder fifty with 20 bhp . . .

Transformation

In 1962 Suzuki's first "oriental MZs" – a 125 cc single and 250 cc parallel twin – produced 22 and 42 bhp respectively at 11,000 rpm. They were so manifestly uncompetitive that the two-fifty was allowed to fade away (pending the arrival of the water-cooled square four two years later) while the one-two-five got the scaling-down treatment and rear exhausts for 1963, although it remained air cooled.

The transformation was dramatic. From the season's dawn in Barcelona to its close at Suzuka, the battle with Honda brimmed over with excitement. Hugh Anderson not only led his team-mates Frank Perris and Ernst Degner to a clean sweep of the TT; he also won the West German, East German, French, Dutch, Ulster, Finnish and Argentine GPs to sew up the world 125 cc championship (manufacturers' too) and force Honda to ditch their twin for a four.

A novel feature of the Suzuki twin was the designer's deliberate refusal to join the crankshafts, either with a Hirth coupling or a common splined gear. Instead, each shaft had a thin gear on its inboard end; running closely side by side, these meshed with a double-width gear on the jackshaft, which

distributed the drive to the clutch and ignition generator.

With two individual and two manufacturers' titles, Suzuki lightweights were riding high, but not for long. Honda's tiny four seemed to escape teething troubles altogether, while Suzuki squeezed their air-cooled twin too hard and bartered their 1963 reliability for their 1964 power increase. Taveri reasserted himself in both the TT and the world championship, but not without a thrashing in the Ulster GP, where a first-lap toss at the hairpin inspired Anderson to one of his characteristically dashing displays of utter invincibility.

Suzuki were as quick to respond to defeat as Honda had been a year earlier. They adopted water cooling; fitted a gearbox-driven pump that took oil from a compartment in the seat back and fed it to the big ends; and they enlisted Mikuni's aid in cleaning up the carburation.

With 30 bhp at 14,000 rpm, nine gears and a top speed of 125 mph, Anderson gave Taveri no chance of retaining his title. Four straight wins at the start of the season laid the foundations of Honda's defeat. Later on, Frank Perris whittled down his team-mate's lead after Anderson missed the East German round, then tumbled on the last lap at Brno. But the New Zealander finally established his unquestionable right to the crown with a phenomenal aquatic win at Monza – in

Nose to tail on the Nürburgring. Winner Hugh Anderson leads his Suzuki team mate Ernst Degner (fourth) in the 1965 West German 125 cc GP. Both bikes are water-cooled disc-valve twins and Anderson went on to relieve Luigi Taveri of the world title

conditions better suited to boating, he even lapped second-man Perris.

Although Honda countered in 1966 with five cylinders to give Taveri his third 125 cc title in five years, it was Yamaha, not Suzuki, who were then shaping up to spearhead the two-stroke challenge. With the refinement of an impeller in their cooling system, they had added reliability to a slight edge in speed, whereas the Suzukis were often no faster than in 1965 yet threw more tantrums. While neither team could outrun Taveri's screaming Honda in the title chase, it was significant that Anderson trailed the Yamaha twins of both Bill Ivy and Phil Read in the TT.

For 1967 Yamaha played a trump card with their tiny vee-four. It suited Ivy's style and stature to perfection and he gave the factory its first title in the 125 cc class. Yet Suzuki were far from disheartened. In the TT, Stuart Graham's great challenge to the victorious Read suggested that the Suzuki twin was no more than 2 bhp down on the Yamaha four – and Suzuki's own vee-four was practically ready for the track.

A few months earlier it had been pushing out 4 bhp more than the twin but its track debut was put back by the need to broaden the power band. Inevitably, that entailed the sacrifice of two of the extra bhp, so the rival fours looked like being very evenly matched once they got to grips.

Regrettably, that exciting prospect was never fulfilled. Suzuki's withdrawal at the end of the year, along with Honda, left the Yamaha four as unchallenged boss and Read won the last 125 cc championship to be run without an FIM limit on gears (six) and cylinders (two).

From dream to nightmare

It was in the heady days of 1963, when Suzuki's all-conquering new air-cooled twin first exploded the myth of Honda invincibility, that they had a brainwave. Why not stick another two cylinders on the front of the engine and blow Honda off in the 250 cc class as well? Of course, masking of the rear cylinders would necessitate water cooling but that was no problem, especially as no impeller was incorporated.

As the 1964 season approached, Hamamatsu rumours of 54 bhp at 12,500 rpm were sufficient to scare Honda clean off the start grid. When the new square four took to the tarmac with a fanfare, invincibility

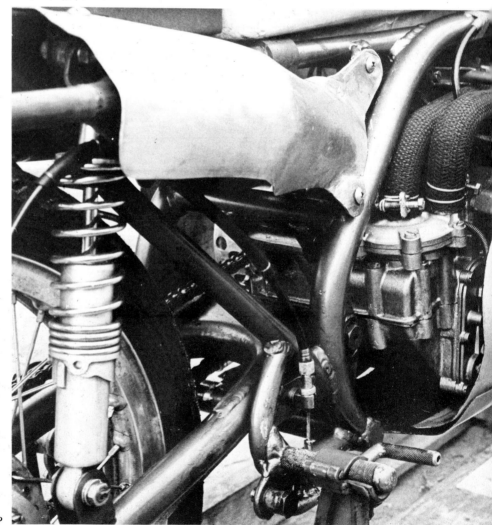

Large gearbox-driven water impeller and hoses on a 125 cc Suzuki twin in the 1967 West German GP

Above: *an early version of Suzuki's nightmare two-fifty, the water-cooled square four. Although based on Hugh Anderson's world championship-winning 125 cc twin, it was never competitive*

seemed just around the corner. Incredibly for such a bold and logical design, it was just about the most abject failure in the history of classic racing.

Only three times throughout the year did it finish in the first six. Best was third place at Clermont Ferrand by Austrian Bert Schneider, who later was sixth in Ulster. At Barcelona's tricky Montjuich Park, one of his favourite circuits, Hugh Anderson could manage no better than fifth, lapped by the winner, Tarquinio Provini on a Benelli four. In the TT, Perris' engine succumbed after only five miles, Schneider's chain broke

Below: *in 1965 Suzuki fitted this cable control to the oil pump of their 250 cc square four so that pump stroke could be varied experimentally*

while he lay seventh on lap 2 and Jack Ahearn's engine failed next lap when he was sixth.

Plug fouling and problems with carburation and ignition dogged the team persistently. When the engine was coaxed up to 12,500 rpm and a temperature of 90 degrees C on a long straight the bike just flew. But no sooner had the rider braked, changed down and scratched round a slow corner than much of the power had evaporated.

Developments included omission of the idler gear coupling the crankshafts, so shortening the engine and causing the front and rear inlet discs to overlap (as in the Kawasaki tandem twins 10 years later). A new duplex frame was made to suit. Carburation was cleaned up and the problem of providing 50,000 sparks a minute eased by doubling-up the ignition unit, halving its speed and fitting four separate high-tension coils.

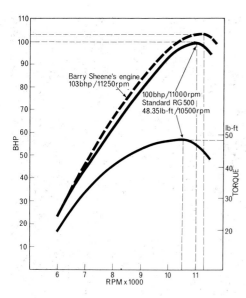

Above: *1976 engine performance curves for a standard RG500 Suzuki (solid lines) and Barry Sheene's works model. The extra 3 bhp came from modified porting, higher secondary compression and square cylinder dimensions, which increased torque from 6,000 rpm upward*

Below: *exploded view of the engine of Barry Sheene's 1976 world championship-winning RG500 Suzuki. Square-four arrangement is necessary because disc-valve cylinders cannot be coupled more than two abreast. Cylinders fire in diagonal pairs and inlet valves spin between fibre discs. Wide gear on underslung jackshaft is driven by four thin gears on inboard ends of crankshafts. Subsequent developments include modified porting, wider squish bands, plated (not sleeved) cylinders, discarding of oil pump (bottom left), a one-piece jackshaft, a two-piece crankcase (giving lower front cylinders) and transmission changes enabling all gear ratios to be varied individually.*

Brake cooling was improved and auxiliary oiling arranged for the big ends. One way and another, the exorbitant weight of 330 lb was trimmed to 286 lb (still excessive for a two-fifty). Otherwise the specification survived: 43 × 42·6 mm bore and stroke; cylinders cast in right and left pairs; squish heads; single piston rings; 22 mm carburettors and three transfer ports. A jackshaft distributed the drive to the ignition and transmission (which gave a choice of five or six speeds). There was a kill-button for upward gear changes.

In terms of results, the effort was ill-rewarded. Perris' third place in the TT, after a plug change, was easily the best performance in 1965. Later, in the Belgian and Dutch GPs, the dashing young Yosh Katayama raised Suzuki hopes by handling the square four like a toy but it was too late. The bike was still far from competitive and the opposition, both four-stroke and two-stroke, was streaking ahead.

If at first you don't succeed . . .

To Suzuki's credit they kept their heads and, when they returned to classic racing 10 years later, it was with a square four, the RG 500, designed by Makoto Hase. However, instead of building a handful of works specials and marketing a detuned version later on, they launched the RG 500 as a catalogue racer

(selling initially for about £4,500), then souped-up a few machines for selected riders.

Hase's faith in the square-four layout was vindicated when private RG500s almost immediately swamped the grand-prix results, while Barry Sheene's factory prepared model took him to a quick brace of world championships, in 1976 and 1977. In 1977, too, Phil Read rode an RG500 to win the Senior TT. By that time, however, the FIM had struck the TT out of the world-championship list – brainwashed by a few riders with a financial axe to grind (notably Read and Agostini, with 16 wins to their credit and no injuries), who complained that the course was too difficult to learn, too dangerous to ride.

The embarrassing problems of the earlier two-fifty were precluded by great interim advances in carburation and ignition, also by forced water circulation. In cylinder and piston layout, the engine was almost pure MZ, except that the Suzuki had a bore and stroke of 56 × 50·5 mm, not 54 × 54 mm. Indeed, with an initial output of 90 bhp at 10,500 rpm, the RG's specific power (180 bhp/litre) was appreciably lower than the 200 bhp/litre which MZ had achieved in Ernst Degner's air-cooled 125 cc single in 1961.

Hase retained the earlier twin-cylinder arrangement of separate left and right crankshafts driving a common jackshaft

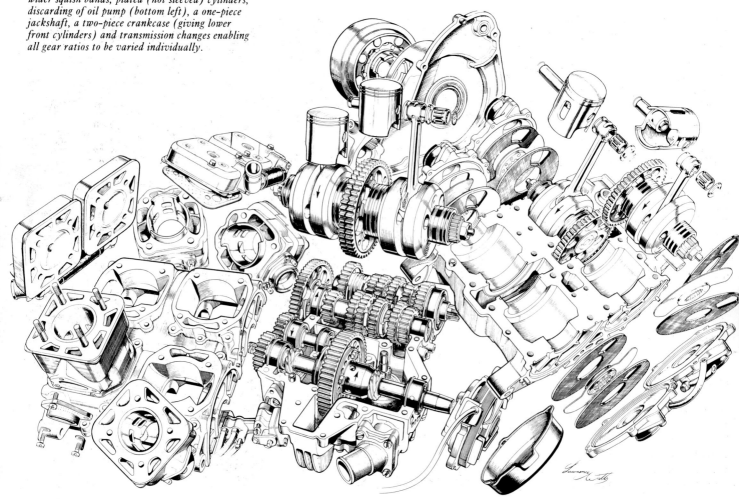

Above: *best result for Suzuki's ill-fated 250 cc square four was third place in the 1965 TT by Frank Perris, seen here speeding through Union Mills*
Right: *the low level of the front cylinders stamps this Suzuki RG500 engine as a 1978 model, when the crankcase was redesigned to simplify gearbox servicing and bring chain sprocket and fork pivot closer together*

through side-by-side thin gears. As in the smaller square four, the cylinders fired in diagonal pairs (two double power impulses every revolution). The jackshaft drove the water impeller and ignition on the left, and the oil pump and six-speed transmission on the right. The carburettor size was 34 mm and the inlet discs operated in fibre sandwiches to prevent seizure and reduce wear. To minimise the build-up of frictional heat in the big ends, they were given ample side clearance and the connecting rods located at the small end instead. Consequently the pump feed proved superfluous and was discontinued.

The chief problems with the earliest models were hairy handling and the suddenness with which the power rushed in when engine speed entered the resonant band. By 1976, however, these traits had been tamed. Standard power had risen to 100 bhp at 11,000 rpm, giving a top speed approaching 170 mph, although weight (315 lb) still seemed in need of trimming.

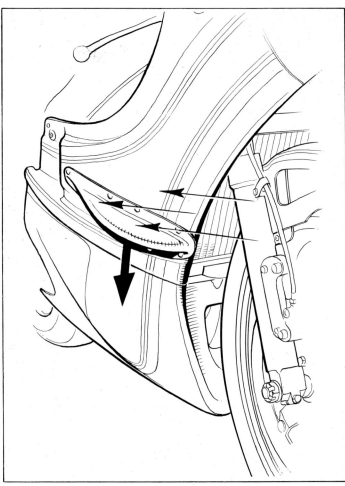

Wings on the sides of the Suzuki works RG500 fairing help keep the front wheel down at speed. Angle is a compromise between down force on the one hand and tyre temperature (plus a possible sacrifice in speed) on the other

During a visit to Japan at Suzuki's invitation that year, I asked Hase in what respects Barry Sheene's RG500 differed from standard. In a nutshell, he said, it had more power, less weight, less drag and better handling.

Three factors contributed to the higher power (at that stage, 103 bhp at 11,250 rpm) – first, modified porting; second, wider squish bands, raising the "trapped" compression ratio from 7·7 to 8·4:1 (in geometric terms, from 14 to 15:1); third a reversion to MZ's square cylinder dimensions, which boosted torque from 6,000 rpm upward. At the same time, a one-piece construction was adopted for the jackshaft, to obviate breakage of the four bolts clamping the two parts of the standard shaft.

A weight saving of 18 lb (bringing Sheene's bike down to 297 lb) was effected by substituting magnesium for aluminium for the crankcase castings, fitting a smaller magneto and having a purge on the cycle parts. Drag was reduced through a slimmer, smoother fairing, and handling was improved by lengthening rear-wheel travel and changing to air springing in the Kayaba front fork.

By 1977, engine power was up to 118 bhp and pneumatic springs had spread to the rear, with a further increase in travel to $5\frac{1}{4}$ in. Within another year peak power was 122 bhp (still at 11,000 rpm) and the crankcase had been redesigned to comprise two major castings instead of three. The benefits from this were easier gearbox servicing, lower front cylinders and closer spacing of the chain-sprocket and fork-pivot axes, so reducing chain snatch with suspension movement.

To cope with the extra speed, the diameter of the two front brake discs was increased to 310 mm ($12\frac{1}{4}$ in) and small "wings" were fitted to the fairing sides to discourage the front wheel from lifting. For the second year running, victory in the Senior TT (by Tom Herron) was wasted in a classic (world-championship) sense. Worse still (for Suzuki), Yamaha regained the world title with the aid of the brilliant and business-like American star, Kenny Roberts, and variable-height exhaust ports to give their piston-ported YZR500 engine some much-needed "driveability".

Clearly, piston control of the inlet port, for all its unwanted symmetry, was dying hard. Equally plain, and not for the first time, was the fact that engine power, despite the wonderful grip of modern tyres, is not the sole decisive factor in the 500 cc class. Light weight and a low centre of gravity; a

small frontal area and slippery shape; and, no less, the ability, temperament and form of the rider can be just as decisive.

Trump and counter-trump

Yamaha's long and distinguished participation in classic racing divides neatly into two distinct phases: 1961 to 1968 and 1970

Limited-dive device on 1979 works Suzuki RG500. When the front brake is applied, a bleed from the hydraulic line to the caliper closes a valve in the fork leg, so restricting compression. The setting is adjustable

Eight screaming cylinders and only 250 cc between them. In the 1968 Ulster 125 cc GP, winner Phil Read leads his Yamaha team mate Bill Ivy

onward. Statistically (in terms of world championships and grand prix victories), the second period has been much the more successful. Technically, however, the first phase is much more significant. In those eight years, when design was much less restricted by the FIM and competition much fiercer, Yamaha clawed their way to supremacy in the 250 and 125 cc classes through sheer technical merit.

It is true that Phil Read's double championship in 1968 (especially the 250 cc) would have carried even more kudos had Honda still been competing. But the whole period was vibrant with excitement, both on the tracks and in the race shops, as riders and engineers trumped and counter-trumped one another's latest moves – and Yamaha contributed their full share to that excitement, especially with their water-cooled, disc-valve vee-fours.

When, after a year's absence, they re-entered the fray, the adventurousness of their designers was curtailed not only by the FIM ceiling of two cylinders and six gears but also by a commercial policy that sought to identify their track machines with the piston-ported, side-by-side twins available on the open market.

Their subsequent grand prix successes reflect several factors. First, with Honda and Suzuki out, there was an immediate drop in the calibre of the opposition. Second, with the help of Professor Gordon Blair's researches at Queens University, Belfast, Yamaha were able to extend the symmetrical inlet phase beyond 200 degrees by maximising the reflected pressure pulse that resists blowback. Third, they appreciated that a slim, nippy lightweight is a good bet against more powerful machines that are handicapped by extra weight and bulk.

The most spectacular proof of the last point was provided outside the classic scene, when the highly talented Jarno Saarinen dominated the 1973 Formula 750 races at

Daytona and Imola on a 350 cc Yamaha twin. In the grands prix, MV had already been feeling Saarinen's pressure for a couple of years. Desperately they stemmed the tide by switching from three cylinders to four for 1972 – and the pressure was further eased when Saarinen was tragically killed at Monza early in 1973. But it only needed Giacomo Agostini to move from MV to Yamaha the following year and the four-stroke game was up in the 350 cc class.

In 1975, Agostini brought Yamaha their first 500 cc championship, too, riding the four-abreast job that was first recognised as an MV-beater when Saarinen won the French GP on it two years earlier. Technically, though, the disc-valve engine still held the aces, provided the layout did not entail excessive width. So it was no real surprise when Barry Sheene's disc-valve Suzuki RG500 and Kork Ballington's disc-valve 250 and 350 cc Kawasaki tandem twins eventually exposed the limitations of Yamaha's policy of basing their grand-prix specials on series-production layouts.

Above: *Proving the advantages of a slim, nippy lightweight against more powerful machines handicapped by extra weight and bulk, Jarno Saarinen dominates the 1973 Formula 750 race at Imola on a 350 cc Yamaha twin.*

Below: *first grand-prix Yamaha seen in Europe, this 1961 125 cc single already had a gearbox-driven pump dribbling oil to the crankshaft bearings. Like the early 50 cc Kreidlers, it had a carb each side of the crankcase*

Achilles heel

One of Yamaha's biggest handicaps on their 1961 debut was the enormous size of their fairings. Nor were the engines up to date. Both the 125 cc single and the 250 cc twin lacked auxiliary transfer ports – and the single had the Kreidler arrangement of a disc valve and carburettor on each side of the crankcase. Already, however, there was a gearbox-driven pump dribbling oil to the big ends.

On the credit side they had, in Fumio Ito, a dashing and fearless rider renowned for his contemptuous handling of big BMW twins, let alone lightweights. It was indicative of Yamaha's initial lack of speed that his sixth place in the Lightweight 250 cc TT and 11th in the 125 cc event were both some 11 mph down on the winners' speeds. With no better results in France and Belgium, the team packed up in mid-season.

It was 1963 before they returned to Europe; and the engineers had clearly made good use of the intervening year. They had abandoned the single and their concentration on the twin had endowed it with a highly competitive turn of speed for no sacrifice of reliability. Indeed, in only his third Isle of Man race, Ito led world champion Redman (in his 13th) for the first two laps of the Lightweight 250 cc TT.

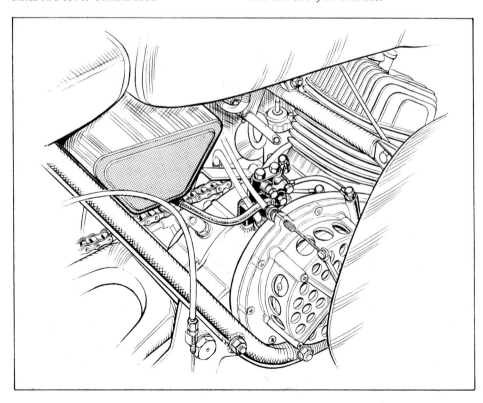

The Island held its breath at the imminent prospect of defeat for the No 1 Honda four. But Ito squandered his chance of immortality in a lackadaisical pit stop and Redman beat him by 27·2 seconds. The Japanese star notched another second place in Holland, won the Belgian GP with a record lap at 117·82 mph and finished the season third in the world championship, behind Redman's Honda and Tarquinio Provini's phenomenal Moto Morini single.

With their twin so obviously worthy of a world championship, Yamaha left nothing to chance and signed Phil Read. Nobody could have exploited the situation better. Shadowing Redman's Honda for most of the race, then using the Yamaha's speed to breeze past in the closing stages, Read eventually relieved Jim of his crown through victories at Clermont Ferrand, Solitude, Sachsenring, Dundrod and Monza.

But the TT exposed the Yamaha's Achilles heel when Read, after making the fastest lap, dropped from second to fourth position before packing up. While the engine was dependable enough on less exacting circuits, the long and arduous Mountain course showed that its winter power boost had increased its susceptibility to various two-stroke ailments, from plug fouling to the big scrunch.

Above: the writing on the wall for the Honda fours. Fumio Ito wins the 1963 Belgian 250 cc GP on a Yamaha twin after chasing Jim Redman home in the TT and Dutch GP. Ito was second again in Japan and finished the title chase third behind Redman and Provini (Moto Morini)

Below: Yamaha's method of equalising pressure on the dual front brakes of the 1963 250 cc twin was to run a single inner wire round a free roller in the handlebar lever. Only one cable adjuster was needed

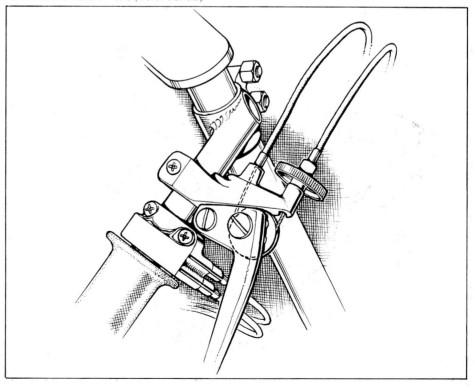

Above: *Yamaha's highly successful air-cooled disc-valve twin was made in a 125 cc version, too. Here is a 1964 model*

Below: *setting a last-lap record on his Yamaha twin, Phil Read blows off Jim Redman's Honda four in the 1964 West German 250 cc Grand Prix at Solitude*

By the penultimate championship round at Monza, there was little separating Redman and Read, and Honda tried to clinch the issue by bringing out their six. Had its challenge not been blunted by misfiring and poor handling, Read's gallant efforts throughout the season might have been frustrated. As it was, he settled the issue there – and only just in time because Jim was uncatchable at the final round in Japan.

Any apprehension in the Yamaha camp about matching the new Honda's speed in 1965 was misplaced – Redman's bad patch and Honda's half-hearted backing saw to that. Read's biggest shock came early at Montjuich Park, where Provini, then on a Benelli four, stretched him to the limit. However, Read's four straight wins at the start of the season took the heart out of the opposition – and three more victories later on gave him maximum points for his second title.

Even so, Yamaha had no illusions about the suspect stamina of their air-cooled twin. Again it had failed miserably in the TT, breaking a crank while Read was leading – although a slightly bored-out version went the full six laps in the Junior race, finishing a poor second to Redman's Honda but comfortably ahead of Agostini's MV.

In view of Suzuki's bitter experience with their square four, Yamaha's answer seemed bold – a water-cooled vee-four with two banks of cylinders spaced at about 60

For 1965, Yamaha changed their 125 cc twin to water cooling and the extra stamina enabled Phil Read to win the TT. The engine was later doubled-up into the world-beating 250 cc vee-four

degrees on a common crankcase. Race-shop confidence was high, however, for the engine was virtually a double-up of a new 14,000 rpm, nine-speed twin, with an impeller in the cooling system – and Read had already proved the stamina and speed of that 30-bhp "guinea-pig" by beating Luigi Taveri's Honda four in the Lightweight 125 cc TT, thus giving Yamaha their first IoM victory.

Once their second 250 cc championship was comfortably secured, Yamaha gave the new four a couple of outings at the end of 1965. Its speed was plain to see but so were its teething troubles – for Read lost a lap at Monza through plug fouling and fell at Suzuka through mettlesome handling.

So the faithful air-cooled twin was brought out of retirement at the start of 1966. For the record, the light-alloy cylinders had a bore and stroke of $56 \times 50 \cdot 7$ mm and, to permit close piston clearances, the bores were said to be not sleeved but anodised – an electro-chemical treatment better known as a defence against corrosion. The squish bands in the heads were annular in shape and compression was quoted as $10:1$. Situated on top of the seven-speed gearbox, the engine oil pump had no fewer than seven feeds.

The weight, including the glass-fibre fairing, was 242 lb and single leading shoes for the two front brakes were deemed adequate. Most unusual was the steering damper, in which a 12-start quick thread at the bottom of the steering stem raised and lowered a large-diameter diaphragm in a shallow hydraulic cylinder as the steering was turned. Performance figures were always difficult to drag out of Yamaha. For what it is worth, 47 bhp at 13,000 rpm was bandied around; if anything, the power figure seems a shade low and the revs a shade high. Top speed was estimated to be about 145 mph.

Blisters!

When the vee-four eventually replaced the twin, Read had another problem to contend with besides its difficult handling and temperament – Mike Hailwood had joined Honda and taken over Redman's six. Read could not possibly have fought harder to keep his crown but he soon learned what it felt like to be the mouse, rather than the cat, in a tactical battle as Mike expoited the Honda's appreciable edge in reliability, cornering and engine braking. Hailwood not only relieved Read of his title in 1966 but kept it the following year.

Naturally enough, Read's handling

Phil Read gives the 250 cc Yamaha vee-four its debut in the 1965 Italian GP at Monza. When on song it was very fast but it was dogged by misfiring

problem was highlighted in the TT. During the 1966–67 winter a lot of the bike's weight had been shed, especially at the front, and so much tamer was the handling on the smooth circuits of the season's early races that the steering damper was discarded. As soon as the bike was given its head round the bumpy Mountain course, however, it wobbled alarmingly.

Read's suspicion that the front end was too light was upheld when some loss of air from the front tyre reduced its tendency to bounce off the road and practically eliminated the wobble. As a palliative, the diaphragm steering damper was reinstalled and progressively adjusted to give the stiffest check. It was not enough and finally a conventional telescopic strut was added, too.

Yet after the race, Read's blistered palms showed what a stranglehold he had had to keep on the steering and why he had lagged nearly $1\frac{1}{2}$ minutes behind Hailwood in spite of having an all-out speed advantage over the Honda six. Stiffer damping, he said, would cause the bike to run wide on corners through lack of steering response. What was wanted was a forward shift in the weight distribution and more sensitivity in the front springing.

Opposite, top: *1978 world 125 cc champion Emilio Lazzarini on his tiny MBA twin in the Dutch TT*

Opposite, bottom: *Dramatic action in the 1978 Dutch TT by Werner Schwarzel and Andreas Huber on Helmut Fath's flat-four two-stroke*

Above: *Helmut Fath's two-stroke masterpiece – a transverse flat-four two-stroke with a scissors-action pair of contra-rotating disc inlet valves for each crank chamber (front and rear). A reduction box on front of crankcase drives belt pulleys at half engine speed and in opposite directions. A short belt drives oil pump. Carburettor adaptors are curved for chassis installation*

Above: *world 250 cc champion on a Yamaha twin for the first time in 1964, Phil Read (right) discusses his prospects with the author now that Honda have switched from four cylinders to six*

Right: *at the Gooseneck in the 1965 TT, the ageing air-cooled twin dwarfs Bill Ivy on his debut as a Yamaha works rider*

Below: *the seven-speed Yamaha air-cooled disc-valve twin on which Phil Read won the 1964 world 250 cc title. Note the two-rate rear springs, single-leading-shoe front brakes (one each side) and diaphragm-type damper beneath the steering head. Weight with fairing was 242 lb and top speed 145 mph*

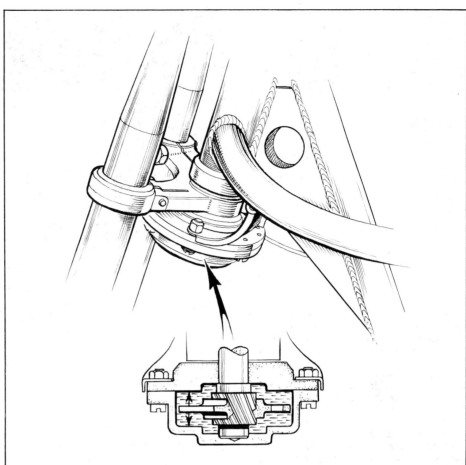

Top, right: *a 12-start worm at the base of the steering stem actuates the diaphragm in this Yamaha hydraulic steering damper*

Right: *details of the adjustable rake angle on the 250 cc Yamaha vee-four. Fitting thick packing pieces between the ears on the frame and the top of the steering head steepens the angle for twisty circuits. Thinner packings give stronger self-centring*

But the Yamaha boffins were using a different approach – adjustable steering geometry. The head lug was pivoted at the bottom and clamped back to the frame at the top. By altering the thickness of packings in the top clamps, the rake angle could be varied a degree or two at a time – both for experiment and to suit different circuits.

For circuits with severe bumps and/or long straights, thin packings gave a shallower head angle and longer fork trail, hence stronger self-centring. For twisty laps such as Assen, thicker packings steepened the head and shortened the trail, making the bike easier to flip from side to side. One of the snags was that, since the fork was telescopic, rake and trail could not be altered independently – a restriction that could have been bypassed by using a leading-link fork with various link lengths.

During those relatively lean two years, Yamaha had the consolation that the two-fifty at least lasted six consecutive laps of the TT in 1967; that Bill Ivy duplicated Read's

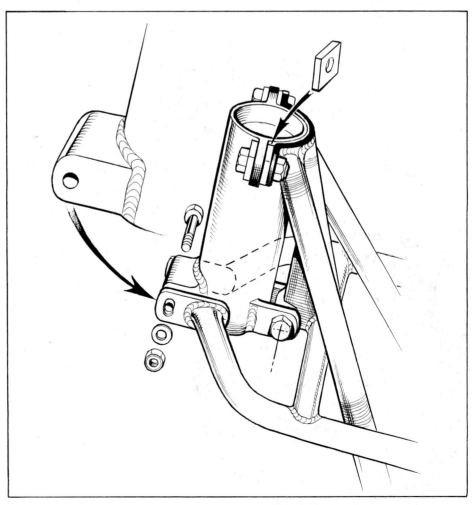

World 125 cc champion for 1979 – Spaniard
Angel Nieto on his Minarelli twin in Yugoslavia

Opposite, top: sign of an experienced two-stroke rider – 1965 Lightweight 125 cc TT-winner Phil Read has two fingers poised over the clutch lever of his water-cooled Yamaha twin. Gearbox drives both oil pump and water impeller. Engine works best between 12,000 and 14,000 rpm

Opposite, lower: with the minimum of weight and bulk to strangle the power of his tiny Yamaha vee-four engine in 1968, Bill Ivy turns the one-and-only 100 mph lap by a one-two-five in TT history

TT victory on the 125 cc twin in 1966; and, sweetest of all, that a half-size version of the vee-four hit the jackpot on its debut in 1967.

With the considerable handling advantage of some 80 lb less weight than its big brother, a lower centre of gravity, a slimmer profile and an appreciable speed advantage over all its rivals, it gave Read his second 125 cc TT win (the factory's third) and enabled Ivy to rob Taveri of the world championship in which he had seemed to have a permanent part share.

More pep was packed into the one-two-five in the winter, and more weight and bulk were trimmed off the two-fifty, so that its handling was transformed. In the circumstances, it was just as disappointing for Yamaha as for Honda that their expected showdown in 1968 never took place because of the latter's withdrawal. As it was, Read took both titles and Ivy almost won both TTs. "Almost" because, although there was no controversy over his 250 cc victory,

with a standing-start lap record of 105·51 mph that was to stand for many years, the 125 cc race was a sensation.

To Ivy's chagrin, team orders were for Read to win, since he already had eight championship points and Ivy had none. Smarting under the constraint, little Bill decided to make his point in an unmistakable way. For $2\frac{1}{4}$ of the scheduled three laps, he flung his 220-lb bike about like a toy, doing a non-stop tap dance on the nine-speed gear pedal to keep the 44-bhp engine spinning within its best rev band of 17,000–18,000 rpm.

Incredibly, he hoisted the lap record to 100·32 mph (where it has remained ever since) and pulled a quarter-minute ahead of Read. A shade over-jetted, Read could not match it. Then Ivy eased the breakneck pace to give Read a chance. Cheekily, he even coasted to a silent stop at Creg-ny-Baa (only four miles from the finish) and asked the astonished crowd who was leading. Told it was Read, he paddled off to finish second.

At 35 × 32·4 mm, bore and stroke of that tiddler were typically a shade oversquare. Top speed was a little over 130 mph. The two-fifty had one gear fewer (eight), cylinder dimensions of 44 × 40·5 mm, weighed a mite under 300 lb, eventually pushed out 73 bhp at 14,000–15,000 rpm and was good for 155 mph. Both engines had seven-feed oil pumps, separate cylinders and crankshafts and the customary jackshaft driving the

clutch on the right and the ignition on the left. Now museum pieces, they were the most exciting lightweights ever raced.

The vacuum and after

In the 1969 world championships, the vacuum left by Yamaha's temporary absence from the tracks was filled by Dave Simmonds' 125 cc Kawasaki disc-valve, side-by-side twin and Kel Carruthers' 250 cc double-knocker Benelli four. But – admirable as were the achievements of both men and their machines – race speeds were down and neither bike had quite the same technical glamour as the Yamaha vee-fours or the yowling Honda fives and sixes.

Even after Yamaha's return in 1970 (when they regained the world 250 cc title through Rod Gould) it took many years for race speeds to regain their former peaks, while technical interest sank into the doldrums. At first the two-fifties were oversquare (56 × 50·5 mm) air-cooled, piston-valve side-by-side twins with no oil pump to supplement the petroil lubrication.

Based on the catalogue TD1C and TD2 models, they were light, slim and nicely streamlined, with the fairing sides united by a smooth belly panel. Hence they made splendid use of what engine power they had and, in the absence of authentic information, wild claims were made for bhp figures comparable to those of disc-valve twins.

Shorn of its fairing, the 1968 Yamaha 250 cc disc-valve vee-four looks extremely busy. Note the two ignition units behind the side-facing carbs, the duplex twin-leading-shoe front brakes, the telescopic steering damper and (just above the hand grip) one of the clamping bolts for the adjustable steering head

Above: *Barry Sheene, Johnny Cecotto, Kenny Roberts and Boet van Dulmen heel into the hairpin at La Source in the 1978 Belgian GP*

Opposite, top: *Graziano Rossi corners his 500 cc square-four Morbidelli at Assen in 1979*

Opposite, bottom: *Works Yamaha 500 cc four for 1979, showing the control box for the so-called Power Valve that regulates exhaust-port height. The control cables come from the tachometer*

Power-house of one of the most exciting two-fifties ever – the eight-speed Yamaha vee-four of 1968. Cylinder blocks (partly masked) were spaced at 60–70 degrees. Bore and stroke were 44 × 40·5 mm. Top power was 73 bhp at 14,000–15,000 rpm. On top of the gearbox is the seven-branch oil pump for the engine

But Carruthers – who preserved his friendship with Benelli when he switched to Yamaha in 1970 – persuaded the Italian engineers to test his TD2 engine on their dynamometer. It gave 45 bhp at 10,500 rpm. Phil Read, who followed Gould as 250 cc champion in 1971, was able to make a direct comparison between the two engine types. His verdict was that his old 1964 disc-valver was appreciably more potent, and more tractable, than the TD2.

On average, the piston-valve engine seems to have lagged some five years and 10 bhp behind the disc-valver, although the latter squandered much of its advantage through extra bulk before the tandem cylinder arrangement was adopted.

Pulse strength

While every high-performance two-stroke of both types stands or falls by the designer's success in getting the inlet and exhaust tracts to resonate at the highest possible speed consistent with adequate tractability and mechanical safety, the piston-valve engine can offset some of the extra power the disc-valver gets from its longer, asymmetric inlet timing by generating a stronger pressure pulse (reflected from carburettor mouth to cylinder port) to resist blowback at the end of the inlet phase.

Even with an inlet duration as long as 200 degrees, a piston-controlled port does not open until 80 degrees after bottom dead centre. At that point the crankcase depression is more pronounced than in the case of a disc-valver (which opens its port only about 40 degrees after bdc) – hence the suction wave is stronger and so is the reflected pressure wave. By suitably tailoring the length of the inlet tract, this pulse can be made to reach the port towards the end of the phase, when the descending piston is doing its best to reverse the gas flow.

The strength of any pressure pulse depends on two factors – the speed (and crispness) of port opening and the pressure differential across the port at the time of opening. Pressure differential was dealt with in the previous paragraph. Speed and crispness of opening are influenced by port shape, disc or piston speed, piston clearance and ring height.

For a simple (and very pleasant) demonstration of these two effects, you can do no better than uncork a bottle or two of still table wine – in which the cylinder port is represented by the mouth of the bottle and the pulse strength by the loudness of the pop as the air rushes into the bottle.

Suppose the cork is $1\frac{1}{2}$ in long and there is a $\frac{1}{2}$ in air space (atmospheric) beneath it. Just before the cork leaves the bottle, the pressure in the neck will have dropped to a quarter-atmosphere (high depression). Pull out the cork as fast as you can (quick port opening) and you will hear the loudest of pops (strongest pulse).

If you finally wriggle the cork out very gingerly, however (slow port opening), the pop will not be nearly so loud (weaker pulse) in spite of the same theoretical pressure differential. Recork the bottle once you have emptied it – then, however briskly you pull the cork, you will get only a quiet pop because (if you are sober enough to appreciate it!) the pressure differential is so low as to be practically non-existent. (Do not incur the expense of champagne for this test – that is pressurised well above atmospheric by bottle fermentation, so the rush of gas is out-

Prepared by Helmut Fath, Phil Read's 1971 world championship-winning 250 cc Yamaha has extra streamlining to reduce the disturbed wake behind the rider's legs. Here Read leads Borje Jansson (Yamaha) in the Italian GP at Monza

ward, not inward, when the cork is pulled.)

Unfortunately for the piston-valver, its stronger inlet pulse only partly offsets the disc-valver's quicker port opening and longer breathing period, while its greater dependence on pulse strength narrows its useful torque spread.

Fath switches

For 1971 Yamaha brought out the faster B series of the TD2 (also of the scaled-up TR2 three-fifty); Gould's machines were factory backed while Read's were prepared by Helmut Fath, who had turned his attentions from four-strokes to two-strokes.

Departures from standard in the B series included wider exhaust ports and shorter pipes, longer inlet duration (through shorter piston skirts) and better big-end cages. Gould's machines also had Spanish Femsa electronic ignition instead of the standard flywheel magnetos.

These developments were not enough for Fath, who further modified the porting; installed a big-end feed while cutting the petroil ratio from 20:1 to 40:1; converted the clutch from wet to dry (for lighter operation and greater immunity from slipping); extended the fairing behind the rider's legs; and fitted Krober electronic ignition on the two-fifty.

On the three-fifty, however, the different vibration characteristics made it necessary to revert to the flywheel magneto. Engine vibration also broke the Cheney frame near

the bottom rear mounting lug during the Junior TT, thereby robbing Read of a TT double in 1971 (he subsequently won the 250 cc race).

By that time Jarno Saarinen's exciting talent was making nonsense of established reputations. Despite his independence, his preoccupation with university studies and the stress of doing his own driving and spannerwork, the charming Finn was beaten only by Read and Gould in the 1971 world 250 cc championship, while scaring MV Agusta by beating Agostini's three in two of the 350 cc title rounds and chasing him home in the championship.

The following year Saarinen proved his calibre beyond doubt by winning the 250 cc title, although Ago's new and faster four kept the Finn at bay again in the 350 cc class. It was the suspect stamina of the bigger Yamaha engine that pointed to the need for water cooling. In the Junior TT, for example, MV did not even bother to field their four, confident that no air-cooled Yamaha could push Ago for the full distance, even on the old three.

On the last of the air-cooled Yamahas of both sizes, a 54 mm stroke had been adopted, with a bore of 54 mm for the TD3 and 64 mm for the TR3 – and these cylinder dimensions were carried over into the water-cooled TZ models. At first, however, Gould's works TZ250 seemed to lack the speed of the best of the earlier models. In the TT, Read beat him by $1\frac{1}{2}$ minutes on a private air-cooled model and was 4 mph faster through the

Despite the 1979 design restrictions in the B2A category, Rolf Biland wins his second sidecar title; passenger on the TTM Yamaha at Assen is Kurt Waltisperg

This view of a 1976 Yamaha TZ250 shows the water impeller in front of the caged clutch. Note the long suspension strut running from the apex of the rear-fork triangle to a point just behind the steering head

Motor Cycle speed trap, where Gould's TZ was only fourth fastest.

In the hands of Chas Mortimer, the 125 cc version of the water-cooled Yamaha won the TT and went on to greater achievements with world championships by Kent Andersson in 1973 and 1974.

Doubling-up

The rear-facing carburettors of the Yamaha twins made it easy to couple two engines abreast without excessive overall width – and this is what they did when challenging MV in the 500 cc class, although they reverted to the earlier cylinder dimensions of 56 × 50·5 mm. Thin gears on the inboard ends of the two crankshafts together drove a double-width gear on the jackshaft, with the clutch on the right.

Had it not been for Saarinen's tragic death at Monza early in 1973, he might well have scooped the title that year on the YZR500, for the combination of his vivacious talent and upward of 80 eager bhp seemed unbeatable. As it turned out, Read took the title for MV that year and the following one. It was not until Ago joined Yamaha in 1975 that the 500 cc four paid off with a world championship.

There followed two years of haughty dominance by Barry Sheene's disc-valve Suzuki four, so that Yamaha were forced to push up their peak revs from 10,500 to 11,500 rpm, relying ever more heavily on natural resonances to offset the restrictions of symmetrical port timing. Inevitably, the exhaust port got higher and higher, the power curve peakier and peakier.

Were it not for the regulation limit of six gear ratios, this might have been more acceptable. As it was, Yamaha sought to broaden the useful power band by introducing an automatic height control for the exhaust port, which they called the Power Valve.

This comprised a speed-sensitive cylindrical shutter in the roof of the port, controlled by cables from the tachometer drive. As engine speed dropped towards the lower end of the useful rev range, the shutter rotated backward, so lowering the effective height of the port. Since transfer streams are angled upward to converge towards the back of the head and fill the cylinder from the top downward, this lowering reduced the escape of fresh gas, to the benefit of torque and fuel consumption.

The Power Valve had its baptism in the Venezuelan GP in March 1978 and proved delicate to set up for the best results. When Yamaha regained the championship at the end of the season, it was difficult to avoid the conviction that they owed at least as much to Kenny Roberts' superb riding as to the slight benefit of the Power Valve.

"It gives me a few more bhp at the bottom end of the rev range," he said. "Without it, there's just nothing at 9,000 rpm and the power comes in with a rush at 9,500. With the valve, there's precious little below 9,500 but at least it's usable. I now have a power range from 9,000–9,500 to 11,500–12,000."

Outstanding Ks

The only other factory to win world championships with piston-controlled induction was Harley-Davidson in Italy (formerly Aermacchi), for whom Walter Villa took the 250 cc title in 1974 and 1975, and both 250 and 350 cc titles in 1976. The two-fifty was virtually a water-cooled copy of the 56 × 50·5 mm Yamaha TD2B and the three-fifty a water-cooled TR2B. Not surprisingly, the engines contained several Yamaha internals.

No other team saw any point in disregarding the disc-valver's superiority in power, tractability and fuel consumption – and two examples of the type stand out from the many whose names appear in the world-championship lists. They are Kawasaki and König.

Notwithstanding the side-by-side arrangement of the cylinders in Dave Simmonds' 125 cc championship-winning Kawasaki twin in 1969, engine designer Nagato Sato rejected that configuration when he laid out the 250 cc twin in 1974. He recalled that the MZ twin of that size had been too wide – and he also recalled Walter Kaaden's experiments with a tandem cylinder arrangement during the later stages of MZ's grand prix involvement.

So Sato accepted the tiny frictional loss in the crankshaft coupling gears as a small price to pay for combining an ultra-slim profile with the benefits of disc valves. Right from the start, even when carburettor size was no more than 32 mm, it was clear that the new Kawasaki had the potential for a world title. What delayed that honour until 1978 (besides the absence of Kork Balling-

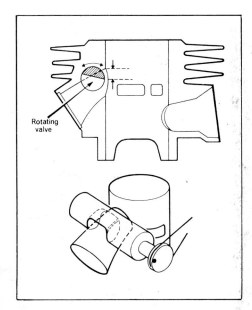

Above: *the section through the cylinder shows how backward rotation of the Yamaha Power Valve lowers the effective height of the exhaust port by the amount between the arrowheads. Also shown is a perspective sketch of the cylindrical valve and its control cables*
Right: *in this view of Johnny Cecotto's works 500 cc Yamaha four (photographed in the Francorchamps paddock in 1979) the control pulley for the exhaust-port Power Valve can be seen through the vent in the fairing flank*

ton's decisive riding talent) was insufferable vibration, even when the engine was rubber mounted.

As it turned out, Kawasaki had been too clever by half in their crankshaft coupling. With only two cylinders, it was understandable that they should want them to fire alternately (as in a side-by-side twin) for the smoothest possible torque. So they coupled the cranks 180 degrees out of phase, with one piston at the top of its stroke while the other was at the bottom. What they overlooked was the effect on mechanical balance. As shown in the diagrams on page 162, with a 100-per cent balance factor in each flywheel assembly, the vertical primary inertia forces at top and bottom dead centres were completely neutralised by the flywheel counterweights, leaving only the much smaller (although double frequency) secondary forces unbalanced. Unfortunately, at both midstroke positions the counterweights acted in unison to set up a double-size horizontal vibration.

While this could have been reduced by lowering the balance factor, that would have left part of the vertical forces unbalanced, so introducing a fore-and-aft rocking couple. Kawasaki's solution was simply to remesh the coupling gears so that the pistons moved in step.

True, the consequent change to a double firing impulse every 360 degrees cost a bit of power but this was negligible. The crucial effect was that the centrifugal forces from the counterweights cancelled one another at midstroke (as in the Velocette Roarer, page 40) – so eliminating all horizontal vibration while still opposing the primary forces at tdc and bdc. (Secondary vibration was unaffected by the change but adequately absorbed by the rubber engine mountings.)

Kawasaki first got the smell of Yamaha blood in the Japanese GP late in 1976, when Takeo Abe finished second to Yamaha's Japanese champion Mori, despite making the wrong tyre choice for the damp track. From then on, it was a case of painstaking development (including a frame rehash) allied to world-class track talent – a combination that paid off handsomely in Ballington's emphatic double title (250 and 350 cc) in 1978 and 1979.

In cylinder porting, as well as dimensions (54 × 54 mm), Nagato Sato followed MZ's lead. He chose a large unbridged exhaust port and, to back up the two main transfer ports, only one steep auxiliary (exactly opposite the exhaust) rather than the proliferation some designers have produced.

Also, by having the front crankshaft run backward and the rear one forward, he ensured that both pistons thrust against the exhaust side of the cylinder, so making the best seal between that port and the crankcase.

On the left, the Mikuni carburettors – angled slightly upward, the better to fill the space between flywheel rims and piston – grew through 34 to 36 mm. The large inlet discs, which were changed from the original steel to 0·040 in (1 mm) thick fibre, overlapped one another so that the whole rear

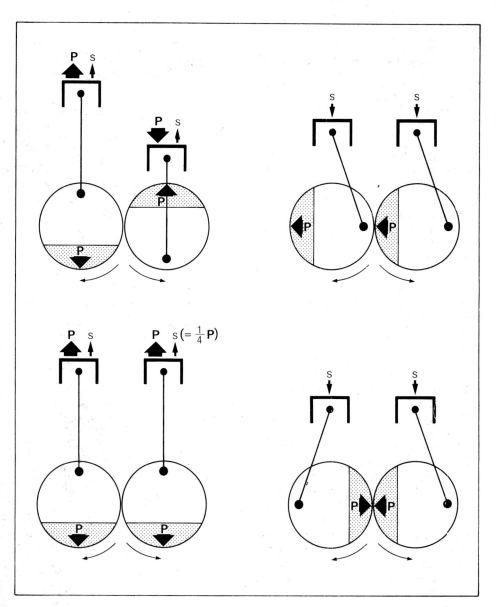

Kawasaki tandem twin with 100 per cent balance factor

Top diagrams: *original arrangement (pistons out of step)* – At top and bottom dead centres the primary inertia forces are exactly opposed by the flywheel counterweights, leaving only the small upward secondary forces unbalanced. At mid-stroke, however, where there are no primary inertia forces, the centrifugal forces from the counterweights act together in a horizontal plane while the downward secondaries are still unbalanced. Overall result: Small secondary vibration in vertical plane at twice engine speed plus engine-speed horizontal vibration four times as large.

Lower diagrams: *successful arrangement (pistons in step)* – At top and bottom dead centres the primary inertia forces are still exactly opposed by the flywheel counterweights, leaving only the small upward secondaries unbalanced. But at midstroke the centrifugal forces from the counterweights cancel one another, leaving only the small downward secondaries. Overall result: Only the high-frequency vertical vibration of the original arrangement, no horizontal vibration

crank chamber and flywheel assembly was offset about $\frac{5}{8}$ in to the left.

On the right the coupling gears, each sandwiched between two main bearings, were only 8 mm wide (about $\frac{5}{16}$ in). Outboard of the bearings were the Kokusan ignition unit (front) and, on the rear shaft, a small gear driving the seven-plate aluminium clutch and a skew gear for the water impeller and tachometer.

At both ends, the connecting rods had caged needle bearings. Each piston had one ring, of keystone (taper) section. Annular squish bands in the head gave a compression ratio of 7:1 from exhaust-port closure (about 13:1 from bdc). The coolant was fed into the head (not the block) but cast-in baffles deflected it down to the exhaust ports before it left from the opposite side of the head – the left. Lubrication was by a 20:1 petrol-oil mix, without any pump feed.

To keep weight down (to 238 lb) magnesium was chosen for the crankcase castings, covers and carburettors, as it was for the seven-spoke Morris wheels. Aluminium was used for the cylinder block and head. The useful power span was from 9,000 to 12,500 rpm, with a peak at 11,600 where rear-wheel power was upward of 55 bhp. (For comparison with crankshaft-measured power, that should be increased by about 10 per cent.) The larger machine was virtually a 10 mm-oversize two-fifty (64 × 54 mm = 347 cc). Its rear-wheel power must have approached 70 bhp and it weighed 247 lb.

Originally, the 250 cc engine was housed in a miniature version of the duplex frame used on the big three-cylinder KR750. Then it was decided to give the new lightweight an

Right: *rear suspension on Barry Sheene's works Suzuki RG500. The fabricated aluminium fork is triangulated below pivot level, so keeping the weight low and necessitating a pair of air struts. The leverage ratio is 4:3*

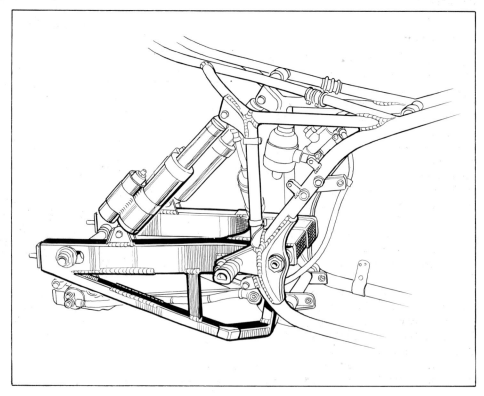

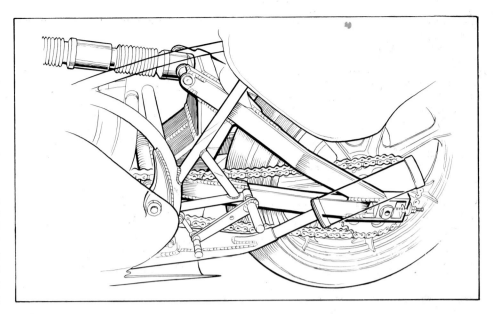

Top: rear suspension on Kenny Roberts' 1978 world champion 500 cc Yamaha four. The fabricated aluminium fork is triangulated above pivot height and operates a single long strut above the engine
Centre: on Eugenio Lazzarini's 125 cc championship-winning MBA twin, the Marzocchi rear shock absorbers have independent damping adjustments for bump and recoil. There are ten settings for each
Bottom: rocker arm in the rear suspension on Kork Ballington's 1978 250 and 350 cc championship-winning Kawasakis transfers fork movement to vertical Koni strut

up-to-date frame of its own – smaller, lighter and providing longer suspension travel. It was the brainchild of Kinuo (Cowboy) Hiramatsu, and had a fairly conventional middle portion – a duplex structure with plenty of gusseting and the steering head additionally stiffened by four struts – but a highly unorthodox and complex rear suspension.

In this, the fork (made from steel tubes at first, then fabricated in aluminium sheeting with rectangular-section arms) was pivoted on two ball bearings. Halfway along the arms, a tubular structure in the shape of an inverted V was attached by two Rose joints, while its apex was connected to the rear end of a bellcrank pivoted on a cross-tube. The front end of the bellcrank actuated the piston rod of a Koni strut, installed upright behind the gearbox and anchored to a cross-tube at the bottom. Overall leverage ratio was about 2:1 and the joints were all heavily loaded – especially at the bellcrank, where the pivot bracket had to be strengthened after fracture.

Also designed by Hiramatsu, the dolphin fairing had the floor of the front opening angled to generate a downthrust on the front wheel at high speed as well as guiding air to the radiator.

The flat fours

In much the same way that Suzuki doubled-up a side-by-side twin into a square four by tacking two more cylinders on the front, so Kawasaki's tandem layout might have lent itself to the square-four treatment by adding two cylinders on the right. There was no comparable progression, however, in the development of the König horizontally-opposed four that put an end to BMW's long supremacy in sidecar racing when Rolf Steinhausen relieved Klaus Enders of the world title in 1975.

The König engine was "borrowed" from the sport of outboard boat racing where it was already a top performer. Its attractions for sidecar racing were both economic and technical. On the economic side, BMW spares were becoming extremely scarce, hence astronomically expensive. In contrast, König engines and spares were in good supply at reasonable prices.

Technically, the engine was not only powerful (85 bhp at 10,000 rpm when it

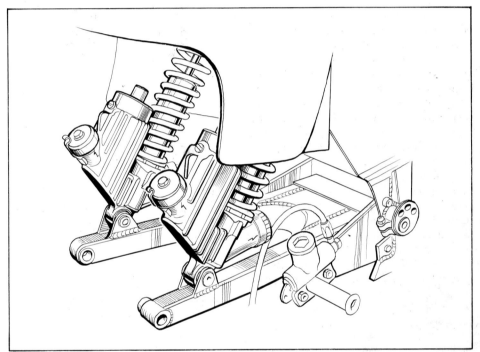

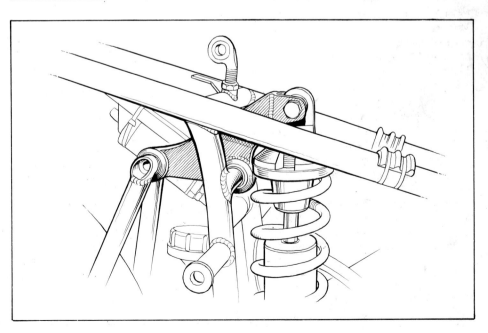

first caught on in 1973) but also light, low and slim. Thus it offered better acceleration and a higher top speed.

Its chief drawback was the complete absence of transmission, so that builders had to fit a separate gearbox and two chains. Also, like all two-strokes, the König was short on engine braking compared with the BMW so that four fade-free brakes were essential – two in the front wheel, one each rear and side.

On the smooth Continental circuits, transmission was no great problem once it had been installed, usually incorporating a six-speed Schafleitner gear cluster in a Norton shell. But on the bumpy TT course it was a different story. There, as Helmut Fath learned some years earlier on the Urs, the combination of a small-diameter, wide tyre and precious little flywheel effect in the crankshaft was a recipe for rear-wheel patter and destructive chain snatch.

The instant the wheel lost contact with the road, the engine revs soared sharply. When

Developed at Rotax by Austrian Harald Bartol in 1978, this 250 cc water-cooled twin has a common disc valve serving both crankcases, König fashion. The large diameter of the disc (which is driven by skew gears) gives extra-quick port opening and closing, while the Lectron carburettors aim their cool, oily mixture straight at the big ends. At the end of a 30-hour endurance test, it was claimed the engine still gave 65 bhp at 11,800 rpm. The unusually broad power band started at 7,500 rpm

contact was regained the grippy tyre bit firmly and the rear chain was subjected to a higher shock loading than it was ever designed to stand. Chief sufferer in the 1973 TT was Jeff Gawley, who snapped $\frac{5}{8} \times \frac{1}{4}$ in rear chains of both leading makes – Renold and Regina.

Softening the suspension to cut down patter was no answer, for that invited wallowing in corners. Steinhausen tamed the problem by using an old-fashioned wire wheel, shod with a 3·50 × 16 in tyre. The larger overall diameter reduced the tendency to patter, and the smaller contact area softened the snatch on landing. He was rewarded with third place (both chains still in perfect adjustment), although his lap speeds were appreciably slower than Gawley's.

As to the engine itself, it was virtually a pair of flat twins side by side in a unit, installed with the crankshaft across the frame. As the pistons on one side moved inward, the others moved outward, so that the left and right crank chambers breathed alternately. They were fed by a 45 mm twin-choke Solex carburettor on top of the crankcase (one choke serving each side), and induction was controlled by a single horizontal disc of large diameter, giving very rapid port opening, hence a strong pulse.

Naturally, the right-hand cylinders fired together and so did the left, 180 degrees

later. So it was convenient to use a common exhaust box (with siamesed pipes) for the out-of-step front cylinders and another for the rear. The power band was none too broad – the engine preferring to work above 8,000 rpm when handling the extra weight and bulk of a sidecar and passenger, although the few König-powered solos could make good use of power from as low as 4,000 rpm.

Mechanical balance was ideal, to the benefit of attachments vulnerable to high-frequency vibration. There were two main bearings on the drive side of the crankshaft, one at the opposite end and a fourth in the middle. Lubrication was by petroil (an old-fashioned 16 : 1) and, because the mixture was directed straight at the big ends, there was no need for the customary oil slots in the connecting-rod eyes – an omission that gave some desirable extra stiffness. The big-end bearings were caged rollers, the small ends crowded.

The drive from the right-hand end of the crankshaft to the inlet disc looked impossibly flimsy but was perfectly adequate. Not only did the light toothed belt have to change direction from vertical to horizontal and back as it circled both pulleys, but the two rollers that effected these changes required the belt to twist through 90 degrees each time (so as to present the smooth side of the belt to the rollers). Similarly flimsy looking but reliable were the two synthetic-rubber

Above: *an early König installation in Rolf Steinhausen's 1972 kneller. Three years later it broke BMW's long hold on the world championship*

Right: *in his home near Heidelberg, Helmut Fath (right) discusses engine design with the author*

bands that drove the water impeller.

Steinhausen added to his 1975 world championship with a repeat the following year – and underlined his claim to the title by winning the TT both years. The König's reign was brief, however. Inevitably, it lost favour as soon as a competitive engine with an integral gearbox became readily available – the Yamaha unit used by George O'Dell (champion in 1977) and Rolf Biland (champion in 1978 and 1979). At the hand-built level, though, König's flat-four layout lived on in another Helmut Fath engine – a much-improved version, with integral transmission, used by Werner Schwarzel to finish third in the 1977 title chase and fourth in 1978.

The incredible Fath

To regard Fath's engine as a König copy, however, is unfair to Fath. Any resemblance began and ended with the flat-four cylinder arrangement – and even that was precisely the layout Fath had had in mind, during his long convalesence in the early 1960s, for a water-cooled four-stroke world beater before BMW declined to provide the necessary transmission parts.

As to the differences from the König layout, the most obvious were the longitudinal position of the crankshaft (with the 56 × 50 mm cylinders across the frame) and an integral six-speed gearbox – with the clutch on the tail of the crankshaft (BMW fashion) but a pair of bevel gears coupling the output shaft to a left-side sprocket for chain final drive. Although Fath preferred shaft drive in principle, he begrudged its extra unsprung weight as well as the difficulty and expense of providing sufficient variation in overall gearing.

From the start, the engine had four separate carburettors. Much as the König

Rear three-quarter view of Helmut Fath's flat-four two-stroke with four 34 mm Mikuni carburettors. The upward inclination of the sparking plugs is to allow room for nozzles in direct-injection experiments

big ends might relish their perpetual shower of oily ingoing mixture, Fath reasoned that a whirling crankshaft directly under each inlet port must impede the gas flow to some extent and prevent both sides of the crank chamber from being properly filled. Accordingly, each inlet passage in the crankcase was curved out towards the space it had to fill, between the flywheel rims and the underside of the piston. Anyway, he rejected the use of oil in the fuel on the grounds that it reduced the octane rating of the fuel. Instead, he fitted a belt-driven, throttle-controlled pump which dribbled oil to the main bearings, big ends and disc bearings in an overall proportion equivalent to a petroil ratio of 30:1.

Inevitably, the use of four carburettors called for two small discs – one for the front

pair of opposed cylinders, the other for the rear pair. And since the cylinders in each pair worked in unison, each disc had two diametrically opposed cutaways – a symmetry that resulted in perfect disc balance.

Naturally, the discs had to run at half engine speed so that each inlet port was opened by one blade of a disc and closed by the opposite blade. The drawback of running the discs at half speed was that port opening was comparatively slow. To Helmut Fath that was no problem – he simply doubled-up each disc (one spindle working inside the other), and ran the two elements in opposite directions so that they had a scissors action across the port and halved the opening time.

This move also meant doubling-up the skew reduction gearing as well as the number of polyurethane toothed driving belts (from two to four) – a rather complex way of producing an additional $2\frac{1}{2}$ bhp.

Unlike the König, the reduction gearing turned the drive from the front of the

crankshaft through 90 degrees so that all belt pulleys rotated in a horizontal plane and there was no need for belt contortions over rollers. To reduce disc friction, incidentally, the valve cover was faced with Teflon (made famous by non-stick frying pans) and a thin Teflon-coated sheet was sandwiched between the contra-rotating discs.

There was no water impeller – circulation (as in MZs) being by thermosiphon action, with the water entering the underside of the cylinder blocks and leaving from the top. Uniquely, however (since each block casting incorporated half the crankcase) the crank chambers themselves were also water cooled, to the benefit of charge density. Typically, Fath had proved this theory earlier by running Phil Read's 250 cc Yamaha engine on the dynamometer and pouring cold water over the hot crankcase from a garden watering can! As he did so the power steadily increased.

Carburettor installation on the flat four was a compromise. Ideally, Fath wanted vertical inlet tracts, to straighten the gas path; but no available carburettor would work satisfactorily with the mixing chamber horizontal, so he had to settle for curved adaptors. Bing carburettors, although giving excellent power on the dynamometer, were too tall for installation in the chassis – so 34 mm Mikunis were substituted, working at their maximum inclination of 35 degrees.

Fath regarded this layout as a stop-gap, however, pending solution of the problems of direct injection, when he would be able to fit vertical air trumpets.

Incidentally, his dynamometer was an old Schenck water brake, installed in a small wooden hut in the woods half a mile from his home in the hills above Heidelberg. A 40-gallon drum on the roof supplied the water and was replenished from a well. There was no exhaust silencing (save for the usual padding round the perforated tail-pipes) – earlier, the BMW and Urs engines were tested with wide open pipes!

Yamaha pistons were fitted at first, for convenience, then replaced by pistons of Fath's own design, which were claimed to prevent any reduction in the cold running clearance as the engine got hot. (The cylinder liners were in aluminium, with a Nikasil finish for the bores.) There was only one ring per piston and wide annular squish bands in the cylinder heads gave a compression ratio of 14·5:1 from bdc (about 8:1 from exhaust-port closure).

The exhaust ports were oval and un-bridged; the side transfers were divided into wide and narrow passages; and, to cool the small-end bearings, there were two small auxiliary transfer ports opposite the exhaust, fed through windows in the piston skirt. Caged needle bearings were used in both ends of the connecting rods while the six-disc flywheel assembly was supported in four roller bearings – the middle two separated by a labyrinth oil seal.

Sparks were initially provided by a Bosch flywheel magneto but the generator (which incorporated two ignition coils, two trigger coils and three more for tachometer, fuel pump and water pump, if required) proved too heavy for the crankshaft taper. So a battery was installed for current and only a trigger unit fitted on the front of the crankshaft.

Fath shunned siamesed exhausts, preferring separate boxes for maximum effect. The results justified his thinking for he got not only 112 bhp at 12,200 rpm (with useful power from 8,200 and peak torque at 10,500) but also a remarkably light fuel consumption of 21 mpg.

Although his dynamometer readings may have been optimistic, speed checks and fastest laps on a variety of circuits suggested Fath's engine was more than a match for the Yamahas. Had he still been young enough to race himself, it is a virtual certainty that he

Above: *for 1979, Morbidelli doubled-up their successful 250 cc disc-valve parallel twin into this water-cooled square four with forward-sloping cylinders*

Right: *typical engine layout of a 50 cc single (1976 Morbidelli) with the cylinder almost horizontal and rubber-bushed mounting lugs. Carburettor size (28 mm) is 70 per cent of cylinder bore (40 mm), giving very deep breathing*

would have scooped another title.

Unhappily, development proved less easy with other drivers involved, especially as they were responsible for the chassis and installation sometimes hampered the engine's breathing. There were, too, personality clashes with some sponsors and drivers. What is beyond doubt, however, is that Helmut Fath – without benefit of academic training but with an exceptional flair for engineering, a first-class apprenticeship at the Kaiser Wilhelm Institute and a tremendously competitive spirit – was unsurpassed as a rider-tuner and one of the most genuine characters to grace the GP scene.

Painstaking progress

The remaining championship-winning two-strokes (Derbi, Bultaco, Morbidelli, MBA and Minarelli) were all water-cooled, six-speed disc-valvers with the maximum permitted number of cylinders, two for the one-two-fives, one for the fifties. Since engine width was no problem despite side-facing carburettors, the twins had their cylinders arranged in the simplest way – abreast. In the singles, the cylinders were horizontal or nearly so.

In basic design, there was no fundamental advance on Walter Kaaden's time-honoured formula, although specific power (bhp/litre) – hammered by the FIM's cylinder restriction in 1969 – resumed its upward climb despite the need to keep power bands wide enough to cope with only six gears.

This steady power increase stemmed from painstaking work on harnessing the inlet and exhaust resonances, along with bearing improvements that took the risk out of sustained ultra-high rpm. With no scope for offsetting their deficiency in power and tractability, the piston-valve 125 cc Yamahas were ousted by Morbidelli in 1975, 1976 and 1977, while Mario Lega (on the bigger Morbidelli in 1977) put an end to the three-year reign of Walter Villa's piston-valve Harley-Davidson in the 250 cc class. Naturally enough, in view of Suzuki's example, Morbidelli doubled-up their larger twin into a 500 cc square four for 1979.

Although the 50 cc minimum cylinder size hampers an engine designer's quest for power, it nevertheless highlights the tiddler's enormous advantage in deep breathing. On Ricardo Tormo's 1978 world 50 cc championship-winning Bultaco, for example, carburettor size (28 mm) was 70 per cent of the cylinder bore (40 mm).

Even on a simple linear comparison, that is equivalent to a $2\frac{1}{2}$ in (63 mm) carburettor on the last of the works Norton 500 cc singles (90 mm bore) – whereas, in fact, its carburettor size was $1\frac{13}{32}$ in (36 mm). On a

1978 world 125 cc champion Eugenio Lazzarini takes his 130 mph MBA disc-valve twin to victory in the Austrian GP on the Salzburgring. Within 10 years, the twin-cylinder two-stroke had matched the 1968 Yamaha vee-four's 44 bhp despite the latter's 5 : 4 overall advantage in relative port size and higher peak revs

volumetric comparison, which is what really matters, the tiddler's breathing advantage is even more spectacular – just over 3 : 1.

Allied to the higher engine speed permitted by its lighter reciprocating parts, this freer breathing accounts for the little Bultaco's specific power of 360 bhp/litre (18 bhp at 15,500 rpm). At that level, Barry Sheene's RG 500 Suzuki would have produced 180 bhp, which is 50 per cent more than it actually gave.

Incidentally, it is because of the high operating range of 50 and 125 cc grand-prix engines that they can more safely reduce friction by using only one ring per piston – the impaired sealing at low rpm is of no consequence. Another slight saving, on the fifties, is driving the water impeller electrically, not mechanically.

Of course, light weight and low drag are especially important in the smaller classes. At 123 lb, the 50 cc Bultaco and Morbidelli were only fractionally over the FIM minimum for the class – as were the 125 cc MBA and Morbidelli at 176 lb. Fairings were either developed in a university wind tunnel or copied from Yamaha, who used tunnel facilities in Japan. Either way, notable

features were the "chin" filling in the wake behind the front wheel and the tail doing a similar job behind the rider's rump.

Spectacle may not be a powerful attraction in the smaller classes but the technical achievements have been remarkable. Tormo's little Bultaco could tank along at 112 mph, yet its overall fuel consumption was a miserly 68 mpg. Eugenio Lazzarini's 1978 world 125 cc championship-winning MBA (good for 130 mph) not only had an aluminium monocoque frame that looked as if it might even cope with a 250 cc engine – it was also claimed to match Bill Ivy's immortal 125 cc Yamaha vee-four for power (44 bhp).

Naturally, we were entitled to expect progress in the 10 years since the vee-four was outlawed – but in power potential a four has a theoretical advantage over a twin of 5 : 4. Peaking around 17,500 rpm, the Yamaha achieved 20 bhp/litre/1,000 rpm. If MBA's claim to have made up the bhp leeway at a peak of only 14,000 rpm was true, they had achieved an incredible 25 bhp/litre/1,000 rpm. When a bike is firmly on top of its heap, however, there is little point in arguing.

THE CHAMPIONSHIPS

European championships

From 1924 to 1937 inclusive, one grand prix each year was allocated the title of European Grand Prix and the championships were based on the results of that meeting alone. During that period nine countries hosted the championships but the Isle of Man TT was not included.

To make the titles more representative in 1938 and 1939, championship points were awarded at eight major grands prix, including the TT. In 1938 the top six finishers scored 6, 5, 4, 3, 2 and 1 respectively but for 1939 only the top five finishers got points, starting with five for the winner and finishing with one for the fifth man.

1924 Italian GP, Monza

250 cc
1 J.Van Geert, Belgium (Rush-Blackburne)
2 H.Höbel, Austria (Puch)
3 R.Karner, Austria (Puch)

350 cc
1 J.H.Simpson, GB (AJS)
2 I.Mariani, Italy (Garelli)
3 M.Saetti, Italy (Bianchi)

500 cc
1 G.Mentasti, Italy (Moto Guzzi)
2 E.Visioli, Italy (Moto Guzzi)
3 T.Simister, GB (Norton)

1925 Italian GP, Monza

175 cc
1 M.Vaga, Italy (Maffeis-Blackburne)
2 Cavedagna, Italy (GD 125)
3 U.Faraglia, Italy (Puch)

250 cc
1 J.A.Porter, GB (New Gerrard-Blackburne)
2 A.Ruggeri, Italy (Garanzini-JAP)
3 M.Maffeis, Italy (Maffeis-Blackburne)

350 cc
1 T.Nuvolari, Italy (Bianchi)
2 M.Maffeis, Italy (Bianchi)
3 E. Self, Italy (Bianchi)

500 cc
1 G.Revelli, Italy (GR-JAP)
2 P.Ghersi, Italy (Moto Guzzi)
3 M.Saetti, Italy (Norton)

1926 Belgian GP, Francorchamps

175 cc
1 R.Milhoux, Belgium (Ready-Blackburne)
2 R.Beckers, Germany (DKW)

250 cc
1 J.A.Porter, GB (New Gerrard-Blackburne)
2 G.S.Davison, GB (New Imperial)

350 cc
1 F.A.Longman, GB (AJS)
2 O.Putz, Austria (Sunbeam)
3 R.Demulder, Belgium (Indian)

500 cc
1 J.H.Simpson, GB (AJS)
2 R.Karner, Austria (Sunbeam)
3 S.Woods, Eire (Norton)

1927 German GP, Nürburgring

175 cc
1 P.Henkelmann, Germany (DKW)
2 A.Geiss, Germany (DKW)
3 A.Müller, Germany (DKW)

250 cc
1 C.T.Ashby, GB (OK Supreme-JAP)
2 W.Winkler, Germany (DKW)
3 H.Höbel, Austria (Puch)

350 cc
1 J.H.Simpson, GB (AJS)
2 F.A.Longman, GB (Velocette)
3 F.Sieder, Germany (Velocette)

500 cc
1 G.W.Walker, GB (Sunbeam)
2 S.Woods, Eire (Norton)
3 C.T.Ashby, GB (Rudge)

750 cc
1 S.Stelzer, Germany (BMW)
2 P.Koppen, Germany (BMW)

1,000 cc
1 S.Giggenbach, Germany (Bayerland-JAP)
2 W.Huth, Germany (Harley-Davidson)
3 H.Kürten, Germany (Andrees)

1928 Swiss GP, Geneva

125 cc
1 H.Lehmann, Switzerland (Moser)
2 R.Brehm, Switzerland (Moser)
3 O.Tenni, Italy (GD)

175 cc
1 A.Panella, Italy (Ladetto-Blatto)
2 R.Brusi, Italy (Benelli)
3 G.Sourdot, France (Monet-Goyon)

250 cc
1 C.T.Ashby, GB (OK Supreme-JAP)
2 J.A.Porter, GB (New Gerrard-Blackburne)
3 O.Geissler, Switzerland (Moto Guzzi)

350 cc
1 W.L.Handley, GB (Motosacoche)
2 A.J.Guthrie, GB (Norton)
3 B.Martinelli, Switzerland (Motosacoche)

500 cc
1 W.L.Handley, GB (Motosacoche)
2 G.E.Nott, GB (Rudge)
3 G.W.Walker, GB (Rudge)

350 cc sidecar
1 S.A.Crabtree, GB (Excelsior-JAP)
2 H.Pfister, Switzerland (Royal Enfield)

600 cc sidecar
1 D'Eternod, Switzerland (Sunbeam)
2 E.Stärkle, Switzerland (Scott)
3 E. Stuzzi, Jugoslavia (AJS)

1929 Spanish GP, Barcelona

175 cc
1 S.Klein, Germany (DKW)
2 R.Brusi, Italy (Benelli)
3 G.Sourdot, France (Monet-Goyon)

250 cc
1 F.A.Longman, GB (OK Supreme-JAP)
2 P.Ghersi, Italy (Moto Guzzi)
3 G.Himing, GB (Zenith-JAP)

350 cc
1 L.H.Davenport, GB (AJS)
2 G.Rowley, GB (AJS)
3 F.Aranda, Spain (New Imperial)

500 cc
1 P.M.Hunt, GB (Norton)
2 G.W.Walker, GB (Rudge)
3 C.J.P.Dodson, GB (Sunbeam)

350 cc sidecar
1 F.G.Hicks, GB (Velocette)

600 cc sidecar
1 D.K.Mansell, GB (Norton)
2 D'Eternod, Switzerland (Sunbeam)
3 F.Naura, Spain (Scott)

1930 Belgian GP, Francorchamps

175 cc
1 J.Goor, Belgium (DKW)
2 E.C.Fernihough, GB (Excelsior-JAP)
3 J.Mawet, Belgium (Bovy-Villiers)

250 cc
1 S.A.Crabtree, GB (Excelsior-JAP)
2 E.A.Mellors, GB (New Imperial)
3 S.G.Gleave, GB (SGS-JAP)

350 cc
1 G.E.Nott, GB (Rudge)
2 A.E.Simcock, Australia (AJS)
3 G.Himing, GB (AJS)

500 cc
1 H.G.Tyrell Smith, Eire (Rudge)
2 G.W.Walker, GB (Rudge)
3 J.G.Duncan, GB (Raleigh)

1931 French GP, Montlhéry

175 cc
1 E.C.Fernihough, GB (Excelsior-JAP)
2 Y.van Goor, Belgium (DKW)

250 cc
1 G.W.Walker, GB (Rudge)
2 C.W.Johnston, Eire (Moto Guzzi)
3 G.L.Boudin, GB (CTS)

350 cc
1 G.E.Nott, GB (Rudge)
2 S.Woods, Eire (Norton)
3 F.Renier, Belgium (Velocette)

500 cc
1 P.M.Hunt, GB (Norton)
2 A.E.Simcock, Australia (OK Supreme-JAP)
3 A.J.Guthrie, GB (Norton)

1932 Italian GP, Rome

175 cc
1 C.Baschieri, Italy (Benelli)
2 T.Benelli, Italy (Benelli)
3 A.Tigli, Italy (MM)

250 cc
1 R.Brusi, Italy (Moto Guzzi)
2 A.Cimatti, Italy (Moto Guzzi)
3 V.Fieschi, Italy (Miller)

350 cc
1 L.Jeanin, France (Jonghi)
2 G.Sandri, Italy (Rudge)
3 F.Renier, Belgium (Jonghi)

500 cc
1 P.Taruffi, Italy (Norton)
2 F.Aranda, Spain (Rudge)
3 B.Mantovani, Italy (Miller)

1933 Swedish GP, Saxtorp

250 cc
1 C.J.P.Dodson, GB (New Imperial)
2 R.Gülich, Sweden (Moto Guzzi)
3 L.H.Davenport, GB (Excelsior)

350 cc
1 J.H.Simpson, GB (Norton)
2 A.J.Guthrie, GB (Norton)
3 R.Jönsson, Sweden (Husqvarna)

500 cc
1 G.Kalen, Sweden (Husqvarna)
2 L.Demeuter, Belgium (FN)
3 Y.Ericsson, Sweden (Husqvarna)

1934 Dutch GP, Assen

175 cc
1 J.Goor, Belgium (Benelli)
2 G.Dickwell, Belgium (Barbe-JAP)
3 W.van Geert, Belgium (Rush-Blackburne)

250 cc
1 W.Winkler, Germany (DKW)
2 L.J.Archer, GB (New Imperial)
3 A.Geiss, Germany (DKW)

350 cc
1 J.H.Simpson, GB (Norton)
2 W.F.Rusk, GB (Velocette)
3 A.G.Mitchell, GB (Velocette)

500 cc
1 L.Demeuter, Belgium (FN)
2 "Noir", Belgium (FN)
3 A.v.d.Pluym, Holland (Husqvarna)

1935 Ulster GP, Clady

250 cc
1 A.Geiss, Germany (DKW)
2 A.R.Foster, GB (New Imperial)
3 J.B.Burney, Eire (Moto Guzzi)

350 cc
1 W.L.Handley, GB (Velocette)
2 E.R.Thomas, GB (Velocette)
3 J.G.Duncan, GB (Norton)

500 cc
1 A.J.Guthrie, GB (Norton)
2 R.Milhoux, Belgium (FN)
3 A.Tyler, GB (Velocette)

1936 German GP, Sachsenring

250 cc
1 H.G.Tyrell Smith, Eire (Excelsior)
2 E.Kluge, Germany (DKW)
3 B.Port, Germany (Rudge)

350 cc
1 F.L.Frith, GB (Norton)
2 O.Steinbach, Germany (NSU)
3 H.Fleischmann, Germany (NSU)

500 cc
1 A.J.Guthrie, GB (Norton)
2 H.P.Müller, Germany (DKW)
3 J.H.White, GB (Norton)

1937 Swiss GP, Berne

250 cc
1 O.Tenni, Italy (Moto Guzzi)
2 N.Pagani, Italy (Moto Guzzi)
3 E.Kluge, Germany (DKW)

350 cc
1 A.J.Guthrie, GB (Norton)
2 F.L.Frith, GB (Norton)
3 E.R.Thomas, GB (Velocette)

500 cc
1 A.J.Guthrie, GB (Norton)
2 F.L.Frith, GB (Norton)
3 O.Tenni, Italy (Moto Guzzi)

600 cc sidecar
1 K.Braun, Germany (DKW)
2 F.Aubert, Switzerland (Norton)
3 M.Hunziker, Switzerland (Norton)

1,000 cc sidecar
1 H.Schuhmann, Germany (DKW)
2 H.Kahrmann, Germany (DKW)
3 P.Weyres, Germany (Harley-Davidson)

1938

250 cc
1 E.Kluge, Germany (DKW), 36
2 B.Petruschke, Germany (DKW), 25
3 H.Gablenz, Germany (DKW), 13

350 cc
1 E.A.Mellors, GB (Velocette), 28
2 J.H.White, GB (Norton), 15
3 S.Wünsche, Germany (DKW), 12

500 cc
1 G.Meier, Germany (BMW), 24
2 H.L.Daniell, GB (Norton), 20
3 F.L.Frith, GB (Norton), 18

1939

250 cc
1 E.Kluge, Germany (DKW), 27
2 B.Petruschke, Germany (DKW), 12
3 {E.A.Mellors, GB (Benelli), 5
   {N.Pagani, Italy (Moto Guzzi), 5

350 cc
1 H.Fleischmann, Germany (DKW), 23
2 E. A. Mellors, GB (Velocette), 19
3 S.Woods, Eire (Velocette), 16

500 cc
1 D.Serafini, Italy (Gilera), 19
2 G.Meier, Germany (BMW), 15
3 S.Vailati, Italy (Gilera), 8

World championships

A points system has been used throughout the world individual championships. For the first year (1949) the leading five finishers scored 10, 8, 7, 6 and 5 respectively and an extra point was awarded for the fastest lap, provided the rider finished.

From 1950 to 1968 inclusive, the first six riders scored – 8, 6, 4, 3, 2 and 1 – and the point for fastest lap was dropped. The number of scoring finishers was extended to ten in 1969, the points being 15, 12, 10, 8, 6, 5, 4, 3, 2 and 1 (still with nothing for the fastest lap).

Up to and including 1976, the championships were calculated on net scores, not gross. A rider's net score comprised his best points in half the grands prix run, plus one, ignoring fractions (ie, 12 grands prix run, best seven to count).

From 1977 onward, however, all events counted (gross scores). Incidentally, a rider's country is that which issues his competition licence, not necessarily his country of birth.

1949

125 cc
1 N.Pagani, Italy (Mondial) 27
2 R.Magi, Italy (Morini) 14
3 U.Masetti, Italy (Morini) 13

250 cc
1 B.Ruffo, Italy (Guzzi) 24
2 D.Ambrosini, Italy (Benelli) 19
3 R.Mead, GB (Mead Norton) 13

350 cc
1 F.Frith, GB (Velocette) 33
2 R.Armstrong, Eire (AJS) 18
3 A.R.Foster, GB (Velocette) 16

500 cc
1 L.Graham, GB (AJS) 30
2 N.Pagani, Italy (Gilera) 29
3 A.Artesiani, Italy (Gilera) 25

Sidecar
1 E.Oliver, GB (Norton) 26
2 E.Frigerio, Italy (Gilera) 18
3 F.Vanderschrick, Belgium (Norton) 16

1950

125 cc
1 B.Ruffo, Italy (Mondial) 17
2 G.Leoni, Italy (Mondial) 14
3 C.Ubbiali, Italy (Mondial) 14

250 cc
1 D.Ambrosini, Italy (Benelli) 30
2 M.Cann, GB (Guzzi) 14
3 F.Anderson, GB (Guzzi) 6

350 cc
1 A.R.Foster, GB (Velocette) 30
2 G.Duke, GB (Norton) 24
3 L.Graham, GB (AJS) 17

500 cc
1 U.Masetti, Italy (Gilera) 28
2 G.Duke, GB (Norton) 27
3 L.Graham, GB (AJS) 17

Sidecar
1 E.Oliver, GB (Norton) 24
2 E.Frigerio, Italy (Gilera) 18
3 H.Haldemann, Switzerland (Norton) 8

1951

125 cc
1 C.Ubbiali, Italy (Mondial) 20
2 G.Leoni, Italy (Mondial) 12
3 W.McCandless, GB (Mondial) 11

250 cc
1 B.Ruffo, Italy (Guzzi) 26
2 T.L.Wood, GB (Guzzi) 21
3 D.Ambrosini, Italy (Benelli) 14

350 cc
1 G.Duke, GB (Norton) 40
2 J.Lockett, GB (Norton) 19
3 W.Doran, GB (AJS) 19

500 cc
1 G.Duke, GB (Norton) 35
2 Alfredo Milani, Italy (Gilera) 31
3 U.Masetti, Italy (Gilera) 21

Sidecar
1 E.Oliver, GB (Norton) 30
2 E.Frigerio, Italy (Gilera) 26
3 Albino Milani, Italy (Gilera) 19

1952

125 cc
1 C. Sandford, GB (MV) 28
2 C.Ubbiali, Italy (Mondial) 24
3 E.Mendogni, Italy (Morini) 16

250 cc
1 E.Lorenzetti, Italy (Guzzi) 28
2 F.Anderson, GB (Guzzi) 24
3 L.Graham, GB (Velocette) 11

350 cc
1 G.Duke, GB (Norton) 32
2 R.Armstrong, Eire (Norton) 24
3 W.R.Amm, Rhodesia (Norton) 21

500 cc
1 U.Masetti, Italy (Gilera) 28
2 L.Graham, GB (MV) 25
3 R.Armstrong, Eire (Norton) 22

Sidecar
1 C.Smith, GB (Norton) 24
2 Albino Milani, Italy (Gilera) 18
3 J.Drion, France (Norton) 17

1953

125 cc
1 W.Haas, W.Germany (NSU) 30
2 C.Sandford, GB (MV) 20
3 C.Ubbiali, Italy (MV) 18

250 cc
1 W.Haas, W.Germany (NSU) 28
2 R. Armstrong, Eire (NSU) 23
3 F.Anderson, GB (Guzzi) 22

350 cc
1 F.Anderson, GB (Guzzi) 30
2 E.Lorenzetti, Italy (Guzzi) 26
3 W.R.Amm, Rhodesia (Norton) 18

500 cc
1 G.Duke, GB (Gilera) 38
2 R.Armstrong, Eire (Gilera) 24
3 Alfredo Milani, Italy (Gilera) 18

Sidecar
1 E.Oliver, GB (Norton) 32
2 C.Smith, GB (Norton) 26
3 H.Haldemann, Switzerland (Norton) 12

1954

125 cc
1 R.Hollaus, Austria (NSU) 32
2 C.Ubbiali, Italy (MV) 18
3 H.P.Muller, W.Germany (NSU) 15

250 cc
1 W.Haas, W.Germany (NSU) 32
2 R.Hollaus, Austria (NSU) 26
3 H.P.Muller, W.Germany (NSU) 17

350 cc
1 F.Anderson, GB (Guzzi) 32
2 W.R.Amm, Rhodesia (Norton) 22
3 R.Coleman, New Zealand (AJS) 20

500 cc
1 G.Duke, GB (Gilera) 32
2 W.R.Amm, Rhodesia (Norton) 20
3 K.Kavanagh, Australia (Norton) 16

Sidecar
1 W.Noll, W.Germany (BMW) 30
2 E.Oliver, GB (Norton) 26
3 C.Smith, GB (Norton) 22

1955

125 cc
1 C.Ubbiali, Italy (MV) 32
2 L.Taveri, Switzerland (MV) 26
3 R.Venturi, Italy (MV) 16

250 cc
1 H.P.Muller, W.Germany (NSU) 19
2 C.Sandford, GB (Guzzi) 14
3 W.Lomas, GB (MV) 13

350 cc
1 W.Lomas, GB (Guzzi) 30
2 R.Dale, GB (Guzzi) 18
3 A.Hobl, W.Germany (DKW) 17

500 cc
1 G.Duke, GB (Gilera) 32
2 R.Armstrong, Eire (Gilera) 26
3 U.Masetti, Italy (MV) 19

Sidecar
1 W.Faust, W.Germany (BMW) 30
2 W.Noll, W.Germany (BMW) 28
3 W.Schneider, W. Germany (BMW) 22

1956

125 cc
1 C.Ubbiali, Italy (MV) 32
2 R.Ferri, Italy (Gilera) 14
3 L.Taveri, Switzerland (MV) 12

250 cc
1 C.Ubbiali, Italy (MV) 32
2 L.Taveri, Switzerland (MV) 26
3 E.Lorenzetti, Italy (Guzzi) 10

350 cc
1 W.Lomas, GB (Guzzi) 24
2 A.Hobl, W.Germany (DKW) 17
3 R.Dale, GB (Guzzi) 17

500 cc
1 J.Surtees, GB (MV) 24
2 W.Zeller, W.Germany (BMW) 16
3 J.Hartle, GB (Norton) 14

Sidecar
1 W.Noll, W.Germany (BMW) 30
2 F.Hillebrand, W.Germany (BMW) 26
3 P.V.Harris, GB (Norton) 24

1957

125 cc
1 T.Provini, Italy (Mondial) 30
2 L. Taveri, Switzerland (MV) 22
3 C.Ubbiali, Italy (MV) 22

250 cc
1 C.Sandford, GB (Mondial) 26
2 T.Provini, Italy (Mondial) 16
3 S.H.Miller, GB (Mondial) 14

350 cc
1 K.Campbell, Australia (Guzzi) 30
2 R.McIntyre, GB (Gilera) 22
3 L.Liberati, Italy (Gilera) 22

500 cc
1 L.Liberati, Italy (Gilera) 32
2 R.McIntyre, GB (Gilera) 20
3 J.Surtees, GB (MV) 17

Sidecar
1 F.Hillebrand, W.Germany (BMW) 28
2 W.Schneider, W.Germany (BMW) 20
3 F.Camathias, Switzerland (BMW) 17

1958
125 cc
1 C.Ubbiali, Italy (MV) 32
2 A.Gandossi, Italy (Ducati) 25
3 L.Taveri, Switzerland (Ducati) 20

250 cc
1 T.Provini, Italy (MV) 32
2 H.Fugner, E.Germany (MZ) 25
3 C.Ubbiali, Italy (MV) 16

350 cc
1 J.Surtees, GB (MV) 32
2 J.Hartle, GB (MV) 24
3 G.Duke, GB (Norton) 17

500 cc
1 J.Surtees, GB (MV) 32
2 J.Hartle, GB (MV) 20
3 R.H.Dale, GB (BMW) 13

Sidecar
1 W.Schneider, W.Germany (BMW) 30
2 F.Camathias, Switzerland (BMW) 26
3 H.Fath, W.Germany (BMW) 8

1959
125 cc
1 C.Ubbiali, Italy (MV) 30
2 T.Provini, Italy (MV) 28
3 M.Hailwood, GB (Ducati) 20

250 cc
1 C.Ubbiali, Italy (MV) 28
2 T.Provini, Italy (MV) 16
3 G.Hocking, Rhodesia (MZ) 16

350 cc
1 J.Surtees, GB (MV) 32
2 J.Hartle, GB (MV) 16
3 R.N.Brown, Australia (Norton) 14

500 cc
1 J.Surtees, GB (MV) 32
2 R.Venturi, Italy (MV) 22
3 R.N.Brown, Australia (Norton) 17

Sidecar
1 W.Schneider, W.Germany (BMW) 22
2 F.Camathias, Switzerland (BMW) 22
3 F.Scheidegger, Switzerland (BMW) 16

1960
125 cc
1 C.Ubbiali, Italy (MV) 24
2 G.Hocking, Rhodesia (MV) 18
3 E.Degner, E.Germany (MZ) 16

250 cc
1 C.Ubbiali, Italy (MV) 32
2 G.Hocking, Rhodesia (MV) 28
3 L.Taveri, Switzerland (MV) 11

350 cc
1 J.Surtees, GB (MV) 22
2 G.Hocking, Rhodesia (MV) 22
3 J.Hartle, GB (MV/Norton) 18

500 cc
1 J.Surtees, GB (MV) 32
2 R.Venturi, Italy (MV) 26
3 J.Hartle, GB (Norton/MV) 16

Sidecar
1 H.Fath, W.Germany (BMW) 24
2 F.Scheidegger, Switzerland (BMW) 16
3 P.V.Harris, GB (BMW) 14

1961
125 cc
1 T.Phillis, Australia (Honda) 48
2 E.Degner, E.Germany (MZ) 42
3 L.Taveri, Switzerland (Honda) 30

250 cc
1 M.Hailwood, GB (Honda) 44
2 T.Phillis, Australia (Honda) 38
3 J.Redman, Rhodesia (Honda) 36

350 cc
1 G.Hocking, Rhodesia (MV) 38
2 F.Stastny, Czechoslovakia (Jawa) 30
3 G.Havel, Czechoslovakia (Jawa) 19

500 cc
1 G.Hocking, Rhodesia (MV) 48
2 M.Hailwood, GB (Norton/MV) 40
3 F.Perris, GB (Norton) 16

Sidecar
1 M.Deubel, W.Germany (BMW) 30
2 F.Scheidegger, Switzerland (BMW) 28
3 E.Strub, Switzerland (BMW) 14

1962
50 cc
1 E.Degner, W.Germany (Suzuki) 41
2 H-G.Anscheidt, W.Germany (Kreidler) 36
3 L.Taveri, Switzerland (Honda) 29

125 cc
1 L.Taveri, Switzerland (Honda) 48
2 J.Redman, Rhodesia (Honda) 38
3 T.Robb, GB (Honda) 30

250 cc
1 J.Redman, Rhodesia (Honda) 48
2 R.McIntyre, GB (Honda) 32
3 A.Wheeler, GB (Guzzi) 19

350 cc
1 J.Redman, Rhodesia (Honda) 32
2 M.Hailwood, GB (MV) 20
3 T.Robb, GB (Honda) 18

500 cc
1 M.Hailwood, GB (MV) 40
2 A.Shepherd, GB (Matchless) 29
3 P.Read, GB (Norton) 11

Sidecar
1 M.Deubel, W.Germany (BMW) 30
2 F.Camathias, Switzerland (BMW) 26
3 F.Scheidegger, Switzerland (BMW) 18

1963
50 cc
1 H.Anderson, New Zealand (Suzuki) 34
2 H-G.Anscheidt, W. Germany (Kreidler) 32
3 E.Degner, W.Germany (Suzuki) 30

125 cc
1 H.Anderson, New Zealand (Suzuki) 54
2 L.Taveri, Switzerland (Honda) 38
3 J.Redman, Rhodesia (Honda) 35

250 cc
1 J.Redman, Rhodesia (Honda) 44
2 T.Provini, Italy (Morini) 42
3 F.Ito, Japan (Yamaha) 26

350 cc
1 J.Redman, Rhodesia (Honda) 32
2 M.Hailwood, GB (MV) 28
3 L.Taveri, Switzerland (Honda) 16

500 cc
1 M.Hailwood, GB (MV) 40
2 A.Shepherd, GB (Matchless) 21
3 J.Hartle, GB (Gilera) 20

Sidecar
1 M.Deubel, W.Germany (BMW) 22
2 F.Camathias, Switzerland (BMW) 20
3 F.Scheidegger, Switzerland (BMW) 20

1964
50 cc
1 H.Anderson, New Zealand (Suzuki) 38
2 R.Bryans, GB (Honda) 30
3 H-G.Anscheidt, W.Germany (Kreidler) 29

125 cc
1 L.Taveri, Switzerland (Honda) 46
2 J.Redman, Rhodesia (Honda) 36
3 H.Anderson, New Zealand (Suzuki) 34

250 cc
1 P.Read, GB (Yamaha) 46
2 J.Redman, Rhodesia (Honda) 42
3 A.Shepherd, GB (MZ) 23

350 cc
1 J.Redman, Rhodesia (Honda) 40
2 B.Beale, Rhodesia (Honda) 24
3 M.Duff, Canada (AJS) 20

500 cc
1 M.Hailwood, GB (MV) 40
2 J.Ahearn, Australia (Norton) 25
3 P.Read, GB (Matchless) 25

Sidecar
1 M.Deubel, W.Germany (BMW) 28
2 F.Scheidegger, Switzerland (BMW) 26
3 C.Seeley, GB (BMW) 17

1965
50 cc
1 R.Bryans, GB (Honda) 36
2 L.Taveri, Switzerland (Honda) 32
3 H.Anderson, New Zealand (Suzuki) 32

125 cc
1 H.Anderson, New Zealand (Suzuki) 56
2 F.Perris, GB (Suzuki) 44
3 D.Woodman, GB (MZ) 28

250 cc
1 P.Read, GB (Yamaha) 56
2 M.Duff, Canada (Yamaha) 42
3 J.Redman, Rhodesia (Honda) 34

350 cc
1 J.Redman, Rhodesia (Honda) 38
2 G.Agostini, Italy (MV) 32
3 M.Hailwood, GB (MV) 20

500 cc
1 M.Hailwood, GB (MV) 48
2 G.Agostini, Italy (MV) 38
3 P.Driver, South Africa (Matchless) 26

Sidecar
1 F.Scheidegger, Switzerland (BMW) 32
2 M.Deubel, W.Germany (BMW) 26
3 G.Auerbacher, W.Germany (BMW) 15

1966
50 cc
1 H-G.Anscheidt, W.Germany (Suzuki) 28
2 R.Bryans, GB (Honda) 26
3 L.Taveri, Switzerland (Honda) 26

125 cc
1 L.Taveri, Switzerland (Honda) 46
2 W.Ivy, GB (Yamaha) 40
3 R.Bryans, GB (Honda) 32

250 cc
1 M.Hailwood, GB (Honda) 56
2 P.Read, GB (Yamaha) 34
3 J.Redman, Rhodesia (Honda) 20

350 cc
1 M.Hailwood, GB (Honda) 48
2 G.Agostini, Italy (MV) 42
3 R.Pasolini, Italy (Aermacchi) 17

500 cc
1 G.Agostini, Italy (MV) 36
2 M.Hailwood, GB (Honda) 30
3 J.Findlay, Australia (Matchless) 20

Sidecar
1 F. Scheidegger, Switzerland (BMW) 24
2 M. Deubel, W. Germany (BMW) 20
3 C. Seeley, GB (BMW) 13

1967

50 cc
1 H-G. Anscheidt, W. Germany (Suzuki) 30
2 Y. Katayama, Japan (Suzuki) 28
3 S. Graham, GB (Suzuki) 22

125 cc
1 W. Ivy, GB (Yamaha) 56
2 P. Read, GB (Yamaha) 40
3 S. Graham, GB (Suzuki) 38

250 cc
1 M. Hailwood, GB (Honda) 50
2 P. Read, GB (Yamaha) 50
3 W. Ivy, GB (Yamaha) 46

350 cc
1 M. Hailwood, GB (Honda) 40
2 G. Agostini, Italy (MV) 32
3 R. Bryans, GB (Honda) 20

500 cc
1 G. Agostini, Italy (MV) 46
2 M. Hailwood, GB (Honda) 46
3 J. Hartle, GB (Matchless) 22

Sidecar
1 K. Enders, W. Germany (BMW) 40
2 G. Auerbacher, W. Germany (BMW) 32
3 S. Schauzu, W. Germany (BMW) 28

1968

50 cc
1 H-G. Anscheidt, W. Germany (Suzuki) 24
2 P. Lodewijkx, Holland (Jamathi) 17
3 B. Smith, Australia (Derbi) 15

125 cc
1 P. Read, GB (Yamaha) 40
2 W. Ivy, GB (Yamaha) 34
3 G. Molloy, New Zealand (Bultaco) 15

250 cc
1 P. Read, GB (Yamaha) 52
2 W. Ivy, GB (Yamaha) 52
3 H. Rosner, E. Germany (MZ) 32

350 cc
1 G. Agostini, Italy (MV) 32
2 R. Pasolini, Italy (Benelli) 18
3 K. Carruthers, Australia (Aermacchi) 17

500 cc
1 G. Agostini, Italy (MV) 48
2 J. Findlay, Australia (Matchless) 34
3 G. Marsovszky, Switzerland (Matchless) 10

Sidecar
1 H. Fath, W. Germany (Urs) 27
2 G. Auerbacher, W. Germany (BMW) 22
3 S. Schauzu, W. Germany (BMW) 19

1969

50 cc
1 A. Nieto, Spain (Derbi) 76
2 A. Toersen, Holland (Kreidler) 75
3 B. Smith, Australia (Derbi) 69

125 cc
1 D. Simmonds, GB (Kawasaki) 90
2 D. Braun, W. Germany (Suzuki) 59
3 C. van Dongen, Holland (Suzuki) 51

250 cc
1 K. Carruthers, Australia (Benelli) 89
2 K. Andersson, Sweden (Yamaha) 84
3 S. Herrero, Spain (Ossa) 83

350 cc
1 G. Agostini, Italy (MV) 90
2 S. Grassetti, Italy (Yamaha/Jawa) 47
3 G. Visenzi, Italy (Yamaha) 45

500 cc
1 G. Agostini, Italy (MV) 105
2 G. Marsovszky, Switzerland (Linto) 47
3 G. Nash, GB (Norton) 45

Sidecar
1 K. Enders, W. Germany (BMW) 60
2 H. Fath, W. Germany (Urs) 55
3 G. Auerbacher, W. Germany (BMW) 40

1970

50 cc
1 A. Nieto, Spain (Derbi) 87
2 A. Toersen, Holland (Jamathi) 75
3 R. Kunz, W. Germany (Kreidler) 66

125 cc
1 D. Braun, W. Germany (Suzuki) 84
2 A. Nieto, Spain (Derbi) 72
3 B. Jansson, Sweden (Maico) 62

250 cc
1 R. Gould, GB (Yamaha) 102
2 K. Carruthers, Australia (Yamaha) 84
3 K. Andersson, Sweden (Yamaha) 67

350 cc
1 G. Agostini, Italy (MV) 90
2 K. Carruthers, Australia (Benelli/Yamaha) 58
3 R. Pasolini, Italy (Benelli) 46

500 cc
1 G. Agostini, Italy (MV) 90
2 G. Molloy, New Zealand (Kawasaki) 62
3 A. Bergamonti, Italy (Aermacchi/MV) 59

Sidecar
1 K. Enders, W. Germany (BMW) 73
2 G. Auerbacher, W. Germany (BMW) 62
3 S. Schauzu, W. Germany (BMW) 56

1971

50 cc
1 J. de Vries, Holland (Kreidler) 75
2 A. Nieto, Spain (Derbi) 69
3 J. Schurgers, Holland (Kreidler) 42

125 cc
1 A. Nieto, Spain (Derbi) 87
2 B. Sheene, GB (Suzuki) 79
3 B. Jansson, Sweden (Maico) 64

250 cc
1 P. Read, GB (Yamaha) 73
2 R. Gould, GB (Yamaha) 68
3 J. Saarinen, Finland (Yamaha) 64

350 cc
1 G. Agostini, Italy (MV) 90
2 J. Saarinen, Finland (Yamaha) 63
3 K-I. Carlsson, Sweden (Yamaha) 39

500 cc
1 G. Agostini, Italy (MV) 90
2 K. Turner, New Zealand (Suzuki) 58
3 R. Bron, Holland (Suzuki) 57

Sidecar
1 H. Owesle, W. Germany (Munch-Urs) 69
2 A. Butscher, W. Germany (BMW) 57
3 S. Schauzu, W. Germany (BMW) 57

1972

50 cc
1 A. Nieto, Spain (Derbi) 69
2 J. de Vries, Holland (Kreidler) 69
3 T. Timmer, Holland (Jamathi) 50

125 cc
1 A. Nieto, Spain (Derbi) 97
2 K. Andersson, Sweden (Yamaha) 87
3 C. Mortimer, GB (Yamaha) 87

250 cc
1 J. Saarinen, Finland (Yamaha) 94
2 R. Pasolini, Italy (Aermacchi) 93
3 R. Gould, GB (Yamaha) 88

350 cc
1 G. Agostini, Italy (MV) 102
2 J. Saarinen, Finland (Yamaha) 89
3 R. Pasolini, Italy (Aermacchi) 78

500 cc
1 G. Agostini, Italy (MV) 105
2 A. Pagani, Italy (MV) 87
3 B. Kneubuhler, Switzerland (Yamaha) 57

Sidecar
1 K. Enders, W. Germany (BMW) 72
2 H. Luthringshauser, W. Germany (BMW) 63
3 S. Schauzu, W. Germany (BMW) 62

1973

50 cc
1 J. de Vries, Holland (Kreidler) 60
2 B. Kneubühler, Switzerland (Kreidler) 51
3 Th. Timmer, Holland (Jamathi) 47

125 cc
1 K. Andersson, Sweden (Yamaha) 99
2 C. Mortimer, GB (Yamaha) 75
3 J. Shurgers, Holland (Bridgestone) 70

250 cc
1 D. Braun, W. Germany (Yamaha) 80
2 T. Lansivuori, Finland (Yamaha) 64
3 J. Dodds, W. Germany (Yamaha) 58

350 cc
1 G. Agostini, Italy (MV) 84
2 T. Lansivuori, Finland (Yamaha) 77
3 P. W. Read, GB (MV) 56

500 cc
1 P. W. Read, GB (MV) 84
2 K. Newcombe, W. Germany (Konig) 63
3 G. Agostini, Italy (MV) 57

Sidecar
1 K. Enders, W. Germany (BMW) 75
2 W. Schwarzel, W. Germany (Konig) 48
3 S. Schauzu, W. Germany (BMW) 45

1974

50 cc
1 H. van Kessel, Holland (Van Veen Kreidler) 90
2 H. Rittberger, W. Germany (Kreidler) 65
3 J. van Zeebroek, Belgium (Kreidler) 59

125 cc
1 K. Andersson, Sweden (Yamaha) 87
2 B. Kneubühler, Switzerland (Yamaha) 63
3 A. Nieto, Spain (Derbi) 60

250 cc
1 W. Villa, Italy (H-D) 77
2 D. Braun, W. Germany (Yamaha) 58
3 P. Pons, France (Yamaha) 50

350 cc
1 G. Agostini, Italy (Yamaha) 75
2 D. Braun, W. Germany (Yamaha) 62
3 P. Pons, France (Yamaha) 47

500 cc
1 P. W. Read, GB (MV) 82
2 G. Bonera, Italy (MV) 69
3 T. Lansivuori, Finland (Yamaha) 67

Sidecar
1 K. Enders, W. Germany (Busch BMW) 66
2 W. Schwarzel, W. Germany (Konig) 64
3 S. Schauzu, W. Germany (BMW) 60

1975

50 cc
1 A. Nieto, Spain (Kreidler) 75
2 E. Lazzarini, Italy (Piovaticci) 61
3 J. van Zeebroek, Belgium (Kreidler) 43

125 cc
1 P.Pileri, Italy (Morbidelli) 90
2 P.Bianchi, Italy (Morbidelli) 72
3 K.Andersson, Sweden (Yamaha) 67

250 cc
1 W.Villa, Italy (H-D) 85
2 M.Rougerie, France (H-D) 76
3 D.Braun, W. Germany (Yamaha) 56

350 cc
1 J.Cecotto, Venezuela (Yamaha) 78
2 G.Agostini, Italy (Yamaha) 59
3 P.Korhonen, Finland (Yamaha) 48

500 cc
1 G.Agostini, Italy (Yamaha) 84
2 P.W.Read, GB (MV) 76
3 H.Kanaya, Japan (Yamaha) 45

Sidecar
1 R.Steinhausen, W. Germany (Busch Konig) 57
2 W.Schwarzel, W. Germany (Konig) 54
3 R.Biland, Switzerland (Seymaz Yamaha) 30

1976

50 cc
1 A.Nieto, Spain (Bultaco) 85
2 H.Rittberger, W. Germany (Kreidler) 76
3 U.Graf, Switzerland (Kreidler) 69

125 cc
1 P.Bianchi, Italy (Morbidelli) 90
2 A.Nieto, Spain (Bultaco) 67
3 P.Pileri, Italy (Morbidelli) 64

250 cc
1 W.Villa, Italy (H-D) 90
2 T.Katayama, Japan (Yamaha) 73
3 G.Bonera, Italy (H-D) 61

350 cc
1 W.Villa, Italy (H-D) 76
2 J.Cecotto, Venezuela (Yamaha) 65
3 C.Mortimer, GB (Yamaha) 54

500 cc
1 B.Sheene, GB (Suzuki) 72
2 T.Lansivuori, Finland (Suzuki) 48
3 P.Hennen, USA (Suzuki) 46

Sidecar
1 R.Steinhausen, W. Germany (Konig) 65
2 W.Schwarzel, W. Germany (Konig) 51
3 H.Schmid, Switzerland (Yamaha) 38

1977

50 cc
1 A.Nieto, Spain (Bultaco) 87
2 E.Lazzarini, Italy (Kreidler) 72
3 R.Tormo, Spain (Bultaco) 69

125 cc
1 P.Bianchi, Italy (Morbidelli) 131
2 E.Lazzarini, Italy (Morbidelli) 105
3 A.Nieto, Spain (Bultaco) 80

250 cc
1 M.Lega, Italy (Morbidelli) 85
2 F.Uncini, Italy (H-D) 72
3 W.Villa, Italy (H-D) 67

350 cc
1 T.Katayama, Japan (Yamaha) 95
2 T.Herron, GB (Yamaha) 56
3 J.Ekerold, S. Africa (Yamaha) 54

500 cc
1 B.Sheene, GB (Suzuki) 107
2 S.Baker, USA (Yamaha) 80
3 P.Hennen, USA (Suzuki) 67

Sidecar
1 G.O'Dell, GB (Yamaha) 64
2 R.Biland, Switzerland (Yamaha) 56
3 W.Schwarzel, W. Germany (Fath) 46

1978

50 cc
1 R.Tormo, Spain (Bultaco) 99
2 E.Lazzarini, Italy (Kreidler) 64
3 P.Plisson, France (Kreidler) 48

125 cc
1 E.Lazzarini, Italy (MBA) 114
2 A.Nieto, Spain (Minarelli) 88
3 P.Bianchi, Italy (Minarelli) 70

250 cc
1 K.Ballington, S. Africa (Kawasaki) 124
2 G.Hansford, Australia (Kawasaki) 118
3 P.Fernandez, France (Yamaha) 55

350 cc
1 K.Ballington, S. Africa (Kawasaki) 134
2 T.Katayama, Japan (Yamaha) 77
3 G.Hansford, Australia (Kawasaki) 76

500 cc
1 K.Roberts, USA (Yamaha) 110
2 B.Sheene, GB (Suzuki) 100
3 J.Cecotto, Venezuela (Yamaha) 66

Sidecar
1 R.Biland, Switzerland (Beo Yamaha) 79
2 A.Michel, France (Seymaz Yamaha) 76
3 B.Holzer, Switzerland (Yamaha) 49

1979

50 cc
1 E.Lazzarini, Italy (Kreidler) 75
2 R.Blatter, Switzerland (Kreidler) 62
3 P.Plisson, France (ABF) 32

125 cc
1 A.Nieto, Spain (Minarelli) 120
2 M.Massimiani, Italy (MBA) 53
3 H.Müller, Switzerland (MBA) 50

250 cc
1 K.Ballington, South Africa (Kawasaki) 141
2 G.Hansford, Australia (Kawasaki) 81
3 G.Rossi, Italy (Morbidelli) 64

350 cc
1 K.Ballington, South Africa (Kawasaki) 99
2 P.Fernandez, France (Yamaha) 90
3 G.Hansford, Australia (Kawasaki) 77

500 cc
1 K.Roberts, USA (Yamaha) 113
2 V.Ferrari, Italy (Suzuki) 89
3 B.Sheene, GB (Suzuki) 87

Sidecar (B2A)
1 R.Biland, Switzerland (TTM Yamaha) 67
2 { D.Greasley, GB (Yamaha) 58
    R.Steinhausen, W. Germany (Yamaha) 58

Sidecar (B2B)
1 B.Holzer, Switzerland (LCR Yamaha) 72
2 R.Biland, Switzerland (LCR Yamaha) 60
3 M.Kumano, Japan (Yamaha) 41

INDEX